Lecture Notes in Computer Science 672

Edited by G. Goos and J. Hartmanis

Advisory Board: W. Brauer D. Gries J. Stoer

Amnon Barak   Shai Guday   Richard G. Wheeler

The MOSIX Distributed Operating System

Load Balancing for UNIX

Springer-Verlag

Berlin Heidelberg New York
London Paris Tokyo
Hong Kong Barcelona
Budapest

Series Editors

Gerhard Goos
Universität Karlsruhe
Postfach 69 80
Vincenz-Priessnitz-Straße 1
W-7500 Karlsruhe, FRG

Juris Hartmanis
Cornell University
Department of Computer Science
4130 Upson Hall
Ithaca, NY 14853, USA

Authors

Amnon Barak
Shai Guday
Richard G. Wheeler
Institute of Computer Science, The Hebrew University of Jerusalem
91904 Jerusalem, Israel

CR Subject Classification (1991): D.4, C.2.4

ISBN 3-540-56663-5 Springer-Verlag Berlin Heidelberg New York
ISBN 0-387-56663-5 Springer-Verlag New York Berlin Heidelberg

© Springer-Verlag Berlin Heidelberg 1993
Printed in Germany

Typesetting: Camera ready by authors/editors
45/3140-543210 - Printed on acid-free paper

Dedicated to our families.

Preface

This book describes the design and internals of the MOSIX distributed operating system. **MOSIX**, an acronym for Multicomputer **O**perating **S**ystem for UN**IX**, integrates a cluster of loosely connected computers into a virtual single-machine UNIX environment. The main property of MOSIX is the *high degree of integration* among the computers, which may include personal workstations, shared memory and non-shared memory multiprocessors, connected by fast communication links. This integration includes network transparency, cooperation between the computers to provide services across machine boundaries, support of dynamic configuration, and system-initiated load balancing by process migration. Another property of MOSIX is the ability to scale up the system configuration to encompass a large number of computers. This is accomplished by using probabilistic algorithms that allow each computer to maintain only partial knowledge about the state of the global system, regardless of the number of computers.

The development of MOSIX was begun in 1981 for a cluster of PDP-11 computers. It was based on UNIX Version 7. Since then, four additional versions of MOSIX have been developed, each version based on the most recent version of UNIX that was available at the time. The latest version is operational on a cluster of workstations, where each workstation is itself a multiprocessor.

We describe MOSIX as it is, rather than as it was meant to be, or as it would be implemented today. The text summarizes some relevant parts of UNIX that provide a basis for understanding MOSIX. Readers interested in detailed descriptions of UNIX should refer to any of the excellent texts referred to in this book. The material presented is intended primarily for readers who are interested in distributed and multiprocessor systems. The reader is assumed to have some knowledge in programming and operating systems, preferably UNIX. Readers without this background will still benefit from the techniques and algorithms discussed.

The book consists of eleven chapters. Chapter 1 gives a brief introduction to MOSIX, placing it in the context of other multicomputer systems. Chapter 2 presents an overview of MOSIX, its characteristics, kernel architecture, and developmental stages. Chapter 3 describes the design of the traditional, non-distributed UNIX file system, followed by Chapter 4, which describes several distributed UNIX file systems and the MOSIX file system in particular. Chapter 5 describes the non-distributed UNIX process structure and the kernel mechanisms that interact with the processes. Chapter 6 presents the MOSIX process, the internal mechanisms that allow process migration in MOSIX, and the details of the distributed interprocess communication mechanisms. The underlying links between the host-specific part of the kernel and the user view of the kernel are presented in Chapter 7.

Chapter 8 describes the load balancing mechanism built into the MOSIX kernel. Scaling considerations, including examples of probabilistic algorithms that are used in MOSIX, are presented in Chapter 9. Chapter 10 presents the performance of the main communication mechanisms of the MOSIX kernel. Chapter 11 discusses distributed applications. It presents a brief description of a language extension for writing distributed programs and gives the performance results of several examples. It concludes with a description of a monitoring facility for distributed applications that is supported by extensions to the MOSIX kernel.

The development of MOSIX has been a cooperative effort of many individuals, but some call for particular mention here. First, we must acknowledge the significant contributions of Amnon Shiloh to the design and implementation of all the MOSIX versions, and for reviewing drafts of the manuscript. Ami Litman made valuable contributions to the design and development of the first version of MOSIX. Special thanks to Danny Braniss for his help and to Avi Barel for the implementation of NSMOS. Thanks are also due to Robert Hofner, Roy Laor, Jonathan Masel, On G. Paradise, Gil Shwed, Yuval Yarom and all of the other participants on the MOSIX team for their contributions. We would like to thank National Semiconductor Corporation (Israel) for their support and equipment contributions, and Jennifer Steiner for editing the manuscript.

The research that led to the development of MOSIX was supported in part by the U.S. Air Force, Office of Scientific Research, sponsored by the HQ Rome Air Development Center and the European Office of Aerospace Research and Development, the Israel Ministry of Science and Technology, the Israel National Council for Higher Education, the Israel Ministry of Defense, National Semiconductor Corporation, and the Israel Academy of Science and Humanities.

The following terms are trademarks: Ethernet (Xerox Corporation), M68000 (Motorola Semiconductor Corporation); NFS (Sun Microsystems, Inc.); PDP-11, Q-Bus, VAX, and VMS (Digital Equipment Corporation); ProNET, ProNET-10, ProNET-80 (Proteon, Inc.); VME532, VR32, NS32000, NS32332, and NS32532 (National Semiconductor Corporation); and UNIX (UNIX System Laboratories).

A. Barak, S. Guday, R.G. Wheeler
Jerusalem, 1993

Contents

Chapter 1

Introduction

Configurations of loosely-coupled multicomputers can be classified as either network systems or distributed systems. In a **network system**, each computer runs its own operating system. Each of these operating systems is augmented by communication facilities that permit interaction with the other systems in the network. In a network system, the user's environment is confined to one (local) computer, with the added ability to access objects that reside on other (remote) computers. This last ability, however, is quite limited, since all network commands must specify the location of each remote object. For example, users access remote objects (e.g., reading a file that resides on another computer) by explicitly using the network name of the computer that has the file. As a result, network operating systems have a limited degree of resource sharing and they are therefore commonly used to connect geographically dispersed and heterogeneous systems.

Distributed systems provide a higher degree of transparency and resource sharing than network systems. Distributed systems can be divided into two categories: user-level distributed systems and distributed operating systems. In a **user-level distributed system**, the support for distribution is provided in a layer of software on top of the (non-distributed) operating system. User-level distributed systems are intended for configurations of machines running different operating systems with the distributed software layer on top. An example of this type of distributed system is the Open Software Foundation's Distributed Computing Environment [17]. **Distributed operating systems**, on the other hand, implement support for distribution in the kernel, and are intended for configurations of machines running the same operating system. The MOSIX system described in this book is an example of a distributed operating system.

In a distributed operating system, one operating system is used by all the computers in the entire network, each computer running its own copy. Distributed operating systems are most commonly used in networks in which all of the computers are from the same manufacturer. Distributed operating systems can also be used in networks of computers from different manufacturers if all of the operating systems have the same functionality (i.e., the same user interface).

The main goal of distributed operating systems is to provide resource sharing over a transparent network. In these systems, the user is provided with a single virtual machine, with transparent network communication, distribution of the workload, and automatic resource allocation.

The architecture of many distributed operating systems is based on the **client/server model**. Among these distributed operating systems, it is possible to distinguish between asymmetrical client/server systems and symmetrical client/server systems. In an **asymmetrical client/server system**, specific machines are assigned service functions (e.g., file servers or name servers), while other machines are used to execute user tasks. Examples of asymmetrical client/server distributed operating systems include the V-System [14] and Amoeba [29].

The main characteristic of a **symmetrical client/server system** is the decentralization of control; each machine is both a server and a client for all of the services. In symmetrical systems, each machine can function as an independent computer, with complete hardware and software facilities, while the entire network behaves like a single computer. The advantages of symmetrical systems over asymmetrical systems include improved cost/performance ratio, better resource utilization, increased availability and reliability, and the possibility to scale up the configuration to large numbers of computers.

The MOSIX system is a symmetrical distributed operating system that integrates a cluster of loosely connected, independent computers into a virtual single-machine UNIX environment. The hardware configuration for MOSIX consists of a cluster of computers, each with its own local memory, that are loosely connected by a local area communication network (LAN). In most configurations that have been developed to run MOSIX, each computer (node) is an independent uniprocessor UNIX system, with complete hardware and software facilities. In the latest configuration running MOSIX, each node is itself a multiprocessor. Each such node may contain up to eight independent processors that share I/O devices and communication controllers over a common bus. In this book, the terms "node" machine, and "workstation" are used to refer to an independent computer. The term "processor" refers to a single Processing Element (PE) within a multiprocessor workstation.

The main characteristics of MOSIX are:

Network transparency – the network is completely invisible to the naive user.

Autonomy – each node is capable of operating as an independent system.

Cooperation – the nodes work together to provide services across the network.

Decentralized control – each processor makes all of its control decisions independently.

Dynamic process migration – processes can be migrated among homogeneous processors.

Load balancing – process migration allows near-optimal assignment of processes to processors.

Dynamic configuration – nodes may be added and removed with minimal side effects.

Increased availability – files and processes can be replicated on different nodes.

Performance – local and remote operations are highly efficient.

Reliability – a limited degree of reliability is provided through the isolation of faults.

Replicated kernel and resources – the system is replicated in each node.

Scalability – the configuration may be scaled up to a large number of nodes.

Compatibility – MOSIX is compatible with AT&T UNIX System V.

More details about these characteristics are given in Chapter 2.

The most noticeable properties for executing distributed applications on MOSIX are its network transparency, the symmetry and flexibility of its configuration, and its dynamic process migration. The combined effect of these properties is that application programs are completely independent of the current state of the system configuration. Users do not need to change their applications due to node or communication links failures, nor be concerned about the load of the various processors. The system automatically attempts to optimize all resource allocation, including migrating I/O-bound jobs to the sites that master the devices they use and migrating heavily communicating jobs to nearby processors so that they benefit from fast services.

The MOSIX kernel is obtained by restructuring the UNIX kernel into machine-dependent and machine-independent parts (modules). The kernel is built as a structure of loosely-coupled modules, where the module interfaces are minimal and well defined [6]. The machine-dependent module provides site-dependent services, such as access to local disks. The machine-independent module provides network-wide services to the application level, such as transparent interprocessor communication. Each MOSIX kernel isolates the users' processes from the specific machines on which they execute, while at the same time providing these processes with the standard UNIX interface [2, 3]. This means that processes execute in a site-independent mode, which allows all system calls to be executed uniformly, regardless of the current location of the requesting process and the site that has the requested object.

The MOSIX kernel is designed to hide the internal network from the user and the application programmer [6]. In order to provide efficient network-wide services, MOSIX kernels interact with each other at the level of kernel remote procedure calls. The MOSIX kernel can be implemented on any reasonable hardware, but the participating processors must be homogeneous, to allow process-migration. This does not exclude MOSIX from being part of wider, heterogeneous networks, where process migration occurs among disjoined sets of homogeneous processors, improving resource sharing and performance.

Another major objective of the MOSIX kernel architecture is high performance. An important consideration in the design of this kernel was the avoidance of the high overhead caused by information hiding. Another architectural consideration was to enable comprehensive debugging of the system on a single machine. This means that, if necessary, any of the known debugging techniques can be applied to the MOSIX kernel. The details of the MOSIX kernel architecture are given in Chapter 2.

MOSIX belongs to a class of modular operating systems, designed as a set of system servers on top of a **microkernel** that provides low-level services (e.g., memory management and interprocess communication). In this type of operating system, the microkernel forms a standard base that can support higher level system-specific interfaces. The specific interface that is supported by MOSIX is UNIX. Examples of other microkernel-based operating systems include Amoeba [29], BirliX [20], Chorus [21], and Mach [46].

There are currently only a few distributed operating systems that support process migration. This is due to the difficulties of managing the migration itself, the need to change the operating system kernel architecture to support migration, the need to change the environment of the process (e.g., its dependence on local kernel tables), and the need to provide access to these resources from other sites. Examples of other operating systems that support process migration include Rhodos [49] and Sprite [15, 30]. For further reading about the design of distributed operating systems see [18]. A comprehensive survey of distributed systems is given in [12].

The motivation behind the MOSIX project is to research and develop operating systems for message passing-based (as opposed to shared memory) distributed systems. This research began in 1981, with the development of the original version of MOSIX for a cluster of PDP-11 computers. That version was compatible with UNIX Version 7 [47]. The second, M68000-based system was compatible with UNIX Version 7 with enhancements from BSD 4.1. Three additional versions have been developed for National Semiconductor's VR32, the VAX family, and National Semiconductor's VME532 multiprocessor architecture. These versions are compatible with UNIX System V Release 2 [2]. The development strategy for all these versions was to use as many ready-made hardware and software components as possible. This strategy enabled the development team to concentrate on such issues as the kernel architecture, probabilistic algorithms, performance, and debugging aids without spending too much effort on hardware design or the supporting software outside the operating system kernel.

Chapter 2

Overview of MOSIX

This chapter presents an overview of the MOSIX system. It begins with a description of some of MOSIX's most notable features followed by a description of the architecture of the kernel. The history of the system's development is then laid out, along with the new features of each of the five versions that were developed.

2.1 The Characteristics of MOSIX

The primary characteristics of MOSIX are network transparency, autonomy of individual nodes, support of dynamic configuration, decentralized data and control, support of a distributed file system, load balancing by dynamic process migration, the use of probabilistic algorithms for system management, and scalability. The following is a description of each of these properties.

2.1.1 Transparency of Local and Remote Operations

In MOSIX the network is completely invisible. The interactive user and the application programmer are provided with a virtual machine that "looks" like a single machine. There is no need and no means for the user to refer to a specific site or to the network itself. When a process issues a system call, it is the responsibility of the kernel on the process' machine to perform network-wide operations to execute the call. Users can access resources on remote machines on the network, interactively access and update remote files, and share devices on remote machines in the same way they would on a single machine. Due to performance considerations, the MOSIX kernels use **remote procedure calls**, called **Scalls**, for internal kernel-to-kernel communication across the network. (See Chapter 7 for further information about Scalls.)

In MOSIX, objects are classified as site-dependent or network-wide. Site-dependent objects (e.g., physical memory segments) are of interest only within the processor on which they reside. Network-wide objects are potentially known beyond one machine boundary, and can be operated on by remote processes. Since the network in MOSIX is invisible and since the system supports process migration, all the objects that are visible to the user are network-wide. These objects include processes, files, directories, pipes, serial lines and terminals.

For a kernel on one machine to operate on a remote object, there must be an unambiguous name for that object. Each (in use) network-wide object has a **universal name** that uniquely identifies that object in the network. These names are invisible to the user and usually are dynamically generated and destroyed by the system. Except processes, all other network-wide objects are static; they do not migrate across machine boundaries and the universal name contains the identity of the machine on which the object resides, as well as other information that permits the retrieval of the object and the validation that a connection was made to that specific object.

2.1.2   Autonomy

Nodes running under MOSIX are capable of operating as independent computers with complete control over their local resources. In order to achieve this autonomy, each node has a complete MOSIX file system and each processor within a node has a copy of the MOSIX kernel.

2.1.3   Decentralized Data and Control

In MOSIX, the system's databases are completely decentralized and the control of all of the internal mechanisms is distributed; that is, there are no master/slave relationships among the nodes, and in particular, there are no server nodes. Each kernel makes all of its control decisions independently and is responsible for all the objects that reside on its machine. Also, no assumption is made about the topology of the network, except that it is connected.

The only exception to the above description is the hardware configuration of the multiprocessor workstation, where one of the processors is responsible for I/O, communication, process numbering, etc. on behalf of all of the workstation's processors. Other than that, the processors are independent.

2.1.4   The MOSIX File System

The MOSIX file system comprises a forest with several disjoint trees. Each tree is a complete UNIX file system, with regular files and devices on the leaves and directory files on the internal vertices. Each user is assigned to one of these trees, and the root of that tree is the root directory of the user. A user always has the same root directory at all login sessions, but different users may have different root directories.

The MOSIX file system uses a super-root (named "/...") as a network-wide root. The super-root is replicated on all the nodes and is supported by the kernel. When addressing a file using an absolute pathname, usually on a tree that differs from the user's root directory, the user prefixes the super-root to the machine name and then adds the usual UNIX path. For example, /.../m2/etc/passwd is the absolute pathname for the password file on Node 2.

In MOSIX, the *inode* (file identifier - see Section 3.2.3) of an open file is held by the site on which the file resides. All remote *open()* calls return a universal pointer to the file. This universal file pointer includes the identity of the machine on which the file resides, and is used for future file accesses. MOSIX does not support file migration. A *garbage collection* facility is used to clean up allocated inode structures should a failure occur on the machine where the process using the inode runs. See Chapter 4 for more information on the MOSIX file system.

2.1.5 Load Balancing

In MOSIX, load balancing is carried out by dynamic process migration [7]. Due to the system architecture, a process running under MOSIX is indifferent to its physical location: a system call that accesses a resource not on the local processor is automatically forwarded by an internal remote procedure call mechanism to the (remote) processor that has this resource. In order to support process migration, the hardware configuration must consist of clusters of homogeneous processors. Process migration is allowed only among processors with the same instruction set, since application tasks may be assigned or migrated arbitrarily among the processors of the cluster. Note that all the other functions of MOSIX could be supported among heterogeneous processors.

In MOSIX, each processor exchanges its local load estimate with a set of randomly selected processors every unit of time (e.g., every second). Load estimates received from other processors are kept in a **load vector** and are "aged" to reflect their decreasing relevance. The algorithms used for load balancing are probabilistic. They are designed to use partial information in providing each processor with the latest, most up-to-date information about the load of other processors. Another goal of these algorithms is to handle processor failures and to respond to dynamic changes in the configuration of the system.

The decision to migrate a process is based on many parameters, including the (past) profile of the process, the amount of local versus remote I/O, the relevant locations of the I/O, the relative load of the sending and receiving processors, the size of the process, etc. After a decision has been made to migrate a process, the chosen processor has the option of refusing (due to local circumstances) to accept the migrating process. Processes that have a history of creating new processes are given migration preference by the algorithm in order to further speed up the even distribution of the load. Processes with a history of specific I/O operations on a set of processors are given priority for migrating to one of those processors.

Several heuristics are used to avoid overmigration. For example, the load balancing algorithm does not migrate a process unless the process has first established **residency** (i.e., it has accumulated a minimum amount of CPU time on the current processor). The actual migration starts by passing the information required to rebuild the page table, followed by the data pages that were changed (i.e., the "dirty pages"), including in-core or swapped out pages. The rest is either mapped to the original file (for demand paging) or defined as containing all zeroes (such as in the case of uninitialized and still unused data).

After a process migrates, it can still be located (by other processes) using a mechanism for locating a migrated process. Chapter 8 gives further information on MOSIX load balancing.

2.1.6   Probabilistic Algorithms

In order to limit the distributed management activities performed by each processor, the internal control algorithms of MOSIX are probabilistic. These algorithms attempt to achieve near-optimal performance at a fraction of the cost required by a centralized algorithm. For example, the load balancing algorithm ensures that each processor has a sufficient, yet limited, amount of information about other processors. This method allows for load balancing interactions between many different pairs of processors, yet at the same time it prevents the flooding of a single processor. Flooding could occur, for example, after a processor joins the network.

Another example of a distributed algorithm is the remnant collection mechanism. Unlike more traditional garbage collection mechanisms, the MOSIX algorithm is designed to remove any remnants of a process that loses its objects or communication links due to a failure in a remote processor. For this reason, all the allocated resources include a timer and a **keep-alive** mechanism that is supported by the kernel. The timer is reset at regular intervals as well as whenever the process and object interact. When the timer expires, the object is removed; it is assumed that the process that uses this object no longer exists.

2.1.7   Dynamic Configuration

MOSIX supports dynamic reconfiguration and node clustering (grouping). Dynamic reconfiguration allows nodes to join or leave the network at any moment without special provisions. There are typically many nodes connected to a MOSIX network. It may sometimes be necessary to partition the network into different groups; for example, by assigning a subset of nodes to a project. The system administrator is provided with tools to reconfigure the network into sub-clusters and to determine the level of intercluster connectivity. There are three possible levels of connectivity: full connection, including process migration (the default connection among nodes in the same cluster); partial connection (remote file access only); or no connection. Another aspect of MOSIX's dynamic configuration is the routine use of remnant (garbage) collection.

2.1.8   Scalability

The issue of scaling is addressed in MOSIX in several ways. First, due to the architectural symmetry, no single machine is used as the provider of any particular service. While this measure alone cannot prevent overloading of any particular processor, it tends to distribute the load of remote operations evenly among the processors. Furthermore, the combination of symmetry and process migration yields a high probability for balanced load distribution and the avoidance of bottlenecks. Another consideration for scaling is the way remote operations are executed. In each remote call in MOSIX, there are at most two processors involved. This means that there is no processor clustering or central decision-making activity that requires more than two processors for any system operation. The third measure is the organization of data and control and the use of partial information, rather than global information, to make system-wide decisions. One example of the use of partial information is the dynamic load balancing facility. Another measure taken for scaling purposes is limiting the overhead of the communication protocols when using the LAN. Scaling considerations in MOSIX are further discussed in Chapter 9.

2.2   The Architecture of the MOSIX Kernel

The basis for the MOSIX kernel is obtained by restructuring the UNIX kernel without changing its interface. The resulting kernel consists of three modules, as shown in Figure 2.1: the site-dependent module, called the **lower kernel**, the site-independent module, called the **upper kernel**, and the communication layer, called the **Linker** [6].

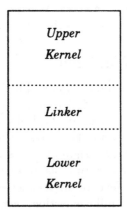

Figure 2.1: MOSIX Kernel Architecture

The lower kernel contains routines that access local resources, such as device drivers for local disks, and routines that access file and process structures. The lower kernel is tightly coupled with the local processor, has complete knowledge of all local objects, and can only access local objects (or objects that have migrated to the processor). The lower kernel does not have any knowledge about processors other than the one on which it executes, and it does not distinguish between requests originating at its local site and requests originating at other processors. The lower kernel module of MOSIX consists of approximately 60% of the original UNIX kernel code.

The upper kernel module executes in a machine-independent mode. It provides the standard UNIX system .call interface to the application level. The upper kernel module does not know the identity of the processor on which it executes, but it does know the locations of all of the objects it handles.

The communication between a lower kernel module and an upper kernel module, which can occur at the same site or between different sites, is performed by the Linker, which provides RPC services.   Since the upper kernel module cannot assume that the execution of a system call is performed on its own (local) site, this organization enforces a clear, well defined interface between the upper kernel and the lower kernel. This also allows for a high degree of information hiding between the two modules, thus further enforcing the use of uniform intermodule mechanisms. Due to performance considerations, the lower kernel, the Linker, and the upper kernel modules are combined in MOSIX into a single module, called the **MOSIX kernel**. Thus from the user's point of view, there is only one system module, which provides all the operating system services.

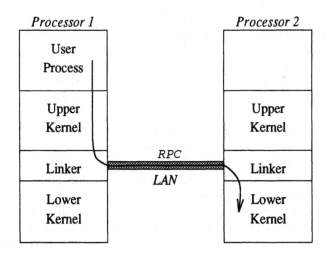

Figure 2.2: A MOSIX Remote Procedure Call

The sequence of events that follows the execution of a remote system call is illustrated in Figure 2.2. When a process executes a system call, the upper kernel module at the process' local site performs the preliminary processing of the arguments. For example, it would call *namei()* to parse a pathname into a universal inode, and check for user permission to access a certain object. Eventually, the upper kernel calls the relevant lower kernel procedure using the Linker's RPC mechanism to complete the service.

In the following example, the remote kernel procedure *proc_name()* is executed with the arguments specified in *param_list*:

$$Sproc\_name(machine\_id, param\_list)$$

The call is passed by the upper kernel module to the (local) Linker, which then decomposes the RPC into the procedure name and the argument list. The Linker examines the first argument of the call to determine where the call needs to be executed (i.e., whether the call is local or remote). If it is a remote call, the Linker encapsulates the call in a message and sends it to the destination processor. If the call can be executed locally, the Linker invokes the local lower kernel procedure directly. On the target machine, an **ambassador process** (a special, kernel mode, server process) executes the appropriate lower kernel procedure for the calling process. The result of the system call is then encapsulated in another message and returned by the ambassador to the calling processor.

Since the information passed between the Linkers is critical, their communication protocol is designed to provide a high degree of reliability. For example, a change of one bit could cause the removal of a file rather than closing it. The communication protocol therefore includes a CRC checksum that is validated by the receiver, a software-initiated acknowledgment message (in addition to the hardware acknowledgment that may be provided by the LAN), message ordering for each pair of processors. These measures can be enhanced to include security and authentication, such as message encryption. More information about the Linkers and the other communication mechanisms of the MOSIX kernel are given in Chapter 7.

In order to support dynamic reconfiguration, each remote access generates a new remote kernel call that returns a special error code if the processor is currently unreachable. The system does not require any special action to incorporate a new node; the first remote call to the dynamically joined node is simply sent by the system in the usual way.

Remote system calls that need to transmit large amounts of data in addition to the result of the RPC use the MOSIX **Funnel** mechanism to copy data from the memory space of one machine to another. The Linker handles the implementation of the Funnels by breaking up large blocks of data into message-size frames at one end, sending the messages over the network, and rebuilding the data in the proper order on the receiving machine. The data is then copied by the Linker of the receiving processor directly to the specified user's address space. For example, for the *read()* system call, the upper kernel module sets up an input Funnel on the local machine before calling the lower kernel part of the *read()* system call. If the system call access a remote file, the Linker routes the call to the target machine, where an ambassador process there calls the appropriate kernel procedure to read the file. As each logical file block is read, the data is placed into the remote end of the Funnel and passed back to the initiating machine's Linker. After the *read()* is completed, the returned status of the system call is encapsulated by the remote Linker and passed back to the calling machine.

The net result of this kernel architecture is that the user's process is completely isolated from the processor on which it is currently running. This isolation requires that (a) all kernel references are made in a machine-independent (universal) mode, (b) a unified naming scheme is used, and (c) the RPC mechanism has good performance. This organization provides the basis for the implementation of a simple process migration mechanism for homogeneous configurations.

2.3   The History of the MOSIX Project

The MOSIX system has been ported to several different machines. This section describes the various porting efforts, the features added with each version, and the motivation behind the ports.

2.3.1   The PDP-11 Version

The original version of MOSIX, then called MOS [6], was developed for a cluster of four PDP-11/23 computers, each with 256KB of memory and a small disk, connected by a 10 Mbit/second ProNET-10 [31] token ring LAN. In MOS, UNIX Version 7 [47] was enhanced to reflect the kernel architecture, as described in the preceding section. Several new modules were written, including the load balancing module, the Linker, the garbage collection facility, and the kernel debugger.

MOS was developed on a PDP-11/45 computer in several iterative stages. Each stage started with a working kernel, enhanced by adding some services. The new kernel was then downloaded to one of the PDP-11/23s for testing and debugging. Upon completion of a stage, the resulting kernel was used to develop the next stage.

The first stage of the project was devoted to the development of an extensive set of software development tools. These tools provided the means for concurrent software development by several system programmers who worked on closely related kernel modules. These tools helped to provide each programmer with a private version of the kernel, while at the same time providing all the programmers with a consistent working version that was not affected by changes made by individuals.

Another tool that was developed was a symbolic kernel debugger. This debugger was used extensively during the development of all versions of MOSIX. The debugger provides a symbolic interface by recognizing routine names, global and local variable names, source line numbers, and source file references. The latest version of the debugger has 25 different functions including:

- The setting and resetting of triggers for kernel activity reports; for example, execution of system calls, system calls that fail, process switching, filenames that are accessed by user processes, communication errors, swapping of processes, etc.

- The raising and lowering of flags to alter the kernel's behavior. For example, there are flags to enable/disable incoming/outgoing remote calls in the communication subsystem, and a flag to use the communication subsystem in loopback mode.

- The altering of process behavior that is controlled by sending signals, waking up processes, or assigning a process to another processor (manual process migration).

- The printing of kernel tables (e.g., the *proc table*) and memory usage.

- The setting and deletion of breakpoints at the beginning and/or end of any kernel C routine or at any source line. When the kernel arrives at a breakpoint, it enters the debugger for further tracing. There is also a debugger command to list all current breakpoints, and a command for listing all routines and variables that match a given string.

- The printing of stack traces by the debugger. The function names and their arguments are printed, with optional printing of the local variables or selected parts of the stack.

- The reading and modifying of kernel data by the debugger, which can access kernel data, given the address or symbolic name. The data can be read or written in several formats, such as bytes, short, long, integer, hexadecimal, and character formats.

The debugger may be entered after a system crash (panic), through an explicit kernel request, upon demand from the console, or at breakpoints. While in the debugger, all interrupts are disabled. Upon exiting, the kernel continues to run exactly where it left off prior to entering the debugger.

2.3.2 The M68000 Version

The M68000 version was developed during the academic year 1983/4. The hardware configuration included a cluster of CADMUS/PCS 9000, M68010-based computers, each with 1MB of main memory, a 70MB disk and a backup tape. Originally, four machines were connected by a ProNET-10 LAN. Three additional machines were added in 1985.

The main enhancements made in this version include modification of the memory management scheme to M68000-based processors, further tuning of the process migration algorithms, development of a replicated file system, and enhancement of the file system. One aspect of the file system enhancement is the use of a special file type that stores the remote machine number in its inode.

When the inode is accessed by the kernel, the inode of the special file is automatically replaced with the inode of the root directory of the remote processor indicated. For example, if the special file */usr/systems/oren* is created as a remote escape to the file system on Node 2, the path */usr/systems/oren/etc/passwd* refers to the password file on Node 2. This change eliminates the need for a special, nonstandard UNIX pathname syntax, and allows the MOSIX file system to have arbitrarily placed links between processors.

2.3.3   The VR32 Version

The VR32 version, called NSMOS [10], was developed in 1987 for a cluster of National Semiconductor NS32332-based computers that were connected by an Ethernet LAN. The main enhancements that were made in NSMOS include compatibility with AT&T UNIX System V Release 2, with virtual demand paging and paging across the network, support of IPC, global administration, enhancements to the process migration mechanisms, and further optimization of file operations. The following is a brief description of some of these enhancements.

Demand Paging

In NSMOS, the existing UNIX System V Release 2 virtual demand paging system was extended to enable remote demand paging for processes that perform the *exec()* system call from a remote file or migrate between processors. As with local files, a process that starts execution from a remote demand paged executable file does not read pages from the file until the pages are referenced. Remote pages are reclaimable either from the local cache or remotely, and modified pages are swapped locally. Remote demand paging proved to be a powerful extension to MOSIX.

Process Migration

One enhancement made to the load balancing scheme is an explicit migration request by a process. This is accomplished by a new system call, *migrate(where, flag)*. The first argument, *where*, is the destination processor number. If it is -1, then the kernel makes the decision about the destination. The second argument, *flag*, specifies the process state in the destination processor (locked, unlocked, or unchanged). After successful completion of the system call, the process resumes its execution on the destination processor. This system call provides application programmers with a tool for implementing parallel algorithms with static assignment of processes to processors.

Global Administration

A system maintenance enhancement allows the system administrator to disconnect a node from the network with tools provided for orderly system shutdown. After evacuation of all of the "foreign" processes to remote nodes, the processor can be disconnected from the network.

The File System

A new function, called the **local processor**, indicated as /.../m0, allows a process to request file creation or access at the node on which it is currently running. This feature is particularly useful for creating temporary files at the local processor (rather than at the default processor, or the processor that has the root directory of the creating process). The concept of the local processor is intended to reduce the overhead associated with remote file operation. The local processor function does not violate the principle of network transparency, since the requesting process is not aware of the identity of the local processor.

2.3.4 The VAX Version

The VAX version of MOSIX was developed in the summer of 1988. It was based on the VAX version of AT&T's UNIX System V Release 2. Due to the similarities between the architectures of the NS32000 and the VAX families, the VAX version was completed in 5 person/weeks. The main enhancements of the VAX version include:

- Enlargement of the configuration to a larger number of processors (up to one thousand)

- Porting of the kernel debugger to the VAX architecture

- Further use of probabilistic algorithms for load balancing and scaling

As of the summer of 1988, the VAX configuration of MOSIX included four VAX 750 computers connected by an Ethernet LAN.

2.3.5 The VME532 Version

The latest version of MOSIX is a multiple node multiprocessor system [9]. Its hardware configuration consists of a cluster of nodes that are connected by ProNET-80 [32], an 80 Mbit/second token ring LAN (see Figure 2.3). Each node consists of 1 to 8 processors that share I/O devices and communication controllers over a VME bus, and supports a large shared memory. The rationale behind this architecture is an improved cost/performance ratio over the single-processor node. The processor is based on National Semiconductor's NS32532, a 25MHz (8 MIPS) microprocessor. Each processor has 4 to 16 MBytes of local memory, a 64 KByte on-board cache, 2 serial lines, a PROM, and an NS32381 floating point unit. The processor board level, called the VME532, is a 2-board set incorporating a full VME bus interface.

Extensions to the VME Version

As with all previous versions, the VME version of MOSIX is symmetrical, where each workstation (node) is an independent computer, with full UNIX capability. This symmetry could be further extended to the processor level if sufficient I/O

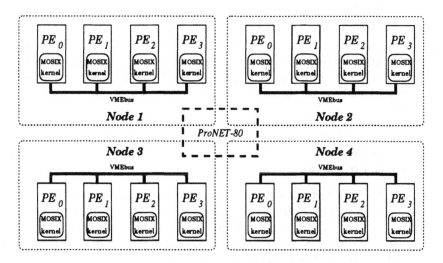

Figure 2.3: A 4-Node, 16-Processor MOSIX Configuration

and communication controllers are available. In order to simplify the organization of the software layer and to use shared I/O and communication devices, a
master/slave organization of the workstation software was preferred. This implies a point of asymmetry, since in each node one processor assumes the role
of a **master,** while the remaining processors are **slaves**; that is, they need the
master processor to perform some of their I/O and communication requests. In
the implementation of this version, a great effort was made to minimize the
above dependency. For example, slave-to-slave (within the same workstation)
communication and load balancing are done without involving the master processor. Also, when data is swapped, DMA transfers are made directly between
the slave processor and the disk, thus reducing the amount of overhead required
from the master processor.

The main enhancements of the VME kernel, also called the "workstation
version," are in the communication interfaces, the Linker level, and in the **boot**
procedure. When the workstation is rebooted, the master processor loads the
kernel from the disk, then copies the kernel to each slave processor, using the
direct addressing mode of the VME532. Also, in the current version a new
process ID (PID) can only be assigned by the master processor.

Other than these, only minor modifications were necessary to enhance the
single machine kernel to the multiprocessor workstation kernel. These modifications resulted from the hardware architecture of the workstation. The main
modifications are:

- Remote swapping that allow slave processors to swap directly to the disk
  in the same workstation. In this case the master processor serves as co-
  ordinator, but the actual addressing and block allocation is done by the

slave. For this purpose, each slave processor has an allocated swap space on the disk.

- A multilevel load balancing scheme between master and slave processors, including master-to-master, master-to-local slave, master-to-remote slave, and slave-to-slave migration (in the same workstation and in different workstations). Each case requires a different set of migration parameters, which are provided by the automatic tuning mechanisms developed for this purpose.

- A two-level Linker for master- and slave-oriented commands, which includes all possible combinations of data transfers and commands between local and remote master and slave processors.

- A TCP/IP package for external communication, including a remote terminal protocol (**telnet**), file transfer (**ftp**), and special services such as remote file copy (**rcp**), remote login (**rlogin**), and remote execution of commands (**rsh**). The application programmer has access to the host-level protocol using a BSD 4.2-like socket software library.

2.4 Summary

MOSIX is a research and development project in distributed operating systems. It explores kernel architectures, internal mechanisms, communication protocols, control algorithms, load balancing, the support of concurrency, and other techniques for the efficient operation of message passing-based multicomputer systems with a large number of processors. This research shows that by using only software mechanisms, it is possible to integrate a cluster of loosely-coupled computers into a virtual single machine computing environment, with performance and global resource allocation that is comparable to a single, large machine with the same combined computing capacity. Unlike tightly-coupled (shared memory) multiprocessing technology, which is based on enhancements at the hardware level and thus cannot be scaled beyond a certain (small) number of processors, the technology presented here can be used to scale the configuration to a large number (e.g., hundreds or even thousands) of processors. This technology also offers a better cost/performance ratio over a single, large machine.

The research also shows that in order to obtain efficient (global) resource allocation, a multicomputer system must include not only software mechanisms for the performance of intermachine operations (e.g., RPC and IPC), but must also have mechanisms for internal monitoring, process migration, and load balancing. Furthermore, when comparing the performance of MOSIX to other multicomputer services, namely NFS and TCP/IP, it is possible to infer that in order for such systems to function efficiently these mechanisms must be part of the operating system kernel.

The unique properties that were first introduced in MOSIX are load balancing by dynamic process migration and the use of probabilistic algorithms to allow scaling the configuration to a large number of computers. Other properties that were developed, but are not unique to MOSIX, include network transparency, support of dynamic configuration, a distributed file system, and the use of decentralized control. In terms of software engineering, MOSIX is a conservative enhancement of UNIX. It preserves the UNIX interface and can be implemented with a relatively small amount of effort. In fact, except for the PDP-11 version, each of the remaining versions were implemented in 6 to 8 person/months.

In spite of different machine and network architectures, the performance of MOSIX consistently shows that different computers can interact efficiently across a network and provide users with a single machine image. The experimental results support the feasibility of constructing multiprocessor workstations in which the internal bus is used as a communication network. Our results also show that several such workstations can be connected by a LAN to provide a high degree of connectivity among users and near-optimal resource utilization.

Chapter 3

The UNIX File System

This chapter presents an overview of the traditional UNIX file system. It emphasizes characteristics of the file system that require modification for a distributed file system, to provide a background for the discussion on distributed file systems that is presented in Chapter 4. For this chapter, we assume that the reader has some familiarity with the UNIX file system.

Disks on UNIX machines are divided into one or more logical partitions. Each of these partitions is a collection of sequential data blocks. Some of these partitions are used as file systems; others may be used for system swapping or paging activity. Each file in a particular file system has at least one full pathname. Pathnames in UNIX are "/"-separated strings of bytes in which every slash-bound component refers to a directory in the file system under which the next component is found. Every full pathname (i.e., a pathname that starts with a "/" character), is interpreted as a path from the unique root of the namespace, through directory nodes, and down to a file leaf. This gives UNIX its hierarchical namespace, discussed in Section 3.1.

Since the MOSIX system is based on UNIX System V Release 2, Section 3.2 reviews the structure of that file system. Where of interest, details of the Berkeley Software Distribution (BSD) file system will be mentioned. The section begins with a brief overview of the UNIX System V Release 2 file system. It continues with a description of the major file system components, and explains their relation to files and directories in the file system. The section concludes with a description of the kernel procedures that manipulate the file system's components.

One of the techniques used by operating systems to reduce the number of I/O operations that need to be performed is to buffer (cache) data. By storing data in main memory, access time to secondary storage systems can be significantly lowered. This approach is used in UNIX to handle file system requests. The organization of the buffer cache, the structure of the individual buffers, and the procedures that direct their interaction with the kernel are described in Section 3.3

The UNIX file system is accessible to user-level processes via a well defined set of system calls. Section 3.4 briefly describes each of these system calls, their implementation, and the kernel data structures they use. The section begins with an overview of two central data structures, the **file table** and the **user file descriptor table**. This is followed by a description of the system calls that manipulate the file system data structures, system calls that handle basic file I/O, and system calls that affect the namespace.

3.1   The Namespace

The traditional UNIX namespace is composed of the root file system tree and any other file system that has been superimposed, or **mounted**, onto some subtree of the namespace. Figure 3.1 shows an example of a UNIX file system namespace.

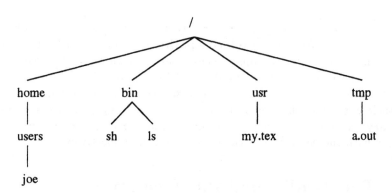

Figure 3.1: A Typical UNIX File System Namespace

The UNIX namespace is dynamic in that, at any directory in the namespace, a file system from some disk partition can be added using the *mount()* system call. Such a directory is called the **mount point** of that file system. After being mounted, the new file system's tree hides the mount point and its descendants from the system's namespace. Mounted file systems can also be dynamically **unmounted** from the namespace via the *umount()* system call. Figure 3.2 shows the namespace resulting from mounting a file system at the */usr* mount point of the file system shown in Figure 3.1. Note that the *my.tex* file has become inaccessible.

Each process in UNIX has an associated **current working directory** and **current root directory**. The current root directory mechanism allows the system administrator to use some subtree of the namespace as his root directory, in effect defining its own namespace to be a subtree of the global namespace. In

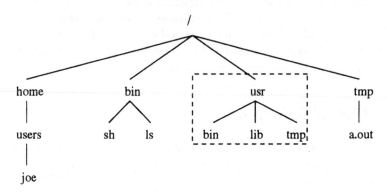

Figure 3.2: Mounting a File System

practice, the current root directory is rarely modified. The current working directory is the point from which **relative pathnames** are searched. The current working directory is often manipulated extensively, so that users' operations can use relative pathnames. On a standard UNIX system, all the users have the same root directory, which points to the real root of the file system, while they have their current working directory initially set during login to their **home directory**. A process can change its current root directory or current working directory with the *chroot()* and *chdir()* system calls respectively.

3.2 The Traditional File System

As previously mentioned, each UNIX file system physically resides on one partition of some disk. Each file system partition contains four basic parts:

- Boot block

- Superblock

- Inode list

- Data blocks

File systems are created by the user-level program **mkfs**. An example of the resulting file system can be seen in Figure 3.3.

The boot block—the first block of the file system—contains code that is used to boot UNIX from the root file system and is therefore not used in non-root file systems. The superblock contains general information about the file system. Following the superblock is the list of all of the inodes allocated to the file system. The remaining part of the disk partition is used for data blocks.

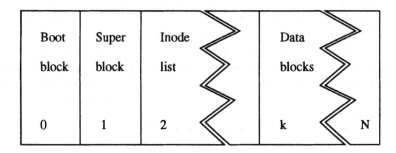

Figure 3.3: Disk File System Structure

When the file system is accessed, copies of the information that resides on disk are brought into main memory. Parts of the file system can therefore exist in two places—on disk and in memory. This results in possible inconsistency between the two copies. The difference between copies of data on disk and in memory, and how inconsistencies are dealt with, are described where relevant in the following sections.

3.2.1   The Boot Block

UNIX traditionally uses the file system's block zero to hold machine-specific code for loading the operating system kernel at boot time. Since the structure of this block is highly implementation-specific, this block requires no further explanation in this context, except for noting that it is empty in most non-root file systems.

3.2.2   The Superblock

The superblock is the main file-system control structure. It includes:

- The size of the file system

- The number of free inodes

- A partial list of free inodes

- The number of free data blocks

- A partial list of free data blocks and a pointer to their rest

- Flags for synchronizing access to the superblock

- Flags that indicate the superblock's current status

Since the superblock is permanently held in memory, it is also used to cache a certain number of free inodes and disk blocks, thereby improving general file system I/O performance. Flags are set to indicate whether the superblock is locked and whether it has been modified since the last disk write. All of these fields are initialized by the **mkfs** program. In the BSD file system [26], duplicate superblocks are stored in different cylinders of the file system's disk partition. This enables the file system check program, **fsck**, to recover file systems with damaged cylinders.

3.2.3   The Inode

The inode is the internal data structure representing a single file, directory, pipe or some other special device. The inode is the focus of all activity in the file system.

On disk, each file in an individual file system is referred to by a **disk inode**. The disk inode contains all of the basic information about a particular file: its type, owner and group identifiers, size in bytes, access permissions, creation time, access time, inode modification time, number of links and indexes of the disk blocks that comprise it. A sample inode is shown in Figure 3.4.

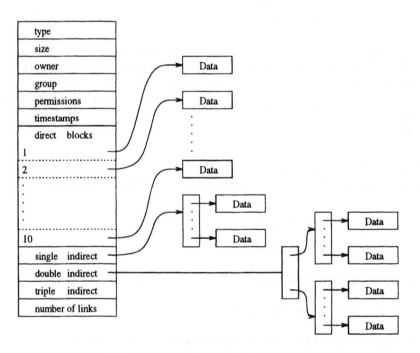

Figure 3.4: The Inode Structure

The number of blocks used to store the inode list depends on the size of the inode and the block size of the file system. The **mkfs** program determines the number of inodes allocated to a particular file system when the file system is created.

Each inode can be uniquely described by the pair <**logical device number, inode number**>. After being accessed, the disk inode is read into a memory-resident inode, which contains several additional fields:

- The status of the inode

- The logical device number of the inode's file system of origin

- The inode's number in its file system

- The inode's reference count (how many processes are currently using the inode)

- Pointers to other memory-resident inodes

The kernel maintains linked lists of the memory-resident inodes for each logical device of the system and a separate list of the free inodes. The memory-resident inode's status reflects the following states:

- Whether or not it has been locked by some process

- If there are processes waiting on the lock

- Whether the inode or data has been updated since the last write to disk

- Whether the inode is a mount point of a file system

System calls that handle inodes use the kernel procedure *iget()* to read a disk inode into a corresponding memory-resident inode structure. *Iget()* searches the list associated with the appropriate logical device for the inode being requested. If the inode is not found, it takes an inode structure from the inode free list, reads the disk inode into the structure, increments the inode's reference count, and then links the inode structure into the proper active-inode hash list. System calls use the kernel procedure *iput()* to release an inode. When closing a file (e.g., with the *close()* system call), *iput()* decrements the reference count of the inode. If the inode or the data has been changed, the relevant information is written to the disk. If both the inode's reference count and its link-count drop to zero, *iput()* also releases all of the file's data blocks, zeroes the file type and returns the inode to the inode free list.

3.2.4 Regular Files and Directories

UNIX imposes no restrictions on the structure of a file; a file is simply a stream of bytes. Regular files and directories are marked as such in the type field of their disk inodes. While directories and regular files are both built in the same way, a directory's data blocks have a fixed format. Each directory entry comprises of a <inode number, filename> pair. A directory may be read as a regular file, but may be written only by the kernel to help maintain file system consistency.

The inode contains a table of pointers to the file's or directory's data blocks. Since the inode is a small, fixed-size structure, it cannot contain pointers to all of a large file's data blocks. Instead, the inode stores several pointers to blocks of pointers to data blocks, as illustrated in Figure 3.4. These blocks are called **indirect blocks**. Traditional UNIX file systems contains singly, double, and triple indirect blocks, which in theory allow for file sizes of over 16 gigabytes. In practice, however, the file size is limited by the number of bits in the inode's offset pointer to 4 gigabytes. Studies have shown that the direct inode pointers suffice for up to 87% of the files in an average UNIX file system [28]. As a result, inodes in BSD do not contain triple indirect pointers. Instead, BSD inodes provide a larger number of direct pointers.

I/O operations on small files are always faster since no indirect blocks need to be accessed. With files that use indirect blocks, one extra read is performed for each level of indirection in order to find the addresses of the data blocks. The actual performance penalty incurred by this scheme is minimized by the fact that the average file size does not require the use of indirect blocks.

3.2.5 The Namei Procedure

The *namei()* kernel procedure maps pathnames, as supplied by user processes, onto inodes. Over a dozen system calls use *namei()*, making it one of the most frequent operations performed by the kernel. In distributed systems, this procedure is often used to also tie remote machines' file systems into a single namespace.

The basic algorithm is quite simple. The inode of the component of the path being searched is referred to as the **working inode**. When passed a full pathname (i.e., a pathname that starts with a "/" character), *namei()* makes the inode of the current root directory the working inode. If the path starts with any other character, the inode of the current working directory becomes the working inode. Then *namei()* reads and compares each directory entry in the working inode's data blocks to the next component of the path. If the next component is found, the current inode takes the value of the matching entry's inode and the algorithm loops. Errors can be returned for several reasons. First, if the next component is not found in the working inode's directory, an error is returned to indicate an invalid path. If the component is found, *namei()* checks for access permission and file type. If the process does not have permission to access any component of the path, an error is returned. When all of the components of the path have been found, the working inode contains the value of the requested inode and is returned.

3.2.6 Inode Manipulations

When creating a new file, a free inode structure is allocated using the procedure *ialloc()*. First, *ialloc()* looks for a free inode in the free-inode list of the superblock of the file system where the file is to be created. If the superblock is locked, it waits until the lock is released. If an inode is not found there, *ialloc()* will search throughout the partition's inode list. Inodes found during this search are used to refill the superblock's cache. If no inodes are found, the superblock is released and an error is returned. When the free inode structure is found, the superblock is unlocked and the procedure *iget()* is used to obtain an inode structure. There is a race condition that requires the inode's status to be checked a second time. If the inode is not free, it is written back to disk, released and another free inode is sought.

When the process has allocated a free inode structure, the inode is initialized to reflect the type of file being created and is immediately written back to disk. This prevents inconsistency between the memory-resident inode and the disk inode. At this point, the number of free inodes in the superblock is decremented and the inode number is returned.

In order to release an inode (e.g., after deleting a file), the *ifree()* procedure is called. It increments the number of free inodes available in the superblock. The type of file is set to zero to indicate a free inode. The (partial) inode list in the superblock is usually also updated.

3.2.7   Disk Block Manipulations

When the **mkfs** program initializes a new file system, all of the free data blocks are arranged into a linked list of blocks, each of which contains pointers to free data blocks and a pointer to the next link in the list. Free data blocks are allocated from the head of the list. The superblock also caches data blocks by keeping the first few entries of this list internally. When the kernel reads the last data block from the superblock cache, the block is treated as a pointer to a list of free blocks and the cache is refilled.

When freeing a data block, the block is added to the superblock cache, if possible, otherwise, the freed block becomes a link block, and the kernel dumps the superblock list into it and writes it to disk. This block then becomes the only entry in the superblock cache.

3.3   UNIX Buffer Caching

Whenever an inode, data or any other block is required, the contents of a disk block must be provided. When the disk is modified, further accesses are necessary to write the new data back to the disk. The rate of data transfer from the disk to main memory is several orders of magnitude slower than the speeds at which the kernel executes operations on data that is already in memory. If the kernel actually executed every requested access, the resulting system response time would be determined directly by the physical speed of the disks.

In an effort to alleviate the problem of data transfer time from the disk and reduce the actual number of disk accesses, the kernel uses a **buffer cache**. The buffer cache contains a pool of internal memory buffers, the **buffer pool**, in which data blocks are stored after being retrieved from the disk. The buffer cache mechanism takes advantage of the tendency of processes to repeatedly access the same areas of a file. For example, many processes spend most of their lifetime executing a relatively small portion of their code, such as a small loop. The buffer cache reduces the number of disk accesses by storing the most recently used data blocks internally. As the size of the buffer cache is increased, the chance of the kernel finding a requested data block in the cache grows and the required number of disk accesses is reduced. Kernel algorithms attempt to maximize the length of time a data block remains in the buffer cache, further reducing the need for disk accesses.

3.3.1 The Structure of a Buffer

A buffer consists of two parts. The first part is the buffer header, containing information that identifies the buffer and its contents. The second part is the actual memory array containing the data from the disk. The basic structure of a buffer header can be seen in Figure 3.5.

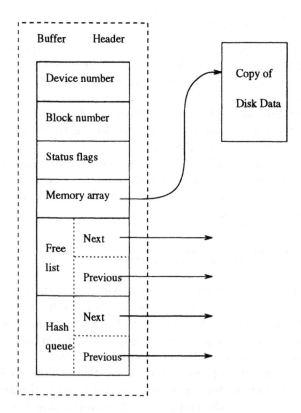

Figure 3.5: A Buffer Header

As shown in Figure 3.5, the buffer header contains a number of fields necessary for the identification and management of the buffer cache. The first two fields contain the **device number** and the **block number**, which uniquely identify the contents of the buffer by specifying the logical file system number and the physical block number of the requested block on disk. The third field contains flags designating the status of the buffer (e.g., the validity of its data, its availability, and system operations that are being or need to be performed). A pointer is used to link the header to the actual memory array. The memory array data corresponds to the data on the logical disk block located in the file system. The size of the memory array must be at least as large as the actual size of the disk block. In order to avoid inconsistency, each logical disk block may reside in at most one buffer at any given time. The buffer header has fields for two sets of pointers that are used to link the headers, forming the buffer cache structures. The first set chains the buffers into the **free list** while the second set is used to link the headers into a device-specific **hash queue**. The free list contains buffers that are not currently being used in an I/O operation. The hash queue organizes buffers so that the data they contain can be found and used. A buffer may be in both the free list and the hash queue. Usually, when all the buffers in the cache have been used at least once, all of the buffers are linked into the hash queue.

3.3.2   Organization of the Buffer Cache

In an attempt to maximize the **hit ratio** (i.e., the proportion of data block requests found in the buffer cache relative to the total number of data block requests), the kernel caches the data blocks in buffers according to the **least recently used** (LRU) algorithm. When a block is read from the disk that is not currently held in the pool, the kernel allocates the buffer with the least recent access to store a copy of the newly read block.

Figure 3.6 shows a typical UNIX System V buffer cache. Double links are shown by bidirectional arrows. Some of the buffers are found on the free list. The free list is a double linked list of buffer headers, containing those buffers that are not currently being used in an I/O operation. The free list links in Figure 3.6 are marked by solid arrows. When the system is booted, all of the buffers are placed on the free list. From this stage onward, whenever the kernel requests a buffer for a data block that is not currently in the buffer pool, the first buffer on the free list is allocated for that purpose. When the kernel has completed using a particular disk-block, it frees the buffer, appending it to the end of the free list. In this manner the kernel ensures that the free list holds the buffers sorted by their last usage times, with those least recently used positioned closer to the head of the free list.

The kernel searches through the buffer headers in an attempt to retrieve the requested data from the buffer cache, thereby saving the cost of a disk access. Although the free list is a convenient structure for ordering the buffers according to the criteria of the LRU algorithm, the free list does not accommodate the necessary operation of specific data buffer retrieval. The hash queue structure

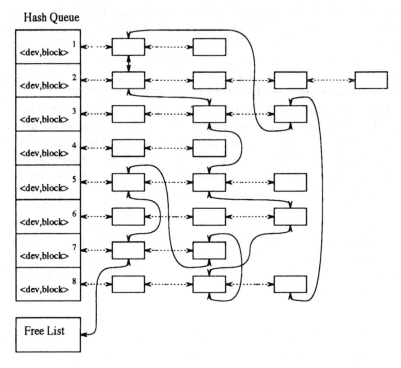

Figure 3.6: Organization of the Buffer Cache

enables the kernel to access buffer headers much more quickly. The headers are mapped onto separate queues by applying a hash function to their device and block numbers. The hash function is selected to be as simple as possible while enabling a uniform distribution of the headers among the queues. The queue itself consists of a double linked list, similar to that of the free list. These links are marked by dotted lines in Figure 3.6. No significance is attached to the position of the buffer on the hash queue.

Buffers can usually be found on either the hash queue, the free list, or both simultaneously. Once the data block has been allocated a buffer, say Buffer A, that buffer is placed on the hash queue for the data block's device. Buffer A's status will be modified to indicate that it is no longer free and it will be removed from the free list. When the kernel frees the buffer, it will be linked to the end of the free list. While on the free list, the data block stored in Buffer A can still be located using the hash function. As buffers are allocated from the free list, Buffer A progresses towards the head of the free list.

3.3.3   Buffer Retrieval

The procedure *namei()*, previously described in Section 3.1, maps a filename onto an inode. The inode holds the addresses for the data blocks of the file, enabling the kernel to retrieve the data blocks using the *getblk()* procedure. When invoked, *getblk()* receives as input arguments the file system number and the block number, and returns a locked buffer that can be used for data. Disk interrupts are disabled in certain sections of the *getblk()* procedure as a consistency safeguard, ensuring that no disk interrupts will be handled during critical sections of the procedure. The hash function is applied and the buffer is linked into the selected hash queue. All further references to a hash queue in this section relate to the target hash queue selected by the hash function. The procedure deals with five possible states that can occur in the buffer cache:

1. The data block is found in a buffer on the hash queue, and the buffer is currently free. In this case, the buffer is marked **busy** using the status flags in the buffer header's field. The buffer is unlinked from the free list and used as is.

2. The data block is found in a buffer on the hash queue, but the buffer is currently locked. The request will sleep until the buffer is released and marked free, after which *getblk()* will be restarted.

3. The data block cannot be found on the hash queue, but a buffer is available from the free list. After searching through the hash queue, the buffer at the head of the free list is unlinked, marked **busy**, removed from the old hash queue, and linked into the hash queue that is appropriate for the new data block.

4. The data block cannot be found on the hash queue, and no buffer is currently available from the free list. In this case, the request will sleep until a buffer becomes available on the free list. Since the kernel cannot guarantee that the specific data block that was requested has not already been allocated a buffer while this request slept, *getblk()* will restart from the hash queue search stage.

5. The data block cannot be found on the hash queue, and the first available buffer on the free list is marked **delayed write**. The delayed write flag indicates that a buffer's contents need to be written to the disk. When buffers thus marked are allocated from the free list, they are unlinked and asynchronously written to the disk. During the period of the asynchronous write, the kernel will continue to process the request, searching for the next available buffer on the free list. When the write completes, the buffer is relinked to the head of the free list and the delayed write flag is cleared.

When allocated to a process, a buffer is marked **busy** and cannot be accessed by other processes. Once a process finish using a buffer, *brelse()* is invoked. *Brelse()*, the complementary routine of *getblk()*, wakes all the processes that wait either for the specific buffer (if any) or just for any free buffer. The buffer flags are set to show that it is free and unlocked and it is linked to the end of the free list. As in the *getblk()* routine, critical sections of *brelse()* are protected from disk interrupts.

Even though it is theoretically possible for a specific process to wait indefinitely as a result of the race conditions that ensue after processes are waked up by *brelse()*, the large number of buffers typically configured in a system precludes the practical possibility of such indefinite starvation.

3.3.4 Data Block Transfer

The buffer cache reduces the number of actual disk accesses and thus increases system response time. Yet eventually some requests will have to access the disk directly to retrieve a disk block that cannot be found in the cache. When the kernel receives a request for a data block that cannot be found in the buffer cache, it passes the request on to the disk driver while the requesting process sleeps until the contents of the block are read from the disk. The disk driver interfaces with the actual disk controller hardware that is responsible for the physical transmission of the data from the disk surface. The data is stored in the buffer that was allocated by *getblk()*. Once the data block arrives, the disk controller initiates an interrupt that result in waking the sleeping process, now free to continue its execution.

The **block read ahead** algorithm, implemented by the kernel procedure *breada()*, attempts to anticipate the kernel's upcoming data block requests. When the kernel receives a request for a data block, it performs a secondary check to ascertain the presence of the next data block in the buffer cache. If the next block is not present, a buffer is allocated on its behalf, after which an asynchronous request is passed along to the disk controller for the next block. The requesting process can continue its execution while the next data block is brought in by the disk-controller. Upon the data block's arrival, the disk-drive will invoke *brelse()* to release the buffer after linking it to the end of the free list. This will enable the buffer to be found through the hash queue, or through the free list, in accordance to the system's demands on the buffer cache.

The kernel algorithm for writing data blocks to the disk allows for three different types of write requests:

Synchronous — The process that originated the request sleeps until after the write request completes and the buffer has been released by *brelse()*.

Asynchronous — Write requests are treated immediately by the kernel, but the requesting process does not sleep pending the output request's completion.

Delayed — In order to minimize the number of write requests that are actually performed, the buffer header is marked **delayed write**, it is linked to the end of the free list, and its lock is released. When accessed by *getblk()* via the hash queue, the buffer is allocated to the requesting process with the delayed write flag unchanged. If accessed via the free list, the request is treated as described in Section 3.3.3 of this chapter.

Since data block transfer to and from the disk can be performed asynchronously, *brelse()* must be capable of being invoked by disk interrupts. To maintain the consistency of the buffer cache's data structures, *brelse()* guards manipulations of these structures by using critical sections.

3.4   UNIX File System Calls

As previously mentioned, user-level processes access the file system via system calls. The file-system calls can be divided into four groups based on the structures that are accessed or manipulated by each call, shown in Table 3.1.

System Call Groups	System Calls
Data Structures	*open()* *creat()* *close()* *dup()* *fcntl()* *access()* *pipe()*
Inodes	*chmod()* *chown()* *stat()* *fstat()*
Input/Output	*read()* *write()* *sync()* *lseek()*
Namespace	*chdir()* *chroot()* *mount()* *umount()* *mknod()* *link()* *unlink()*

Table 3.1: File System Calls

The first group consist of system calls that manipulate kernel data structures. The kernel contains the central **file table** data structure and a per-process

user file descriptor table, with pointers to the above file-table. The system calls that manipulate these structures are *open()*, *create()*, *close()*, *dup()*, *fcntl()*, *access()* and *pipe()*. The second group consist of system calls that manipulate inode properties: *chmod()*, *chown()*, *stat()*, and *fstat()*. The third group consists of system calls that handle the basic file I/O and are the most frequently used system calls in UNIX. These system calls are *read()*, *write()*, *lseek()* and *sync()*. Accordingly, the calls in this group are described in detail. The last group of system calls is composed of system calls that manipulate the namespace: *chdir()*, *chroot()*, *mount()*, *umount()*, *mknod()*, *link()*, and *unlink()*.

3.4.1 File System Data Structures

Each process has an associated **user file descriptor table**. In UNIX, all access to an open file is done through a **file descriptor**, which is a simple index into this structure. Each entry points to an entry in the **kernel file table**. This kernel structure which is allocated per *open()*, *create()* or *pipe* system calls, consists of an inode pointer, offset, permissions and a reference count. This two-layered approach allows several processes to read or write a file synchronously. The *open()* system call receives the following arguments: the pathname to the file to be opened or created, flags indicating the access mode (e.g., read, write, or append), and access permissions used when creating a new file. The *create()* system call receives only the filename and the permissions; the access mode is assumed to be "write" since the file is to be created. Both system calls allocate a kernel file table entry and request that the file's inode be read into memory if it is not already present.

The *close()* system call deallocates the file descriptor's entry in the user file descriptor table and decrements the reference count in the kernel file table. If the reference count reaches zero, the entry in the kernel table is also deallocated and the file's inode is freed. With an understanding of the above, the mechanisms of the other system calls that manipulate these kernel data structures are quite simple. The *dup()* system call receives a file descriptor as an argument. *Dup()* returns the lowest numbered free entry in the user file descriptor table after setting it to point to the given entry in the kernel file descriptor table. This system call allows user processes to redirect I/O operations from one file descriptor to any other file descriptor. This feature is used extensively by **sh**, **csh**, etc. The *fcntl()* system call receives as arguments a file-descriptor, a function code and an optional extra argument, depending on the function code. For example, the **F_DUPFD** function-code duplicates a user-file-descriptor and returns the new descriptor to the file. The new file descriptor number will be the lowest free descriptor at, or above the file descriptor number supplied as the extra argument.

The last call which allocate two file descriptors for interprocess communication is *pipe()*. Its argument is a pointer to an array of two file descriptors. After a successful call to *pipe()*, a free inode from the system's **pipedev** file system and two file-table entries, both pointing to that same inode, are allocated. One of the file-table entries is opened for reading from the inode; the other is opened for writing to it. The inode itself is marked as a pipe inode and all of its data blocks are allocated as for a normal file. After opening both file descriptors, storing them in the array, and marking the inode accordingly, the system call returns. In accordance with the procedure for closing a normal file, if the reference count drops to zero, *close()* wakes up any processes sleeping on a read from the pipe inode and they return with zero bytes read. If, during the life of the pipe, a process attempts to write into the pipe at a time when no processes hold it open for reading, an error signal is generated.

3.4.2   Inode Manipulating System Calls

The second set of system calls consists of the calls that manipulate one of the fields of the inode. The *chown()* system call's arguments are the path to the file, a user identifier, and a group identifier. After using the *namei()* procedure to translate the pathname into an inode, the value of the inode's owner and group identifiers are changed to those of the arguments of the call and the inode is released. Similarly, the *chmod()* system call receives as arguments the pathname and desired mode and updates the mode field of the inode.

Two other system calls, *stat()* and *fstat()* access the inode directly. *Stat()* receives as arguments a pathname and a buffer, while *fstat()* receives as arguments a file descriptor and a buffer. The fields of the structure pointed to by the buffer argument are filled with the values of the inode's fields. *Stat()* uses *namei()* to translate the pathname into an inode; *fstat()* accesses the inode directly through the file descriptor.

3.4.3   I/O System Calls

Four basic system calls perform all of the I/O in UNIX: *read()*, *write()*, *lseek()* and *sync()*. *lseek()* simply adjusts the value of the file offset held in the kernel file table to a given value relative either to the beginning of the file, the current position or the end of the file. Since only kernel data structures are accessed, the *lseek()* system call is one of the faster system calls. The *sync()* system call updates the contents of all the modified blocks in the buffer cache onto the physical disk.

The *read()* system call is used to read a specified number of bytes from a given file descriptor into the user's buffer. *Read()* first checks the permission field of the file descriptor's kernel file table entry and stores both the amount argument and the file's current offset. The corresponding inode is then locked for the duration of the system call.

For each block of the file that must be read to fulfill a read request, the following steps must be taken:

- Call the *bmap()* procedure to compute the disk block that needs to be read

- Compute the offset within that block and how many bytes need to be read

- Use the appropriate procedure (either *bread()* or *breada()*, depending whether the next logical block is already known without needing to read new indirect blocks first) to read a block of data from the disk into the kernel buffer

- Copy the data into the user's buffer

After the requested data has been read, the inode is released and the file offset in the file descriptor table is adjusted accordingly. The system call returns the number of bytes actually read.

The *write()* system call first verifies the validity and write-permission of the file-descriptor, then it loops, in a similar way as *read()*, until all the user's data is written to the file. If the file grows, new blocks are allocated as required for the new data and indirect blocks that contain pointers to the new data blocks.

3.4.4 Namespace Manipulating System Calls

The remaining system calls modify the namespace of the system. Besides the *open()* and *create()* system calls mentioned previously, special files are created by *mknod()*. Each physical device in a UNIX system has a **major device number** and a **minor device number**, which indicate the type of device and the specific unit of a certain device type. These are supplied as arguments to *mknod()* along with flags indicating access permissions. With the exception of **named pipes**, only the superuser is allowed to create special files.

The system call *link()* receives two pathnames as its arguments. The call is used to make the first pathname argument accessible via the second pathname argument. *Link()* adds a second directory entry of the form **<inode, new name>**, where *inode* is the inode of the existing file. Since directory entries always point to an inode in the same file system, the created link cannot span different file systems (this can be done, however, with BSD's "soft" links).

In UNIX System V Release 2 and other early versions of UNIX, directories are created by a user-level routine that calls *mknod()* and *link()*, thus creating a directory entry and linking it into the file system. One call to *link()* is used to create a second name (".") within the new directory for the directory itself. A second call to *link()* adds a directory entry ("..") pointing to the parent of the newly created directory. In BSD, creating directories is handled by a separate *mkdir()* system call.

As mentioned in Section 3.1, the *mount()* and *umount()* system calls are used to respectively incorporate and remove entire file systems from the namespace. After verifying that the call was made by the superuser, both system calls retrieve the inode of the special file. At this point, *mount()* ensures that the file system has not been previously mounted (that is, that the reference count is exactly 1), and then uses the procedure *namei()* to fetch the inode of the directory that is to be the file system's mount point. If all the initial checks succeed, an empty slot in the kernel's **mount table** and an empty file buffer are allocated. The superblock of the file system is read from disk and is copied into the free buffer.

After various fields in the superblock are initialized, the major and minor device numbers of the special file are listed in an empty slot of the mount table, along with a pointer to the buffer, a pointer to the root inode of the file system's "/" directory, and a pointer to the mount point of the file system.

Umount() continues by fetching the mounted directory's inode from the mount table and locating the device. It verifies that no process is using **any** inode on the device and for **any** purpose (in which case, unmounting is refused and an error is returned) and writes the buffer cache to disk. At this point, the root inode of the device is released and all of the device's inodes are flushed to disk. If any of the above operations fail, the system call returns with an appropriate error status.

The *chdir()* and *chroot()* system calls differ from the previous calls, because they affect only the calling process and possibly also its descendants. Both calls receive a directory-pathname. *Namei()* is called to locate the inode, which is then checked to actually be a directory and that it is accessible by the calling user. If so, that directory becomes the next current (*chdir*) or root (*chroot*) directory for subsequent calls to *namei()* by this process and its descendants. Note that *chroot()* may only be called by the superuser.

3.5 Summary

This chapter introduced the UNIX file system, kernel structures used when accessing the file system, and the major kernel routines that perform the accesses. A detailed description of the traditional UNIX file system can be found in [3, 23]. The design of the BSD fast file system for UNIX is described in [26]. A study of high performance file system design is presented in [43]. [3] also contains a detailed description of the kernel structures that serve the file system.

Each UNIX machine has a namespace that is dynamically determined by the file systems that are currently mounted on the root file system. Each file system has four major components: the boot block, the superblock, the inode list, and data blocks. Each component stores a different level of information. The inode holds data relevant to specific files or directories. The data blocks themselves store information relevant to specific files. Individual files are accessed through their inodes. Each time an inode is either allocated or freed, the data in the superblock is adjusted accordingly, retaining consistency with the status of the inodes on the disk.

The kernel attempts to reduce the number of disk accesses by caching data buffers in the buffer cache. The buffer cache is composed of a buffer pool, a hash table, and a free list. Before accessing a data block on the disk, the kernel attempts to locate the data block in the buffer cache. Once modified, data blocks may be written to the disk synchronously, asynchronously, or marked as delayed write.

Chapter 4

Distributed UNIX File Systems

In the past few years, distributed file systems have become a standard feature of various versions of UNIX; for example, SUN Microsystems' Network File System (NFS) [48, 36, 45, 35], AT&T's Remote File System (RFS) [34, 4], and the Andrew File System (AFS) [27, 38, 42]. Each of these systems must deal with the following issues: extending the traditional UNIX namespace to encompass some part of a remote site's namespace, error recovery and garbage collection, and the amount of information that should be hidden from the users. This chapter examines these issues and several possible solutions. After presenting several strategies for the design and construction of distributed file systems for UNIX, the chapter gives the details of the MOSIX distributed file system implementation, followed by a detailed description of the MOSIX system calls that are related to the file system.

4.1   Extending the Traditional Namespace

As described in Chapter 3, a traditional UNIX system namespace is the union of its mounted file systems. File systems are added and removed from the namespace via the *mount()* and *umount()* system calls. In a distributed file system, the namespace must be extended to allow access to some part of a remote site's namespace. In the past, a variety of methods have been used to achieve this goal.

The traditional UNIX **uucp** program was one of the earliest attempts to extend the UNIX namespace. **Uucp** provides access to remote files through electronic mail. To copy System A's password file, */etc/passwd*, to the current directory on System B, the user on System B activates the program as follows: **uucp A!/etc/passwd**. In recent versions of **uucp** the user may choose to explicitly route the request through Systems B and C by invoking **uucp B!C!A!/etc/passwd**.

The **uucp** system has several failings:

- The user must have explicit knowledge of the interconnections between various computers to reach systems not registered in the program's database

- Access to remote sites is performed in batch mode through a special subset of commands

- **Uucp** does not incorporate the remote site's namespace smoothly into the traditional UNIX namespace.

Berkeley's 4.2BSD introduced support for immediate access to remote files. As in **uucp**, to access remote files in 4.2BSD, users execute a special set of programs such as **rcp**. The BSD approach, shown in Figure 4.1, uses the *hostname:pathname* syntax to name a remote file.

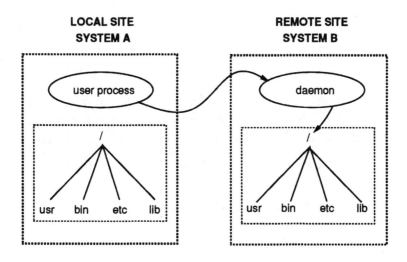

Figure 4.1: The Berkeley Distributed Namespace

To copy the */etc/passwd* file from System B to the current directory at System A, a user types **rcp B:/etc/passwd passwd**. The **rcp** process, activated on the local site, interacts with a daemon process (a special, server process that provides a system-related services) on System B. The daemon process provides the local **rcp** process with the information needed to extend the local namespace so that it includes that of System B. Implemented over local area networks, BSD's utilities provide immediate access to remote files.

4.1.1 The Virtual Super-Root Approach

The Newcastle Connection UNIX United project [13] shows that the escape from the local namespace does not require deviating from UNIX traditional file system semantics. In UNIX United, each site's file system tree becomes a subtree in the global file system. Each system's local namespace become a subtree of the virtual super-root directory. This allows users of UNIX United to view the network as a single tree in which each file has at least one absolute pathname.

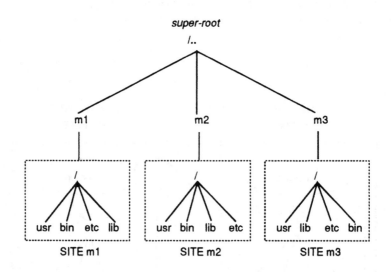

Figure 4.2: The Newcastle Connection Distributed Namespace

In Figure 4.2, the super-directories *m1*, *m2*, and *m3* are virtual entities, supported by the Newcastle Connection software layer. Climbing upwards towards the virtual super-root from any local root directory, "/", is accomplished by prepending the ".." escape to the local root. Thus, /../m1 refers to the root of the site indicated by *m1*.

In this way, the global file system retains the traditional UNIX namespace style. However, the "/.." identifier gains a new and nonstandard meaning other than that found in a conventional UNIX system. In general, this method implies that legal pathnames, those of the super-directories, do not refer to actual directories. The UNIX United project is implemented as a user-level library. By relinking existing programs with the new library, remote files can be accessed transparently over the local network.

Several other systems, including MOSIX, also use the super-root mechanism to extend their traditional namespaces. The MOSIX super-root directory (*"/..."*) is a virtual directory with a non-uniform structure. The root directory of each site in a MOSIX system has an entry in the virtual super-root. For example, the entry for the root directory of Site 17 is */.../m17*.

The virtual nature of the MOSIX super-root leads to anomalies when trying to list the contents of the super-root directory. For example, the command **ls /...** returns an access error code. The contents of a specific site's root directory can be listed by the command **ls /.../m17**.

The use of a virtual super-root, despite its nonstandard behavior, allows MOSIX to dynamically adapt its namespace in response to changes in the number of active sites without any intervention on the part of the system administrator. Since the package is implemented in the kernel, existing programs can access files transparently without becoming aware of the *"/..."* notation. For example, in MOSIX a user types **cp /.../m17/etc/passwd passwd** to copy the password file from Site 17 to the current working directory.

4.1.2   A Special File Approach: Remote Directory Links

The most common method of distributing the UNIX namespace over a local area network uses **remote directory links**. The remote directory link is a special file type that points to some subtree of a remote site's namespace. The system administrator "weaves" together a distributed namespace by manually creating remote directory links for each site. These remote links allow for greater flexibility in arranging the distributed namespace. Each site can have a different set of links, in effect creating a unique namespace for each node in the network.

Remote directory links created at one site define that site's global namespace. Other sites in the network are free to define different global namespaces. As in the current MOSIX implementation, the connections between the remote systems are dynamic and do not require reinitialization in the case of remote node failures.

SUN Microsystems' Network File System (NFS) is a popular distributed file system. In NFS [48] and AT&T's Remote File System (RFS) [34], any remote subdirectory may be linked under any local directory. A special version of the *mount()* system call turns a local directory into a mount point for a remote file system. This scheme introduces a high level of flexibility in the configuration of the file system. Since any point in a mounted subdirectory can become a mount point, "spaghetti" file systems with remote connections looping unpredictably through the network may be created. The failure of a remote site can cause the disappearance of a set of subdirectories.

Both of the above types of remote directory links introduce a new kind of cyclical pathname to the traditional namespace. Special care must be taken to avoid infinite loops when writing and using programs (e.g., when using the standard **find** utility to create a list of every directory in the namespace). The UNIX community's previous experience with BSD's **symbolic links**, which introduced a similar pitfall, mitigates the problem to some degree.

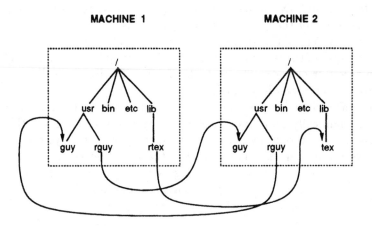

Figure 4.3: The NFS Distributed Namespace

In both methods, maintaining a fully connected network is required in order to provide every file in the system with an absolute, but not necessarily unique, pathname. One additional problem associated with such systems is maintaining UNIX's ".." semantics. For example, in Figure 4.3 a user at Machine 1 might perform the following series of commands:

% cd /usr

% cd rguy

% cd ..

In keeping with the spirit of the traditional UNIX namespace, the user's current working directory should be /usr on Machine 1. This requires the system to store not only the current working directory, but also the path taken in reaching it. NFS retains that information. By failing to provide a remote directory link from Machine 2 back to Machine 1, the system allows a user to change the current working directory irreversibly, not being able to return to machine 1 without supplying an absolute pathname. Some experimental versions of MOSIX also had the above problem and the user would end up in Machine 2. That approach was abandoned in favor of the "..." approach. The current method employed in MOSIX seems preferable in this respect, since the entire set of mount points is automatically available at every node in the system. To some degree, the NFS style of namespace can be emulated in MOSIX by using symbolic links.

4.2 Classifying Distributed File Systems

The variety of distributed file systems has led to a profusion of criteria by which they can be classified. This section presents three major criteria that are useful for comparing distributed file systems.

4.2.1 Site and Operating System Dependencies

Distributed file systems can be classified into **homogeneous** and **heterogeneous** systems. In a homogeneous system, all of the individual machines are identical in both architecture and operating system. A heterogeneous system can run on a variety of architectures or operating systems.

Fully heterogeneous systems, such as NFS, make no restrictions on the type of hardware or operating system. A typical NFS site can provide transparent access to the disks of a DOS-based personal computer's file system, a VAX running VMS, and any number of UNIX systems. NFS supports this type of network by making the following requirements:

- Each system must provide a local implementation of NFS's system calls. The subset of system calls implemented avoid UNIX-specific behavior where possible

- Data must be formatted identically before being transmitted on the network. That means that non-compatible hosts must send each data type in a fixed format with the same number and order of bytes. When receiving a packet, data is translated from the global format into the local system's format.

Clearly, homogeneous distributed file systems are easier to implement than heterogeneous ones. In a general purpose network, the complexity of heterogeneous distributed file systems is offset by the vastly increased accessibility of various sites' file systems.

The MOSIX system is, to a great degree, a homogeneous system. Its basic design philosophy envisions a large number of loosely connected processors, each of which provides binary compatibility for the MOSIX dynamic load balancing mechanism, but the different systems are not required to have identical hardware. The processors may have varying CPU speeds, amounts of physical memory, types of disks, etc. Since file system calls do not rely on binary compatibility, these calls can and have been used experimentally on a heterogeneous network of VAX machines and NS32532 workstations. This allows separate groups of MOSIX machines on the same local area network to share files.

4.2.2 Implementation Levels

The level of the implementation provides another useful criterion for categorizing the various distributed file systems. Systems like the Newcastle Connection [13] are implemented on top of user-level remote procedure calls. The majority of modern implementations, including MOSIX, are done at the kernel level.

User-level implementations are generally slower than kernel implementations. Since user implementations require relinking with new libraries, if not total recompilation of existing programs, the user can choose whether or not to make use of the distributed package. Kernel implementations do not require recompilation of existing programs and are completely transparent to processes that access a remote file. Also, a kernel implementation is usually more efficient because it manages its own network transactions, avoiding the heavy overhead inherent in a layered approach.

4.2.3   Garbage Collection

Another important feature of a distributed file system is the method used to handle **orphaned** system objects; for example, a local file table entry, opened from a remote site that has since crashed. Two basic techniques are used: running **garbage collection** processes or using **stateless protocols**. MOSIX detects an orphaned file table entry by periodically running garbage collection routines. These routines scan kernel structures, such as the file descriptor table, removing objects that have not been accessed over a predetermined period of time. The MOSIX garbage collection algorithm, described in Chapter 9, is implemented by attaching timers to each remote object. The timers are reset whenever the object is accessed. After the specified amount of time has elapsed, the garbage collection mechanism disposes of the object.

Systems like NFS avoid the problem of orphaned objects by using stateless protocols. Stateless protocols guarantee that each invocation of a system call is independent of any other invocation. No resources are held remotely at the end of a call (e.g., an entry in a remote file descriptor table). Each call passes information associated with the request (e.g., the current offset within the file, its user and group numbers, etc.) along with the request itself.

The benefit of a stateless system is that no error recovery or garbage collection is necessary. When a remote server crashes, a user-level process can choose to wait for the server's recovery, after which it continues to access an "open" file as if the crash had never occurred. A disadvantage of stateless systems is that special care must be taken when handling requests from untrustworthy remote systems who might pass the server a read request with forged permissions attached. A further disadvantage of stateless protocols is the waste of network bandwidth caused by the retransmission of associated data with every request.

4.3   MOSIX File System Implementation

The MOSIX file system implementation provides a UNIX System V interface to a user-transparent, distributed file system. In MOSIX, **universal pointers** are pointers that uniquely specify an object in the distributed environment. For example, a **universal inode structure** for the */bin/ls* file on Site 1 contains the site identification number of 1, a pointer to the inode in Site 1's inode table, and the version number of the inode. MOSIX's upper kernel handles only site-independent versions of kernel structures (e.g., universal pointers to inodes or universal pointers to file descriptor entries). Standard kernel data structures, such as the inode table or the file descriptor tables, are maintained by the lower kernel on each site. As a result, purely local actions, such as the maintenance of the UNIX buffer cache, are virtually unchanged from the standard UNIX implementation.

4.3.1   Universal to Local Mapping Routines

Before describing the central file system routines, the set of routines used by the kernel to map universal pointers to site-specific structures must be understood. The two types of universal structures are **universal inode structures** and **universal file structures**. As mentioned previously, universal inode structures contain the site number, a pointer to the file's entry in its local inode table, and a version number. A universal file structure contains the same fields, with a pointer to a file descriptor table entry in place of the inode pointer. By using universal structures, MOSIX circumvents the need to modify the standard file system data structures.

Each type of pointer has a set of utilities that map universal pointers onto local ones and vice versa. The kernel procedure *fp2fnm()* is used to map a local file pointer onto a universal file structure. The conversion process is straightforward: the universal version adds the local site number, the local entry's version number, and its offset in the local file table. The procedure *fnm2fp()*, in addition to performing the reverse mapping, verifies that the version numbers of the universal and the local pointers are identical. This prevents processes from using an open universal file table pointer to a remote file that was opened prior to the remote node's crash and recovery. The procedures *ip2inm()* and *inm2ip()* perform the same mappings for inode pointers.

Two additional remote kernel procedure calls, *Siinc()* and *Sidec()*, are used to update the reference count of an inode at its local site. With these basic procedures, the system calls described in the following section manipulate universal objects.

4.3.2   The MOSIX Buffer Cache

The MOSIX buffer cache is unchanged from that of UNIX System V since all objects local to a certain site (e.g., inodes, file descriptor tables, and the buffer cache itself) are only manipulated by the lower kernel of that site.

The *sync()* system call, which uses the *update()* kernel routine to flush the buffer cache, has only a local version. The semantics of the *sync()* system call has been changed so that only the calling process' home site updates its disks with modified data. An extended system call, *fsync()* (not to be confused with BSD's *fsync()*), can be used to update the data to the disks of particular machines.

---

fsync (filename)

/ Upper Kernel fsync() – on calling process' machine */*

```
{
        map filename to universal inode structure;   /* namei() */
        if (inode is super-root) {
                if (superuser)
                        update all active processors
                                with disks;                    /* Supdate() */
                return;
        }
        update inode's processor;                              /* Supdate() */
}
```

fsyncl (universal inode)

/ Lower Kernel fsyncl() – on inode's machine */*

```
{
        map universal inode onto local;               /* inm2ip() */
        decrement the inode's refrence count
                and unlock the inode;                 /* iput() */
        sync all local file systems to disk;          /* update() */
}
```

Procedure 4.1: Fsync System Call

Fsync(), described in Procedure 4.1, takes a pathname as an argument. When a superuser process passes *fsync()* the MOSIX super-root, all of the systems in the network flush their buffer caches to disk.

When passed any other valid pathname, only the buffer cache of the file's host site is flushed. User applications generally call *sync()* in order to ensure that their buffers will be scheduled to be written to disk. In MOSIX, a user process attains this by calling *fsync()* once for each site that hosts one of the process' files that is opened for writing.

4.3.3   *Namei()* and the MOSIX Super-Root

The MOSIX style of virtual super-root provides one important advantage over the remote directory approach—a dynamic distributed namespace. The kernel attempts to contact the specified processor with each request. As sites join and leave the network, the namespace grows and shrinks accordingly. This eliminates the need for having the system administrator configure and update the mapping tables.

In MOSIX, *namei()* maps pathnames onto universal inode structures. Only upper kernel procedures call *namei()*. The MOSIX version of *namei()*, shown in Procedure 4.2, receives a *pathname*, a *mode*, and an *option* flag as its arguments. The pathname argument specifies the file using either an absolute or a relative path. The mode specifies which function returns characters from the pathname, either the *uchar()* procedure, which fetches a character from the user's space, or the *schar()* procedure, which fetches a character from the system's space. The option argument specifies whether to return the universal inode structure of the file itself or its parent directory.

Namei() begins by determining the initial point from which to start the search. The search may be started from either the process' current working directory or its current root directory. After checking the validity of the options defined for the given pathname, the usage count of the base directory is incremented using the *Siinc()* routine. If a communication error occurred in the *Siinc()* procedure, The *check_failure()* routine is invoked to clear any other file or directory references which the process may hold on the failed machine and send it a special, SIGLOST, signal.

In the main loop of the procedure, each section of the path is searched for in the directory pointed to by the previous section of the path. First, the component of the pathname currently being searched for is stored. Once again, *namei()* checks to see if errors have arisen. If so, the usage count on the directory being searched is decremented with *Sidec()* and the procedure exits. If the current directory being searched is the root of a site and the component is "..", the component is ignored and the search restarts with the next segment of the pathname. If the end of the pathname is detected while searching for the parent directory, *namei()* returns a pointer to the parent and exits. In this case, if the parent directory is the super-root, an error is returned since MOSIX defines the super-root to be parentless. At this point of the main loop, three possibilities remain. If the directory being searched is the super-root, the *dotdotdot()* procedure is called to *read* the super-root directory, returning a pointer which can only be either the super-root itself or the root of some site's namespace. If the directory being searched is a root of a site's namespace **and** the remaining path is of the form "/...", the current search directory is set to the super-root and the search restarts from the top of the loop. The third possibility is a normal pathname segment. In MOSIX, the search for a regular segment of the pathname is done by the remote kernel procedure *climb()*. A description of *climb()* can be found in Procedure 4.3.

Sclimb() receives a universal inode structure to the directory being searched and the component of the pathname currently being searched for. Like all remote kernel procedure calls, this procedure is always executed by an ambassador process on the host site of the inode being searched. It maps the universal inode of the directory onto a locked local inode pointer. Using the standard UNIX

universal inode namei (pathname, mode, option)

/ Upper Kernel namei() – pathname to universal inode routine */*

```
{
    if (illegal path)
        return error;
    if (absolute pathname)
        base = process' current root directory;
    else
        base = process' current working directory;
    if (pathname is "/" and looking for parent directory)
        return error;
    if (super-root not base)
        increment usage count for base's inode;/* Siinc() */
    if (communication error occured at Siinc())
        recover from communication error with
            current/root directory;;          /* check_failure() */
    while (pathname not empty) {
        store next pathname component;
        if (error) {
            decrement base's inode usage count; /* Sidec() */
            return error;
        }
        if (component is ".." and current search directory is root)
            continue;                         /* next component */
        if (end of pathname and looking for parent directory)
            if (search directory is super-root)
                return error;                 /* permissions error */
            else
                return inode of current search directory;
        if (current search directory is super-root)
            parse super-root component;       /* dotdotdot() */
        else if (path is "/..." and current search directory is a root)
            set current search directory to super-root;
        else                                  /* Regular case - use Sclimb() */
            get inode for the current filename component;
    }
}
```

Procedure 4.2: Namei

---

universal inode climb (universal directory inode,
                      filename single component string)

/* Lower Kernel namei() – on inode's machine */

```
{
        map the universal inode structure              /* inm2ip() */
                onto a locked local inode pointer;
        map the component name via the inode directory /* scand() */
                onto an inode number;
        if (inode is a file system root and
                inode's parent directory ".." is needed) {
                search the mount table for the current inode device;
                get inode of the directory that the file system is mounted on;
                loop back to the beginning of the search;
        }
        release current inode;                         /* iput() */
        get inode of the found entry;                  /* iget() */
        unlock the obtained inode;                     /* prele() */
        map inode name onto a universal inode structure; /* ip2inm() */
        return the new universal inode structure;
}
```

Procedure 4.3: Lower Kernel Climb

System V Release 2 *scandir()* procedure, the directory is searched for the requested portion of the pathname. If the search is successful, *scandir()* returns the number of the component's inode. If the inode is the root of a mounted file system, the search is continued using its mount point. Once found, the directory inode is released and the component's inode retrieved. The inode lock is released and the local inode pointer is mapped onto a universal inode structure and returned.

After the call to *Sclimb()* completes, *namei()* verifies that no error occurred. If the end of the pathname has not been parsed, *namei()* continues its search from the top of the loop. The kernel procedure *dotdotdot()*, shown in Procedure 4.4, parse the MOSIX root directory and returns either MOSIX super-root (again) or a machine's root directory, such as */.../m17*.

The MOSIX *namei()* scheme requires multiple remote kernel procedure calls, one for each remote section of the pathname. This process facilitates precise fault detection in case of a remote site failure. One possible way to avoid the overhead associated with remote kernel procedure calls is to place the entire search loop in the lower kernel portion (the *climb()* procedure). This saves on the number

---

universal inode dotdotdot (pathname component)

/* Upper Kernel dotdotdot() – map super-root to universal inode */

```
{
        if (component is ".", ".." or "...")
                return super-root universal structure;
        if (component is of form mN) {              /* N is decimal */
                if (1 ≤ N ≤ maximum number of processors)
                        return universal structure of root directory of machine N;
                else if ( N == 0 )
                        return universal structure of root directory
                                of current machine;
        }
        return error;
}
```

Procedure 4.4: DotDotDot

of remote procedure calls required to parse a pathname by allowing *namei()* to pass the remaining fraction of the pathname to the remote site for parsing. The same remote site would process the segment of the pathname that is part of its local namespace. If it encountered the super-root, the parsing would be passed on, with each site receiving an ever smaller pathname. Finally, a universal inode structure would be returned to the calling process. MOSIX prefers to pay the performance penalty of mutiple remote calls in order to maintain tight control during the parsing of the pathname.

4.4 MOSIX File System Calls

This section describes the MOSIX system calls relating to the file system. It is intended for readers who have some familiarity with the UNIX file system calls.

As in standard UNIX, the MOSIX system calls related to the file system can be divided into four categories: calls that manipulate file system kernel data structures, calls that manipulate inodes, calls that perform basic input and output operations, and calls that manipulate the system namespace (see Table 3.1). In MOSIX these groups of system calls can be further divided into three groups: system calls with no dedicated remote implementation, system calls with Scall (see Section 2.1.1) versions that use the Funnel mechanism (see Section 2.2), and system calls with Scall versions that do not use the Funnel mechanism.

4.4.1   File System Data Structures

As mentioned in Chapter 3, the following system calls manipulate the file system data structures: *open()*, *creat()*, *close()*, *dup()*, *fcntl()*, *access()*, and *pipe()*. In MOSIX, all objects local to a certain site, including the file system data structures, reside on that host site. If the file resides physically on a non-local site, the MOSIX Linker transparently routes the lower portion of the system call to the remote file's site.

```
copen (filename, mode, arg)

/* Upper Kernel copen() - common code for open() and creat() */

{
        if (neither READ mode or WRITE mode set)
                return error;
        get new/existing universal inode for file;              /* namei() */
        allocate a new user file descriptor entry;              /* ufalloc() */
        if (error) {
                decrement inode count;                          /* Sidec() */
                return error;
        }
        call copenl for file descriptor;                        /* Scall */
        if (error)
                return error;
        if (opening a remote terminal device) {
                special handling;
        }
        store returned values in user area;
}
```

Procedure 4.5: Upper Kernel Copen

The *open()* and *create()* system calls demonstrate the simplicity of the MOSIX implementation. As in standard UNIX, a single kernel routine is used by both system calls (except for trivial front-end routines which adjust the arguments). *Copen()*, shown in Procedure 4.5, first verifies a valid *mode* parameter. The *namei()* procedure is then used to retrieve either the file's or its parent directory's universal inode structure. *ufalloc()* is called to allocate a new file descriptor: note that this is a local operation since the user file-descriptor table is attached to the process. If no free file-descriptor was available, the inode's reference count is decremented and the procedure exits.

The lower kernel portion of the *copen()* procedure, *copenl()* (not shown), is invoked via an Scall on the site where the inode physically resides. The *copenl()* procedure returns a structure containing the universal file structure and the device number of the process' controlling terminal. If the device being opened is a "remote terminal device" (a special kind of device used for the "remote" program, which should not be confused with opening a terminal's serial line on a remote machine), special handling is required. If *copenl()* succeeds, the new entry in the user file descriptor is assigned the returned universal file structure. *copenl()* receives as its arguments relevant information about the requesting process, the specific request, and the universal pointer to either the inode being opened or its parent directory.

---

dup (file descriptor)

/* *Upper Kernel dup() – on calling process' machine* */

```
{
      if (file descriptor is invalid)
            return error;
      allocate new user file descriptor;              /* ufalloc() */
      call dup2(file descriptor, new file descriptor);
}
```

dup2 (from, to)

/* *Upper Kernel dup2() – duplicate file descriptor* */

```
{
      increment reference count for file table entry;      /* Sfinc() */
      if (error) {
            check and recover if it is
                  a communication error;                /* check_failure() */
            return;
      }
      copy file pointer to the new entry;
}
```

Procedure 4.6: Dup System Call

The implementation of the *dup()* system call (shown in Procedure 4.6) is straightforward because *dup()* manipulates only the user file-descriptor table in the *u area*; the system call does not require a dedicated lower kernel portion. After checking the validity of the file descriptor being duplicated, a local procedure call is made to the procedure *ufalloc()*. This kernel procedure allocates a new slot in the process' file descriptor table. Next, the local *dup2()* procedure is invoked. Its calling arguments are the numbers of the original file descriptor and the new file descriptor. It uses the *Sfinc()* remote kernel call to increment the reference count of the file's entry on its host site. if successful, *dup2()* copies the original universal file structure into the newly allocated slot and returns.

The *fcntl()* system call first validates the file-descriptor argument, then splits according to its function code. The **F_GETFD** and **F_SETFD** functions only access local, per-process, flags and do not issue any Scalls. **F_DUPFD** acts very similar to *dup()* and calls *dup2()*. **F_GETFL** and **F_SETFL** issue an Scall to *fcntll()* in order to access the file-table entry. **F_GETLK**, **F_SETLK** and **F_SETLKW** issue an Scall to access the lower-kernel file-locking subsystem, which is not described here.

The *access()* system call (with a kernel version, called *saccess()*), shown in Procedure 4.7, is used to check if the process that invoked the system call is allowed to access a given file. The real user and group identifiers of the invoking process and the type of access requested are compared to the permissions field of the file's inode. The rest of the system calls (e.g., *open()* and *create()*) use the process' effective identifiers when checking for access permission or modify permission. This allows *setuid* processes to ascertain whether or not the user executing them would be granted access to a certain file.

Saccess() receives the filename and the access mode as arguments. The call starts by storing the effective user and group identifiers of the calling process. These fields of the *u area* are then set to the real user and group identifiers. At this point, *saccess()* calls the *namei()* procedure to map the filename onto a universal inode structure. If an error is detected, the call simply returns. If the universal inode structure is that of the super-root, the only valid request is "execute" permission. In this case, no Scall is required since the super-root is a virtual inode. In the general case, the upper level system call executes a remote kernel call, *accessl()*. Finally, *saccess()* restores the saved user and group identifiers, and returns.

The lower level procedure is executed on the site of the inode. As usual, the first action taken is the mapping of the universal inode structure to a local inode pointer. The procedure calls the lower kernel procedure *access()*, an internal kernel procedure used to check a specifically requested permission against the given inode's permission field.

The *pipe()* system call (see Procedure 4.8) creates a pipe, a standard UNIX interprocess communication (IPC) mechanism, using file system data structures. The *pipe()* system call receives an array of two integers as its argument. The first cell of the array will contain the file descriptor used for reading from the pipe; the second cell will contain the file descriptor used for writing. The *ufalloc()* procedure, called twice, is used to allocate two new file descriptors in the process' file descriptor table. If the allocation succeeds, the lower kernel portion of the system call, *pipel()*, is called on the master processor of the process' current workstation. If for some reason the local master cannot set up a new pipe, then the pipe is set up on a randomly selected master processor. Upon the

```
    access (filename, mode)

    /* Upper Kernel access() – on calling process' machine */

    {
        save effective user and group ids;
        set effective user and group ids to the real user and group id;
        map filename to universal inode;                        /* namei(); */
        if (no error in namei) {
            if (super-root) {
                if (mode is not execute)
                    set error;
            } else
                Saccessl to invoke lower portion of access;    /* Scall */
        }
        restore effective user and group ids;
        return;
    }

    accessl (universal inode, mode)

    /* Lower Kernel accessl() – on inode's machine */

    {
        map universal inode onto local inode pointer;          /* inm2ip() */
        if (read access requested)
            check for read access;                             /* access() */
        if (write access requested)
            check for write access;                            /* access() */
        if (execute access requested)
            check for execute access;                          /* access() */
        release inode;                                         /* iput() */
    }
```

Procedure 4.7: Access System Call

pipe (array of 2 file descriptors)

/* Upper Kernel pipe() – on calling process' machine */

```
{
        if (allocation of two file descriptors failed)        /* ufalloc() */
                return;
        Spipel to invoke lower portion of pipe;               /* Scall */
        while (failed and number of tries not exceeded) {
                invoke Spipel() on a randomly selected
                        remote machine;                        /* Scall */
        }
        if (failed)
                return;
        set argument array entries to those of created pipe;
        return ;
}
```

struct of two file descriptors pipel()

/* Lower Kernel pipel() – invoked on specified machine */

```
{
        allocate new pipe inode on pipe file system device;
        allocate file table entries for reading and writing;
        set inode link count to 2;
        release inode lock;                                    /* prele() */
        map file pointers to universal file structures;        /* fp2fnm() */
        return  the two universal file structures;
}
```

Procedure 4.8: Pipe System Call

successful completion of *pipel()*, the newly allocated file descriptors are copied into the appropriate cells of the argument array, after which the *pipe()* system call returns.

The lower portion of pipe, *pipel()*, allocates a new pipe inode on the pipe device, a file system which is usually selected when the kernel is compiled. New file table entries for reading and writing are allocated and the inode's link count is set to two. After releasing the inode, the local file pointers are then mapped onto universal file structures and returned.

The last system call in this group is *close()* (see Procedures 4.9 and 4.10). The upper kernel portion of *close()* checks that it was passed an existing and open

```
    close (file descriptor)

    /* Upper Kernel close() - on calling process' machine */

    {
            check that file descriptor exists and is open;
            Sclosef to invoke lower portion of close;          /* Scall */
            if (error while closing)
                    return  bad file-descriptor error;
    }
```

Procedure 4.9: Close System Call

file descriptor before calling its lower kernel portion, *closef()*. Before returning, the *close()* procedure convert all errors to the "bad file descriptor" error (for UNIX compatibility).

The lower kernel *closef()* procedure starts by mapping the universal file structure to a local file pointer. If the file table entry is being used by other processes, the reference count is decremented and the process returns. If not, the routine needs to close the file table entry entirely. The reference count of the entry is set to zero and the entry is added to the free list of file-entries. If the file being closed is a block device, the entry may be freed only if it is not a mounted file system. If it is, the inode is released and the call returns. If the file is any kind of special file, block or character, the procedure takes note of the device-specific close routine for later use. Inodes that are pipes have a special routine, *closep()*, that is used to perform the IPC aspect of closing. In the default case, that of a regular file or directory, the inode count is decremented and the procedure returns.

The rest of the lower kernel procedure handles the case of special files. If the device was not open, the inode is released and the procedure returns. A special flag, **IOPEN**, marks an inode of an open special device to ensure that it is closed only once, when all file-references to the device are cleared. If the current inode doesn't hold this flag, or if the inode is held by another file entry or if this flag can be transferred to another open inode that reference the same special device, no further processing is required. If the file is a block device, the inode is checked once again to ensure that it has not been mounted since the last check. All of the memory resident inodes read from the device are scheduled to be written back to disk and then the device-specific close function is called. In the case of a character device, the preselected device close routine is called. Finally, the inode is released and the routine returns.

```
closef (universal file structure, process id, boot count)

/* Lower Kernel closef() – on universal file structure's machine */

{
    map universal file structure to local file pointer;    /* fnm2fp() */
    if (other processes still using file)
        decrement file reference count and return;
    lock file's inode;                                     /* plock() */
    clean out file table entry and add it to free list;
    switch (inode type) {
        case Character Device:
            func = device close function;
        case Block Device:
            if (device is mounted as disk)
                release inode and return;
            else
                func = device close function;
        case Pipe:
            if (called by process)
                close pipe;                                /* closep() */
        default:
            decrement inode count and return;              /* iput() */
    }
    if (device was not opened or already closed)
        release inode and return;                          /* iput() */
    clear open flag of inode's status field;
    if (any other file entries reference the same device) {
        transfer the open flag to that inode's status field;
        decrement inode count return;                      /* iput() */
    }
    if (block device) {
        if (device is mounted as disk)
            release inode and return;                      /* iput() */
        flush all of the device's blocks;                  /* bflush() */
    }
    call device close function selected previously;
    release inode;                                         /* iput() */
}
```

Procedure 4.10: Lower Kernel Close

4.4.2 Inode Manipulating System Calls

This section describes system calls that manipulate inodes. This group of system calls includes calls that change the values of an inode's fields, such as *chmod()* and *chown()*, and calls that read the inode, such as *stat()* and *fstat()*. Since none of this group moves dynamically sized data like the input/output system calls, the kernel does not need to use Funnels. This results in relatively low overhead for this group of system calls when performed remotely.

The first two system calls described here are *chmod()* and *chown()*. As explained in Chapter 3, *chmod()* and *chown()* change the inode's permission field and owner field. The *chmod()* system call, shown in Procedure 4.11, is passed a *filename* and the new value of the permission field. *Chmod()* begins by using *namei()* to retrieve the inode of the file. If the call to *namei()* succeeds, the upper kernel portion concludes its work by invoking the lower kernel portion of *chmod()*, called *chmodl()*. If the call to *namei()* fails, the procedure returns.

Chmodl() receives the universal inode structure and the new mode. The universal inode structure is mapped onto a local one using *inm2ip()*. After performing some further tests, to prevent breaching the UNIX security policy, the inode's permission field is actually modified. *Chmodl()* concludes by releasing the locked inode with the *iput()* procedure.

The *chown()* procedure call is almost identical to *chmod()*. Its arguments are the file's pathname, the new owner identifier, and the new group identifier. The upper kernel portion of the call is the same as that of *chmod()* with the exception of a call to *chownl()* instead of *chmodl()*. As in *chmodl()*, *chownl()* allows only the superuser or the owner of the inode to modify the inode's owner. At this point, the inode's owner and group fields are set to the calling arguments. If the invoking user is not the superuser, the set-user-identification and set-group-identification bits are cleared. After marking the inode as modified, it is released with the *iput()* procedure.

The system calls *stat()* and *fstat()* read the current status of an inode. *Stat()*, shown in Procedure 4.12, receives two arguments: a pathname for the file and a pointer to the user structure to be updated with the status of the inode. First, *stat()* calls *namei()* to retrieve the universal inode of the file. If the inode returned is that of the virtual super-root, the procedure returns a forged structure with predetermined values. In the normal case, the lower kernel procedure *statl()* is called to actually read the current values of the various inode fields. In any case, *copyout()* is used to copy the structure from the kernel data space into the user's data space before returning.

The lower kernel procedure *statl()* maps the universal inode pointer onto a local one before calling *stat1()* to actually fill in the user structure with the current status of the inode. The inode is released with *iput()* and the *statl()* procedure returns.

The system call *fstat()*, which receives an open file descriptor in place of the pathname, is nearly identical to *stat()* and warrants no further discussion.

chmod (filename, mode)

/ Upper Kernel chmod() – on calling process' machine */*

```
{
      locate and retrieve the universal inode;        /* namei() */
      if (namei fails)
            return;
      Schmodl to invoke lower portion of chmod;  /* Scall */
}
```

chmodl (universal inode structure, mode)

/ Lower Kernel chmodl() – on inode's machine */*

```
{
      map the universal inode structure
            onto a local inode pointer;              /* inm2ip() */
      if (not owner of file and not superuser)
            return;
      if (not superuser) {
            turn off shared-text bit in mode;
            if (process group ≠ inode group)
                  turn off set-group-id bit in mode;
      }
      clear all the read, write, execute bits;
      set new modes;
      mark inode as modified;
      if (inode is program text and shared-text bit not set)
            release shared-text region;              /* xrele() */
      release inode;                                  /* iput() */
}
```

Procedure 4.11: Chmod System Call

```
    stat (filename, status structure)

    /* Upper Kernel stat() - on calling process' machine */

    {
          locate and retrieve the universal inode;          /* namei() */
          if (device is super-root)
                set stat to preset super-root stat;
          else
                Sstatl to invoke lower portion of stat;     /* Scall */
          copy the stat structure into the user structure;  /* copyout() */
    }



    statl (universal inode structure)

    /* Lower Kernel statl() - on inode's machine */

    {
          map the universal inode name
                onto a locked local inode pointer;          /* inm2ip() */
          read status of inode;                             /* stat1() */
          release local inode;                              /* iput() */
          return stat structure;
    }
```

Procedure 4.12: Stat System Call

4.4.3 I/O System Calls

The *read()*, *write()*, and *lseek()* system calls define UNIX's input/output interface. The *read()* and *write()* calls are of special interest for two reasons:

1. They are the most frequently used system calls and consequently have a large influence on system performance.

2. Both system calls allow the user to define the amount of data being read or written. The uncertainty over the amount of data being transferred necessitates the use of the Funnel mechanism, described in detail in Chapter 7.

The *lseek()* system call is one of the faster system calls since it simply adjusts the offset pointer in the specified file's file table entry. The upper kernel portion of *lseek()*, described in Procedure 4.13, receives an open file descriptor, the number of bytes the user wants to move, and a flag. Depending on the value

```
lseek (fdes, offset, origin)

/* Upper Kernel lseek() - on calling process' machine */

{
      map file descriptor to universal file structure;      /* getf() */
      if (origin is invalid) {
            send a signal;                                   /* psignal() */
            return;
      }
      Sseekl to invoke lower portion of lseek;               /* Scall */
}

seekl (fnm, offset, origin)

/* Lower Kernel seekl() - on file descriptor's machine */

{
      map universal file structure to file pointer;          /* fnm2fp() */
      retrieve the inode of the file pointer;
      if (origin is absolute)
            new offset = offset;
      if (origin is relative)
            new offset += current file pointer offset;
      else if (origin is extension)
            new offset += file size;
      if (new offset less than 0)
            return error;
      file pointer offset = new offset;
      return new offset;
}
```

Procedure 4.13: Lseek System Call

of the flag, the file position offset is moved either absolutely, from the current position, or from the end of the file by the indicated number of bytes.

The upper kernel portion of the system call maps the given file descriptor onto a universal file structure, checks that the flag has a valid value, and then calls its lower kernel counterpart, *seekl()*. The lower kernel portion translates the file descriptor into a local file descriptor and retrieves the inode associated with it. The absolute file offset is computed from the value of the flag and the number of bytes specified. Next the system call verifies that the newly computed file offset points to a legal byte in the file. Before returning, the offset in the file table entry is set and the procedure returns the modified offset value. Thus, *lseek()* is a very fast system call. It does not need to allocate new entries in data structures, call *namei()* to parse a pathname, or move data.

The MOSIX implementations of both the *read()* and *write()* system calls use Funnels to transfer data that needs to be read or written between sites. The upper kernel portions of both system calls are presented in Procedure 4.14. After successfully setting up the local end of an input Funnel, *read()* calls the *rdwr()* procedure with a flag indicating that the file descriptor is to be **read** from.

A special mechanism allows the *write()* system call to be interrupted and then restarted. In that case, it should avoid retransmitting bytes that were already sent, so the starting address and the amount of bytes to be written are adjusted prior to calling the *rdwr()* procedure with a **write** flag. If *rdwr()* returns an error to *write()* indicating that the process attempted writing to a pipe whose other end was not open for reading, *write()* sends the appropriate signal to the invoking process. Both high-level procedures return the amount of bytes successfully processed.

The *rdwr()* procedure, described in Procedure 4.15, is the common part of both the *read()* and *write()* system calls. It converts the user-supplied file-descriptor index to a universal file structure, then it calls *rdwrl()*. If *rdwrl()* produces a communication error, the *check_failure()* routine is called to clear all other file and inode references to the failed machine and send a SIGLOST signal to the process.

Rdwrl() receives the universal file structure, the arguments of the *read()* or *write()* system call, a flag indicating read or write mode, the maximum file-size limit (for writing), the process group and controlling terminal. The universal file structure is mapped onto a local one. If no errors occur, the ambassador process sets its environment to match the calling process' file-size limit, process-group and controlling-terminal. The file table is read in order to access the file's inode. Before calling the specific routines used to read or write an inode, *rdwrl()* sets the offset according to the mode argument and the file type. The lower kernel procedure *rdwrl()* then releases the inode and updates the count argument. The number of bytes actually processed is returned to the upper kernel routine.

One of the UNIX operating system's central abstractions is that of the UNIX file, which may represent character or block devices, named pipes, directories, or real files. The two lower kernel procedures used to read and write inodes, respectively shown in Procedure 4.16 and Procedure 4.17, are responsible for

```
int read (file descriptor, data buffer, count)

/* Upper Kernel read() – on calling process' machine */

{
        set input funnel;                                          /* setinf() */
        if (funnel setup did not succeed)
                return;
        invoke common read/write procedure with read flag;    /* rdwr() */
        return total number of bytes read;
}


int write (file descriptor, data buffer, count)

/* Upper Kernel write() – on calling process' machine */

{
        if (call reentered after remote sleep)
                adjust count and offset accordingly;
        set output funnel;                                         /* setoutf() */
        if (funnel setup did not succeed)
                return;
        invoke common read/write procedure with write flag;   /* rdwr() */
        if (pipe-write-error detected)
                send error signal to process;
        return total number of bytes written;
}
```

Procedure 4.14: Read and Write System Calls

translating the operations on the abstract file into the appropriate action for the specific file type. They are two of the most complex of the system calls discussed in this chapter.

The *readi()* procedure starts by verifying the validity of the offset and count arguments. If the inode represents a character device, the procedure simply calls the device-specific read routine and then returns.

If the inode represents a pipe, several steps must be taken. Unlike a regular file, where the beginning of the file is unaffected by the act of reading, the beginning of a pipe is always reset to point to the next unread portion. Pipes are also limited to a relatively small amount of data. When a very large read request is performed on a pipe, the request is broken down in *readi()* into individual read requests of the maximum size. Another divergence from the behavior associated

```
    rdwr (file descriptor, count, mode)

    /* Upper Kernel rdwr() - on calling process' machine */

    {
        map file descriptor to universal file structure;      /* getf() */
        if (mapping failed)
            return;
        invoke Srdwrl and set the return value to its result; /* Scall */
        if (failure occured) {
            check and recover if it is
                a communication failure;              /* check_failure() */
            return 0;
        }
    }

    int rdwrl (universal file structure, count, mode, limit,
            origin, pgrp, ttyd, ttyp)

    /* Lower Kernel rdwr() - on file's machine */

    {
        map the universal file structure
            onto a local file descriptor pointer;         /* fnm2fp() */
        if (failure occured)
            return error;
        copy the caller's environmenta values into the local environment];
        extract inode structure from file table;
        if (file is a regular file or a directory) {
            lock inode;
            set offset to end-of-file if mode is append;
        }
        else if (pipe) {
            lock inode;
            set offset to zero;
        }
        if (reading inode)
            call inode reading routine;                   /* readi() */
        else
            call inode writing routine;                   /* writei() */
        release inode;                                    /* iput() */
        adjust file offset by the number of bytes processed;
        return the number of bytes read or written;
    }
```

Procedure 4.15: Common Read/Write Procedures

```
readi (inode pointer, offset, count, user area information)

/* Lower Kernel readi() - on inode's machine */

{
      check validity of offset, count ;
      if (character special device) {
            call device-specific read routine to read;
            return;
      }
      if (pipe) {
            while (no data in pipe to be read) {
                  if (delay mode not set)
                        return;
                  if (no pipe writers and delay mode set)
                        sleep until someone writes to pipe;
            }
            set larger read request to maximum pipe size;
            set offset to point to read section of pipe's data blocks;
      }
      do {
            get block number of first block;          /* bmap() */
            set offset to offset within block;
            extract device number from inode;
            if (non-existent block) get empty block and clear its buffer;
            else
                  read data block(s);                 /* bread()/breada() */
            if (error occured during read) set bytes read to zero;
            if (something was read) move data read into funnel;
            if (pipe and no more bytes to read in the current disk-block) {
                  decrease size of inode, adjust pipe's pointers and offsets;
                  turn off delayed write bit so that the read portion
                        will not be written to disk;
            }
            release data block and set accessed flag on inode;
      }
      while (data needs be read and no errors);
      if (pipe) {
            adjust offset pointers by bytes read;
            if (someone is waiting to read pipe)
                  enable writing and awaken processes;
      }
}
```

Procedure 4.16: Lower Kernel Read an Inode

with normal files happens when the pipe has no data. Depending on the file-descriptor's option-flags, the process may either wait until another process writes to the pipe or return immediately with no bytes read.

As shown in Procedure 4.16, in the first case (there is no data and the user does not want to wait), the procedure simply returns. In the latter case (the user is willing to wait), the inode is released and the process sleeps until someone writes to the pipe. When some process writes data to the pipe, the sleeping process wakes up, relocks the inode, and proceeds to read the inode. The last pipe-specific preparation taken is to set the read offset to the beginning of the pipe's unread data.

The main loop of the *readi()* procedure is executed by all inode types except for character devices. In the loop, the first action figures out the number of the next block to be read, the offset within the block, and the device number to read the block from. If the *bmap()* procedure returns a negative address for a regular file or a directory, the kernel fetches an empty buffer not associated with any particular device, and zeros the newly allocated buffer. If *bmap()* returns a negative address for any other type of file, the read fails and the procedure exits. Normally, the address points to an actual disk block. Depending on the type of inode, the kernel reads the block with the *bread()* or the *breada()* procedure. Both procedures read the physical block into a memory resident buffer. The *breada()* procedure reads the next logical block of the file, as well as the current block. After successfully reading a block of data, the procedure *iomove()* transfers the data read to the Funnel or, in the case of a local read, to the process data segment. In the case of a remote read, the Linker on the calling site receives each block from the Funnel and transfers it to the appropriate user address. At the end of the main loop, the data block is released and the inode is marked as accessed. If the inode represents a pipe, the size of the inode and the read offset are adjusted by the number of bytes read. The procedure continues until the requested amount has been read or until an error is detected. After the end of the main loop, *readi()* adjusts the pipe-related inode fields.

Procedure 4.17 shows the procedure for writing to an inode. Since the procedure is very similar to that of *readi()*, the following elaborates only the significant differences. After computing the physical address of the disk block and the offset within the block, the procedure reads the block into a buffer. If the amount being written completely overwrites the existing physical block, the *getblk()* procedure is used to get the buffer from cache for the logical block and no disk access is required. The *iomove()* procedure is used to move the data that is being written into the buffer. *Iomove()* moves one logical block either through the Linker from the calling site or from the local process address space. After all of the data has been written, but prior to returning from writing to a pipe, *writei()* wakes up processes that were sleeping on an empty pipe and reiterates as long as there is more data to write beyond the pipe's accommodation capacity.

```
writei (inode pointer, offset, count, user area information)

/* Lower Kernel writei() – on inode's machine */

{
        check validity of offset;
        if (character special device)
                call device-specific write routine and return;
        if (pipe) {
pipe:       while (no room in pipe for new data) {
                        if (no readers on pipe and delay mode not set)
                                return;
                        release inode and sleep until someone reads the pipe;
                        lock inode;
                }
                set largee write request size to max number of bytes left in pipe;
                set offset to pipe's write offset;
        }
        while (data left to write and no errors ) {
                get block number of first block;              /* bmap() */
                set offset and extract device number from inode;
                if (write request is same size as buffer)
                        assign buffer for the given block;     /* getblk() */
                else
                        read disk block into cache;            /* bread() */
                move data from user area to kernel buffer;   /* iomove() */
                write buffer to disk;
                if ((regular file or directory) and (offset > inode size))
                        set inode size to offset;
                if (pipe)
                        increment pipe size by count, resetting if necessary;
                turn on modified flag on inode;
        }
        if (pipe) {
                adjust offset pointers by bytes written;
                if (someone waiting to read pipe)
                        enable reading and awaken processes;
                if (no errors and data left to write)
                        goto pipe;
        }
}
```

Procedure 4.17: Lower Kernel Write an Inode

4.4.4 Namespace Manipulating System Calls

In MOSIX, both the *chdir()* system call and the *chroot()* system call allow a process to change its specific namespace. By passing *chdir()* a valid directory pathname, a process changes the starting point from which *namei()* begins its search. The UNIX *chroot()* system call, while much less frequently used, allows a process to change the root of its namespace to some subtree of itself. In MOSIX, the *chroot()* system call is used to substitute the root of a remote workstation's namespace for the current one.

---

chdir (directory name)

/ Upper Kernel chdir() – on calling process' machine */*

{

    pass the current working directory to
        the common chdir/chroot procedure;   */* chdirec() */*

}

chroot (directory name)

/ Upper Kernel chroot() – on calling process' machine */*

{

    if (not superuser)   */* suser() */*
        return;
    pass the current root directory to
        the common chdir/chroot procedure;   */* chdirec() */*
    set process origin to root directory machine;

}

Procedure 4.18: Chdir/Chroot System Calls

Both *chdir()* and *chroot()*, shown in Procedure 4.18, act as front ends to the *chdirec()* kernel procedure. The *chdir()* system call invokes *chdirec()* with two arguments. The first argument is the filename that was the original calling argument for *chdir()*. The second argument is an inode pointer to the inode of the current working directory, present in the process *u area*.

The implementation of *chroot()* is very similar to *chdir()*, except that the caller must be the superuser. After returning from *chdirec()*, *chroot()* changes the process' root to the newly selected root file system. In the event that *chdirec()* returns an error, the process' root remains unchanged.

The *chdirec()* kernel procedure, shown in Procedure 4.19, receives two arguments: a filename and a universal inode pointer. It begins by retrieving the inode of the given file using the *namei()* kernel procedure. Once the inode has been successfully retrieved, *chdirec()* determines whether the new inode is that of the super-root. unless it is, the lower portion of the kernel procedure, *chdirecl()*, is called on the inode's host site. Unless the old inode was the super-root, its usage count is decremented by *idec()*. Once an inode has been successfully retrieved, *chdirec()* replaces the inode pointed to by the calling argument with the new inode, effectively modifying the process' namespace.

---

chdirec (directory name, pointerr to, universal inode structure)

/* *Upper Kernel chdirec() – common code for chroot() and chdir()* */

```
{
        get inode for directory given;                    /* namei() */
        if (inode is not the super-root)
                invoke Schdirecl on directory's machine;   /* Scall */
        if (old inode is not the super-root)
                decrement usage count for it;              /* Sidec() */
        copy new directory universal inode into argument structure;
}
```

chdirecl (universal inode)

/* *Lower Kernel chdirecl() – on inode's machine* */

```
{
        map universal inode to local inode pointer;        /* inm2ip() */
        if (inode is not a directory)
                release inode and return error;            /* iput() */
        if (no search permission on inode)                 /* access() */
                release inode and return;                  /* iput() */
        release inode lock;                                /* prele() */
}
```

Procedure 4.19: Chdirec System Call

The lower kernel routine, *chdirecl()*, is also shown in Procedure 4.19. *Chdirecl()* is invoked on the inode's site and receives only one argument – a universal inode pointer. The routine maps the universal inode pointer onto a local inode pointer using the kernel routine *inm2ip()*. It then performs a few tests to see whether the given inode actually represents a directory and if so, whether the directory is accessible to the user. If either of the tests fails, the inode is released and the appropriate error value is returned. If both tests pass, the inode lock is released by the kernel routine *prele()*, and the *chdirecl()* routine returns.

Two of the least frequently used system calls are *mount()* and *umount()*, the two system calls that allow the superuser to graft and prune entire file systems from the current namespace. Unlike NFS-type systems, the MOSIX implementation of *mount()* disallows the mounting of a remote file system on a local directory.

---

mount (special filename, directory name, flag)

/* Upper Kernel mount() – on calling process' machine */

```
{
    if (not superuser)
        return;
    convert special filename into universal inode structure;   /* namei() */
    convert directory name into universal inode structure;   /* namei() */
    if (directory inode and disk inode are not on the same machine) {
        release inodes;                                        /* Sidec() */
        return;
    }
    Smountl to invoke Lower Kernel portion of mount;           /* Scall */
}
```

Procedure 4.20: Mount System Call

The upper kernel *mount()* system call, shown in Procedure 4.20, receives as its arguments a special file name, a directory name, and a flag. The special filename is the pathname for the file system's block device. The directory name is the pathname of the mount point on which the file system is to be mounted. The flag indicates whether the file system is to be mounted read-only or read/write. *Mount()* first checks whether or not the owner of the invoking process is the superuser. If not, it immediately returns. Next, *mount()* maps both the special filename and the mount point onto universal inode structures using the *namei()* kernel routine. Once the mapping has been successfully completed, the site numbers of both the universal inodes are compared to verify that both are on the same site. If so, the lower kernel portion of the system call, *mountl()*, is invoked. If the site numbers are different, both inodes are released and the *mount()* system call returns.

When invoked, *mountl()* receives the two universal inode structures retrieved by *namei()* and the original flag. *Mountl()* (not shown) begins by converting the universal inode of the special file into a local inode pointer. Once mapped, the inode is checked to see if it is actually the inode of a block device and is therefore mountable. *Mountl()* next performs a similar mapping for the mount point, testing whether the mount point is a directory, whether the inode is currently being accessed by another process, and whether the inode is that of the root. If any of these tests fail, then the inodes are released by *iput()* and an appropriate error message is returned.

After completing the preliminary checks, *mountl()* attempts to find a free entry slot in the mount table. If no free entry can be found or if the special file is already mounted, the inodes are released by *iput()* and an appropriate error message is returned. Mount table entries contain the following fields: a status flag, the device number of the special file, a pointer to the mount point inode, a pointer to the superblock buffer, and a pointer to the inode of the root directory of the mounted file system. Once a free entry has been found and the file system is verified as not alread mounted, the mount entry flag is marked "busy" and the system call proceeds. In accordance with the device type of the special file, a device-specific *open()* function is called. An empty buffer is allocated to store the superblock of the file system being mounted. At this point, a local Funnel is set up for the use of the *readi()* procedure as it reads the superblock into the new buffer. Since *readi()* assumes the existence of a Funnel, a Funnel must be set up even though no data is being transferred between sites. After reading the superblock, the mount table entry's superblock pointer is set to the address of the buffer and the Funnel is closed.

If either the superblock's type or magic number are incorrect, then all of the previous mappings are undone and an error is returned. If everything checks out, all of the lock flags for the copy of the superblock in the buffer are released, the superblock inode cache is freed, and *mountl()* proceeds. The value of the read-only field in the buffered superblock is set to that of the flag argument. *Iget()* is called to retrieve the root inode of the newly mounted file system. If retrieved successfully, the inode of the mount point is set to indicate that it is currently mounted upon, *mountl()* releases all the locked inodes, and returns.

The *umount()* system call, described in Procedure 4.21, is used to remove a mounted file system from the current namespace. Its only argument is the pathname of the special device to be unmounted. After checking that the request is being made by the superuser, *namei()* is used to convert the pathname into a universal inode structure. The upper kernel *umount()* system call concludes by calling its lower kernel counterpart, *umountl()*, also shown in Procedure 4.21.

Umountl() begins by using the *getmdev()* routine to check the device being unmounted. This routine maps the universal inode onto a local one via *inm2ip()* and checks that the device is in fact a block device. The local inode is then released and the device structure associated with the block device is returned to *umountl()*. The device returned is searched for in the mount table. If the device is not located in the mount table, or if any inode on that device is being used, the file system is not unmounted, and *umountl()* returns an error.

In order to preserve file system consistency, the following steps are taken before clearing the mount table entry associated with the device:

umount (device name)

/ Upper Kernel umount() – on calling process' machine */*

{
    if (not superuser)
        return;
    convert filename of device into
        universal inode structure;   */* namei() */*
    call Sumountl on device machine;   */* Scall */*
}

umountl (universal inode structure)

/ Lower Kernel umount() – on device's machine */*

{
    check the device being unmounted;   */* getmdev() */*
    locate device's mount table entry;
    if (not found)
        return;
    remove file system's unused sticky text entries; */* xumount() */*
    write buffer cache to disk;   */* update() */*
    release root inode;
    flush all inodes on device;   */* iflush() */*
    if (active inodes detected while flushing)
        return;   */* failed */*
    remove text labels of that device;   */* lumount() */*
    if (device not in use as a block device)
        call routine to close device;
    flush all buffers to disk;
    release superblock buffer;   */* brelse() */*
    clean mount table entry;
}

Procedure 4.21: Umount System Call

- All of the device's sticky text segments are removed from memory.

- All of the device's inodes are scheduled to be written to disk. If the flushing process finds a busy inode, the *umount()* fails and an error is returned.

- All of the special MOSIX text labels are removed.

- All of the buffers associated with the device are scheduled to be written to disk.

In addition to the above steps, *umountl()* calls the device driver's *close()* routine (unless the file system's device is in use as a block device). At this point, *umount()* releases the mounted-on inode and the buffer that has been used to hold the superblock since the file system was mounted. Before returning, the mount table entry is cleared.

The *mknod()* system call, used to create special files, is shown in Procedure 4.22. It receives three arguments: a path, a mode, and a device. The path is used to determine the pathname of the file to be created. The mode of the file determines the file's protection bits as well as other special file bits. The device represents the major and minor numbers of the device and is meaningful only in the case of block special or character special files.

Mknod() first verifies that its caller is the superuser, unless the file that it is attempting to create is a (named) pipe. Then, *namei()* is used to retrieve the universal inode of the directory in which the special file is to be created. If successful, *mknod()* calls its lower kernel counterpart, *mknodl()*, also shown in Procedure 4.22, via an Scall.

Mknodl() is called with a number of arguments. It receives the universal inode retrieved in *mknod()*, the file mode and device numbers given to *mknod()*, the intended filename, and the user process' creation mask. The universal inode structure is immediately mapped onto a local inode pointer by a call to *inm2ip()*. Once mapped, the kernel routine *scand()* is used to verify that the intended filename does not already exist within the target directory. The directory permissions are then checked by *access()* to verify that they enable writing by the invoking process. If any of the tests fail, the inode is released and the routine returns with the appropriate error condition.

When all of the preliminary tests have been completed, *mknodl()* proceeds to create the actual file. The kernel routine *mknode()* is called to initialize the new inode, setting the general fields in accordance with the arguments passed to *mknodl()* and values from the user's ID and group ID. If the new inode is to represent a special file, its device field is set to the value of the device arguments passed by *mknod()* and a flag is raised to indicate that the inode has been modified. After all the inode's fields have been properly initialized, the kernel routine *iput()* is invoked to release the inodes of the directory and the special file respectively.

The *link()* system call shown in Procedure 4.23 creates a new pathname to an already existing file. It has two arguments: the target (i.e., a previously existing file to which a new pathname will be created) and the new linkname.

mknod (filename, file mode, device)

/ Upper Kernel mknod() – on calling process' machine */*

```
{
    if (not creating a pipe-device and not superuser)
        return;
    get universal inode structure of directory of new file;  /* namei() */
    if (error)
        return;
    Smknodl to invoke Lower Kernel portion;          /* Scall */
}
```

mknodl (universal inode structure, file mode, device, filename,
          creation mask)

/ Lower Kernel mknodl() – on inode's machine */*

```
{
    map universal inode structure to local inode pointer;  /* inm2ip() */
    if (error)
        return;
    if (filename already in directory)               /* scand() */
        set error condition;
    else
        check for write access in directory;         /* access() */
    if (error detected)
        release inode and exit;
    initialize new inode;                            /* mknode() */
    if (initialization error)
        return;
    if (the new node is a special file) {
        set inode device field to value of device;
        set flag to indicate changed inode;
    }
    release directory and file inodes;               /* iput() */
}
```

Procedure 4.22: Mknod System Call

link (target, linkname)

/* *Upper Kernel link() – on calling process' machine* */

```
{
      map target to universal inode;                    /* namei() */
      map linkname's parent to universal inode;         /* namei() */
      if (inodes are located on different machines) {
            release both inodes;                        /* Sidec() */
            return;
      }
      Slinkl to invoke Lower Kernel portion of link;    /* Scall */
}
```

linkl (target inode, linkname parent inode, filename)

/* *Lower Kernel linkl() – on inode's machine* */

```
{
      map target's universal inode to local inode;      /* inm2ip() */
      if (inode is maximally linked) {
            release inode pointer;
            decrement usage counter;
            return;
      }
      if (user is non-root and link is to a directory) {
            release inode pointer;
            decrement usage counter;
            return;
      }
      set modification flags, increment link-count,
            and sync inode to disk;                     /* iupdate() */
      release target's inode pointer;                   /* iput() */
      map linkname's parent onto an inode pointer;      /* inm2ip() */
      verify uniqueness of linkname and access rights;
      verify that the target and linkname are on the same file system;
      write a linkname entry into the parent directory; /* wdir() */
      release parent inode;                             /* iput() */
}
```

Procedure 4.23: Link System Call

The kernel routine *namei()* is immediately invoked twice by *link()*. The first invocation maps the target to its universal inode structure; the second maps the linkname's parent to its universal inode structure. The site numbers within the universal inodes are then examined to verify that both the target and the linkname are on the same site. If this is not the case, then the kernel routine *idec()* is invoked via an Scall to release both inodes, and *link()* returns. Otherwise the kernel proceeds to invoke *linkl()*, the lower kernel portion of *link()*, via an Scall.

Linkl() is called with a number of arguments. It receives both of the inodes that were retrieved by *namei()* in *link()*, and the intended filename for the new link. The first action taken is the mapping of the target's universal inode onto a local one by *inm2ip()*. Once retrieved, the number of currently existing links to the inode are checked, thus ascertaining that the intended link does not pass the system limit. If it does, then the inodes are released, their usage counters decremented, and *linkl()* returns the appropriate error. Another possible error occurs if the caller is not the superuser and the target is a directory. Next, the kernel routine *iupdate()* is invoked to modify certain fields in the target's inode in accordance with the new link and update the disk-inode. Once this stage has been completed, the target's inode is released and the linkname's directory inode is processed.

Using the kernel routine *inm2ip()*, the local inode is retrieved, after which its uniqueness and access rights are verified. *Linkl()* then verifies that both the target and the linkname are located on the same file system. Once this has been done, a linkname entry is written into the parent directory by the kernel routine *wdir()*. *Linkl()* concludes by releasing all the inodes via *iput()*.

As shown by the previous discussion of the *link()* system call, a UNIX inode may have several names within a file system. The *unlink()* system call (not shown) removes one such name from the file system. If the inode has no other links, then both the inode and its data blocks are freed as well. The MOSIX kernel performs all of the file system data structure manipulations on the site of the file system. Complexities arising from race conditions are not unique to MOSIX and will not be discussed here.

The *unlink()* system call receives as an argument the name of the file to be removed. Using the *namei()* kernel routine, *unlink()* retrieves the inode of the parent directory of the given filename. Once retrieved, the lower kernel routine *unlinkl()*, is invoked via an Scall. A side effect of the call to *namei()* is that the last component of the filename is saved for later use: this component is passed as one of the arguments of *unlink()*.

Unlinkl() receives the universal inode retrieved by *namei()* in *unlink()* and the last component of the filename. The universal inode is mapped onto a local inode by *inm2ip()* and the *scand()* routine is used to determine the inode number of the filename. If an error occurred or the process does not have write access to the directory, the call fails.

4.5 Summary

This chapter presented several strategies for the design and construction of distributed file systems for UNIX. (A comprehensive survey of distributed file systems can be found in [37].) The chapter began by showing how to extend the traditional UNIX namespace, followed by a classification of different distributed file systems. Then the chapter presented the details of the MOSIX distributed file system implementations, followed by explanations of the MOSIX file system calls.

Chapter 5

The UNIX Process

In the UNIX operating system, Processes can be defined as independent streams of computation which, as far as the kernel is concerned, compete over the machine's resources. All UNIX processes are created by invoking the *fork()* system call (except for the *init()* process, which is handcrafted at boot time). This chapter presents an overview of the UNIX process, the mechanisms that control processes, and the system resources used by processes. It provides a background for understanding MOSIX processes, which will be described in Chapter 6.

The memory allocated to UNIX processes can be divided into three logical parts:

Text The text section contains the machine-language code to be executed by the machine on behalf of the process.

Data The data section contains a representation of data preset to initial values. It also includes the amount of space to be allocated by the kernel for uninitialized data (known for historic reasons as *bss*).

Stack The stack area usually contains procedure-based, downward growing, data frames.

All processes are executed independently of any other process on the system. Different processes might share text regions of the same executable file, and processes might share data regions by using the interprocess communication (IPC) mechanism of shared memory, but they do not share their stack regions.

The UNIX kernel provides processes with a working environment supporting the mechanisms and memory required by the process. Understanding the allocation of physical memory to processes is essential for a complete grasp of the kernel's interaction with processes and is described in section Section 5.1.

The basic structure of a UNIX process is similar for every process in a given system. Each process is allocated a fixed-size entry in the *process table*. Further information, which the kernel needs on behalf of the process only while it runs, is stored in a per-process *u area*. These structures are described in Section 5.2.

Each process can be said to execute in its own **context**. The components of the context and the circumstances that require the kernel to either save or restore a process context are explained in Section 5.3.

The organization of processes within the system requires that processes exist within one of nine possible logical states at all times. Section 5.4 presents the logical states, explaining the implications that govern the transition of a process from one state to another.

Section 5.5 presents the scheduling policy used by UNIX, and gives a brief explanation of the system clock mechanism on which the policy is based. The last section in the chapter, Section 5.6, contains a brief overview of the system calls that allow the user to manipulate processes, and through them, system resources.

5.1   Organization of the System Memory

Within the text section of a UNIX process, instructions may reference three different types of addresses: text addresses, data addresses, and stack addresses. Text addresses may consist of machine instructions, while data addresses contain constants and static variables, including all global variables. The generated addresses do not refer directly to physical memory, since this could severely limit multi-tasking. As an example, two processes with overlapping address-spaces could not reside in memory at the same time (an extreme such case would be several copies of the same program). Furthermore, this would require processes to fit completely in the existing physical memory, which can be much smaller than required for a large program. Finally, there are issues of protection and segregation of faults, so when a process access an address outside its address space, either erroneously or maliciously, other processes, as well as the kernel's own code and data-structures, must not be affected. Therefore, processes run in a virtual address space. Virtual addresses are translated, in turn, into physical address locations by the machine's memory management unit (MMU) under the kernel's control, so that no memory conflicts can occur.

5.1.1   Regions

The virtual address space of a process is divided into logical **regions**. Each region is a distinct object composed of a contiguous portion of the virtual address space that can be either shared or protected. The text, data, and stack sections of the **u area** are usually allocated their own regions. Since regions can be either shared or protected, this scheme allows several processes to execute the same program by sharing a single text region, or to purposely modify common variables through a **shared-memory region**.

To facilitate the use of regions, the kernel contains a region table from which entries are allocated for each active region in the system. Each process is allocated a private **per process region table** known as a **pregion table** for short. *Pregion table* entries are composed of a pointer to a region table entry, a permissions field, and the starting address of the region table entry's virtual address for the table's owning process. The permissions field specifies the type of access the process is allowed: read-only, read/write, or read/execute. If a region is shared, it may have different virtual addresses in different processes.

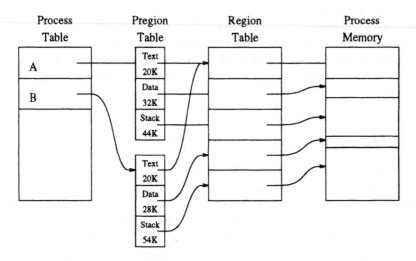

Figure 5.1: Process Data Structures

In Figure 5.1, two processes, Process A and Process B, are sharing their text regions via separate mappings from their *pregion tables* to a single entry in the region table.

An entry in the region table contains the following fields:

- A pointer to the inode of the file whose contents are currently residing in the region (if any)

- The type of the region – text, data, stack, or shared memory

- The region's size

- An array of page table entries

- The region's status, which is some combination of:

    - locked (for atomic operations)

    - in demand

    - being loaded

    - valid

- The number of processes currently referencing the region

The region scheme makes no assumptions regarding either the system's memory management policies or the memory management implementation. In this manner, systems that use paging as well as systems that use segmentation can benefit from the use of regions.

Operations on Regions

The following operations apply to regions. The involved region is locked for the duration of the operation to insure atomic operations:

Allocation Regions are allocated by the *exec()* system call in order to create new text, data and stack regions for the process; by the *shmget()* system call to allocate a shared-memory region and in MOSIX, also to allocate space for migrating processes. In any case, the *allocreg()* routine is called. For demand-paged text or data regions, the inode reference count is incremented.

Freeing *freereg()* is called when a region is not needed any more, to release the region entry. For demand-paged text or data regions, the inode reference count is decremented.

Attaching *attachreg()* connects a region to a specified address within the process address space. The region's reference-count is incremented.

Detaching Regions can be detached following one of three system calls: *exec()*, *exit()*, and *shmdt()*. Each of these system calls invokes the *detachreg()* kernel routine. *detachreg()* detaches a region from a process address space. The region's reference-count is decremented. Usually, when the region's reference count drops to zero, the region is also freed (using *freereg()*), but in some cases, including shared-memory regions and text-regions where the inode's sticky-bit is set, the region remains.

Modifying Regions may require modification, i.e. Expansion or shrinking. In this case the *growreg()* kernel routine is called by the *sbrk()* system call or when the process stack-size needs to be expanded and adjusts the appropriate region and its associated page tables to the requested size.

Loading During the *exec()* system call, an executable file is read into memory, loading the process regions according to the virtual addresses specified in the file. The actual loading of the file is performed by the kernel routine *loadreg()* to load non demand-paged text and data into a region's memory.

Duplicating When a new process is created via the *fork()* system call, the kernel is required to duplicate the regions of the calling process. This operation is performed by the *dupreg()* kernel routine. The routine returns a pointer to a new region, whose page table(s) are initially mapped to the same pages as the original region. Common memory pages are marked as **shared** until one of the resulting processes needs to modify them, in which case two copies will be made.

5.1.2 Pages

Pages are equal sized blocks of physical memory whose actual sizes are defined by the hardware, typically ranging from 512 bytes to 8K bytes. Every addressable memory location falls within one page or another and can therefore be accessed by a data tuple of the form <**page number, byte offset in page**>. Since the CPU can address all of the physical memory with the same ease, physical pages of memory do not need to be assigned contiguously or in any particular order.

In Figure 5.1, the pointers from the region table to the area marked as "Process Memory" are actually pointers to a page table. The page table is composed of entries containing physical page numbers and machine-dependent information controlling the access to the specific page. Unauthorized accesses to memory areas, such as writing data to a page of memory that is part of a text region, or attempting to access areas outside of the process virtual address space, result in a hardware exception.

5.2 Organization of the Process

The kernel uses a fixed size data structure, known as the **proc table**, to organize existing processes. Upon creation, each process is allocated an entry in the process table. Each process table entry points to a *pregion table*, whose entries point to entries in the region table, which ultimately lead to virtual addresses, as previously illustrated in Figure 5.1.

Each process also owns another memory area known as the **u area**. While the process table entry contains data that needs be accessible to the kernel at all times, the *u area* contains data that must be accessed only when the process is active. This scheme allows the kernel to save memory by not allocating *u areas* for unused process slots. Present day memory capacities have weakened the need for this separation.

5.2.1 Process Table

The *proc table* data structure is composed of a fixed number of process table entries that contain the data needed by the kernel to access and manipulate processes. Figure 5.2 shows the types of fields in a *proc table* entry.

The first group of fields in the *proc table* entry denotes the process state. These fields show whether the entry has been allocated, and if so, whether the process is running, sleeping, etc.

The second group of fields stores the process memory assignments including the the address of its *u area*, a pointer to the process *pregion* entry and the process overall size. These allows the kernel to swap the process between memory and secondary storage.

The third group of fields contain the user identification that control the permission of other processes to send signals to the process.

The fourth group of fields stores the (unique) process identification number (PID), it's process-group, parent process, etc. In this manner, relationships

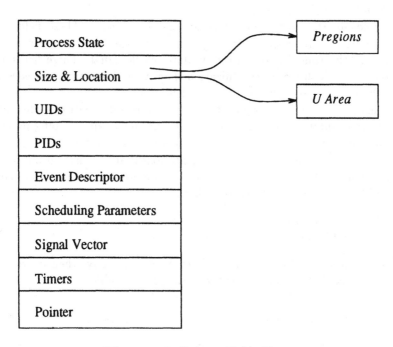

Figure 5.2: Process Table Entry

between processes can be preserved; processes can be aware of the process that created them, or of processes that they created. Similarly, processes can specify a group of processes to which they belong. This allows other processes that are not directly related to them to interact with them via signals.

The fifth group is a field that contains an event descriptor, an address for coordinating between processes. By storing specific addresses in these fields, it is possible to suspend processes pending specific events, such as I/O completion or resource availability.

Various scheduling parameters compose the sixth group of fields. These parameters enable the system scheduler to manipulate active processes according to the scheduling policy. This group consists of at least two fields. The first field is the priority assigned to the process by the system. The priority depends on the total run time accumulated and the time passed since the last CPU burst. The second field consists of the user-assigned priority. In some cases (such as batch jobs) users may wish to assign a lower priority to some of their processes, thereby reducing the load that the processes contribute to the system.

The seventh group is a field that contains a signal vector, A bit-map of signals that the process has receive. Processes can receive signals while swapped out, so it is important that signals be stored in the *proc table* entry. Since the signals are represented by bits, it is not possible to log the number of signals of a given type that a process has received.

The fields in the eighth logical group are the timers. These fields store data regarding the times spent residing in memory, the total time passed since creation, and the time remaining for an alarm clock signal. These fields allow the system to track the resource utilization of active and dormant processes, and provide the basis for scheduling priority calculations.

The last group consist of a link to other process table entries. This allows linking all the running processes into a single run-queue and sleeping processes into hash-chains, according to the event they are waiting for.

While other fields may exist in implementations that have not been described here, they tend to fall into one of the above categories or are implementation-specific and are therefore not discussed here.

5.2.2 The U Area

The *u area*, shown in Figure 5.3, is allocated dynamically when a process is created and linked to the process entry in the process table.

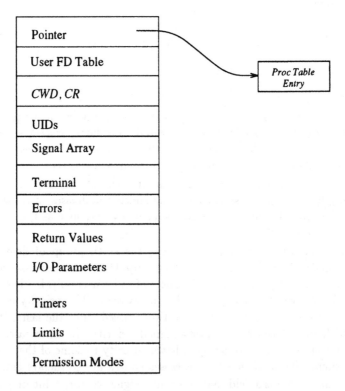

Figure 5.3: The *U Area*

The *u area* can be partitioned into twelve logical groups of fields.

The first group consist of a pointer to the process *proc table* entry.

The second group is the user File-Descriptor (FD) table. This structure, first introduced in Section 3.4, serves as the system interface between the process and the file system.

The third group of fields contain the process root and current working directories. These can be changed by invoking the *chdir()* and *chroot()* system calls, as mentioned in Section 3.4.

The fourth group contains the real user and group IDs of the process.

The fifth group consists of the signal array. This array is composed of the actions that the user wishes the kernel to take when the process receives the corresponding signals. An action can either be a default action, ignoring the signal, or a routine to be called.

The sixth group of fields identify the terminal associated with the process and its controlling device.

The seventh group of fields contains the errors incurred during a system call. This group sometimes consists of an error counter as well as a field that stores the last error encountered. This is similar to the eighth group, which stores the values returned by system calls.

The ninth group contain I/O parameters such as the file offset, the remaining bytes to read/write, the file mode, etc. These are used as hidden arguments to various I/O routines.

The tenth group consists of timers that record the amount of time that the process has spent in user mode and kernel mode. Additional fields store the sum of the times spent in these modes on behalf of all of the processes forked from this process.

The eleventh group of fields contains the limits imposed on the process for system resources. These limits can restrict the size of a process, the size of a file it can attempt to write, or other resources such as the total execution time.

The last group consists of the *permissions mode* field. This field stores the default access mode settings for files created by the process, and is referenced by the appropriate kernel routines.

5.3 Process Context

The user address space, its contents, the kernel data structures relating to the process, and the contents of the hardware registers relating to the execution of the process, all constitute the **context** of the process. Accordingly, this context is composed of three parts: **user-level context**, **system-level context**, and **register context**.

The process table entry and the *u area* of a process form the static part of the system-level context. The dynamic part is composed of *pregion* entries and the stack of the process context layers, which contain information enabling the kernel to suspend or resume the execution of the process. When a system-call or an interrupt occurs, the kernel pushes a context layer into the stack. This layer is later popped on completion of the system call and return to user-mode or after the interrupt is handled. By this definition, the number of context layers cannot exceed the number of interrupt levels plus one.

5.3.1 Interrupts

When an interrupt occurs, a context layer is pushed into the process stack. All interrupts, regardless of their cause, are handled in the following manner:

1. The current activity is saved by pushing a new context layer.

2. The source of the interrupt is identified and the appropriate handler is located via the interrupt vector.

3. The interrupt handler is invoked by the kernel.

4. Upon completion of the interrupt handler, the previously stored context layer is popped, and the process can resume its execution.

It is important to note that higher level interrupts block lower level interrupts. In such cases, the handling of the lower level interrupt is deferred until the handling of the higher level interrupt has been completed. In the event that a low-level interrupt was being handled when a high-level interrupt was generated, the handling of the earlier interrupt is suspended and the processor execution level is raised to prevent lower level interrupts from being handled. An example is presented in Figure 5.4.

This figure shows one possible chain of events that occurs when a system call is executed. A process issues a system call resulting in the kernel pushing a context layer, saving the user's context. Next, a disk interrupt occurs. The kernel immediately raises the interrupt priority to equal that of the disk interrupt and pushes the current context of the system call. Once this has been completed, the disk interrupt handler is invoked. The next interrupt to occur is the clock interrupt, which push the disk-interrupt's context and invokes the clock interrupt handler. Following the clock interrupt, a second disk interrupt is received. This interrupt is blocked, and will not be handled until the handling of the first disk interrupt is complete.

A process context is not affected by an interrupt, but the process may be indirectly affected when the interrupt handler modifies kernel structures that affect the reminder of the process execution.

5.3.2 System Calls

A system call can be thought of as a special kind of interrupt, which allows a set of library routines to be executed in kernel mode. The system call itself is passed to the kernel as an index, identifying the kernel routine and the number of it's argument. When complete, the rersult(s) of the routine or the error code are passed back to the user via register values.

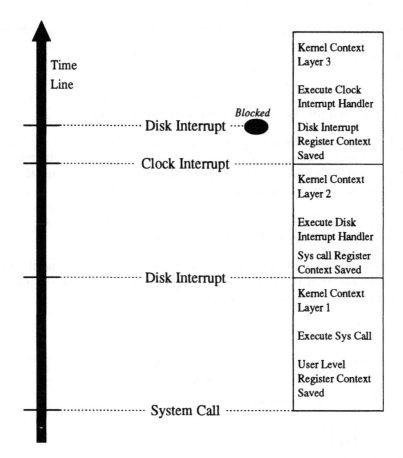

Figure 5.4: An Interrupt Sequence

5.3.3   Context Switch

The suspension of a process execution on behalf of another process is known as
a **context switch**. When performing a context switch, the kernel must ensure
that it will be able to resume the suspended execution unaltered it in any form.
Thus, context switches are allowed in only one of five circumstances:

1. When a process puts itself to sleep

2. When a process exits

3. When a process is about to return to user mode following a system call,
   but is not yet eligible to run

4. When a process is about to return to user mode following an interrupt,
   but is not yet eligible to run

5. When a process suspends itself for tracing (or stopped by a signal on BSD)

In general, it is possible to see the action of the context switch as follows:

1. Save the current context.

2. Locate the process to be executed.

3. Restore that process context, and resume its execution.

The numerous actions that must be undertaken when performing a context switch generate a non-negligible overhead. When devising a comprehensive scheduling policy, this overhead plays a significant part in determining the point at which a context switch is no longer desired.

5.4 Process States

A process can be in one of eight states at any time from its creation until it exits. Strict guidelines limit the transition of the process from one state to another. The eight states are shown in Figure 5.5.

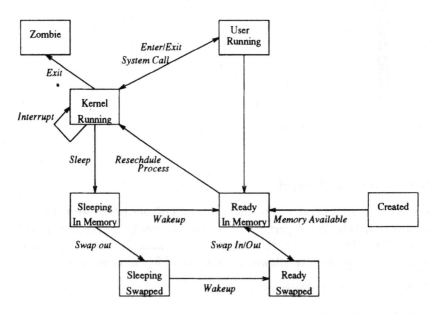

Figure 5.5: Process States and Transitions

The process begins its life cycle from the state of **Created**, shown in the lower right-hand corner of the figure. When the parent of the process finished initiation its child, the child process enters the state marked **Ready In Memory**. A process may move back and forth between the **Ready In Memory** and **Ready swapped** states as it is being swapped in or out, as shown by the bidirectional arrow between the state representations. A process that is ready and swapped out can only transit to a state in which it is ready and swapped in. A process that is ready in memory can either be swapped out or continue its execution by entering the **Kernel Running** state as determined by the scheduler.

Processes that are marked as **Kernel Running** execute in kernel mode, which may be temporarily suspended as a result of an interrupt, returning after the appropriate handler has completed. Such processes can also sleep (e.g., pending I/O events), in which case they are **Asleep In Memory**. Processes that are asleep in memory can be waked up, in which case they return to the **Ready In Memory** state and can proceed as previously described. These processes can also be swapped out, in the state of **Sleeping Swapped**. This state can be changed only as a result of a wakeup, whereupon the process enters the **Ready Swapped** state explained previously. Processes in the **Kernel Running** state can become marked as **User Running** following a system call return. They can revert from **User Running** to **Kernel Running** by invoking a system call or receiving an interrupt.

Finally, a process can enter the **Zombie** state. All processes that invoke the *exit()* system call, as well as processes that were killed by a signal enter this state. These processes no longer exist, but statistics concerning their resource usage and their exit code remain for use by the parent process.

5.5 Scheduling Processes

The UNIX kernel is responsible for allocating time to the various processes, using a scheduling policy. Each process is assigned a priority, which is adjusted periodically by the clock interrupt handler to reflect the relative time spent in execution.

5.5.1 Scheduling Policies

Processes that have been preempted are assigned a low priority, while the process with the highest priority is the process currently selected for execution. This method of scheduling is known as a **round robin policy** wherein each process is cyclically granted a timeslice. The simple round robin policy does not suffice, since there may be factors other than the relative time spent in execution that will impose further constraints on the scheduling. For example, processes that were preempted at a user-level priority should be assigned one class of priorities, as opposed to processes that were preempted while awaiting kernel resources. To facilitate this division into classes, the UNIX system has several priority queues, composed of three priority groups:

User-Level Priorities This level consists of processes that wish to run in user mode.

Low-Level Kernel Priorities This priority level consists of processes with priorities above a threshold value, dividing kernel-level priorities from user-level priorities. Processes at this level can be interrupted by signals.

High-Level Kernel Priorities Processes at this level, in contrast to low-level kernel priorities, continue to sleep upon receipt of a signal.

This scheme is known as **multilevel feedback** and, when implemented in conjunction with the round robin policy described earlier, provides the basis for a comprehensive **round robin with multilevel feedback** scheduler.

The kernel assigns priorities or adjusts them, in one of three instances:

1. The process is about to sleep at some priority, in which case a fixed priority is assigned based on the reason that the process is about to sleep.

2. The process is returning from kernel mode to user mode, causing the kernel to assign the process a low priority and penalize it for its current consumption of CPU resources.

3. The process is in user mode and a predefined period of time has passed, causing the clock handler to modify the process priority.

5.5.2   Process Priorities

The dynamic modifications to a process priority are based on a decay function that is applied to the process' CPU usage. Commonly, in UNIX System V Release 2, the decay function is

$$decay(CPU) = CPU * 3/4,$$

where CPU is an accumulator of CPU usage for each process, decaying at a constant rate every second.

The numerical representation of the priority is the reverse of its common notion: the lower the value - the higher the priority and higher values represent lower priorities. The priority is calculated as follows:

$$priority = CPU/2 + (base\ user\ level\ priority) + (user\ defined\ nice\ value).$$

The *base user-level priority* is the threshold priority level mentioned above, which cause the user-level priority to always be less than the kernel priorities. The *user-defined nice value* is a numerical value ranging from -20 ...+20 set by the user via the *nice()* system call and stored in the *proc table* entry. As the priority of a process in the user-level queues increases, the process begins to move towards the highest level queue. While the process remains at a user-level priority, the process will be constrained by the threshold value and will not be able to join a kernel-level priority queue.

Slice 1

Priority	CPU	Process
60	0	A
60	0	B
66	0	C

Slice 2

Priority	CPU	Process
60	0	B
66	0	C
71	22	A

Slice 3

Priority	CPU	Process
66	0	C
68	16	A
71	22	B

Slice 4

Priority	CPU	Process
66	12	A
68	16	B
77	22	C

Slice 5

Priority	CPU	Process
66	12	B
74	16	C
75	31	A

Slice 6

Priority	CPU	Process
71	23	A
72	12	C
75	31	B

Figure 5.6: A Scheduling Example

Figure 5.6 depicts a sample scheduling for three processes, A, B, and C, during six consecutive timeslices, along with their priority and CPU usage at the onset of each slice. The three processes within each slice are shown in order of descending scheduling priority, the top process being the process about to be executed during the slice. The three processes were consecutively created in alphabetic order, and have the same *base user-level priority* of 60. Process C has had its *user-defined nice value* set to +6, which will demonstrable affect Process C's scheduling.

In Slice 1, the process about to be executed is Process A. This is in accordance with the rule that the total length of time spent in the queue shall be a secondary criteria, applied when two or more processes have the same priority level. The process which waited longer shall then be executed first. At this stage, Process C's nice value has had no impact on its scheduling. From Slice 2 through Slice 6, the CPU usage is calculated using the simple decay function and added to the *base user-level priority* as previously described. Under the scheduling policy, Process A received 3 slices, Process B received 2 and Process C received only one slice. If the calculation was continued, Processes A and B would continue to differ by no more than a single timeslice, while the difference between them and Process C would steadily grow larger.

5.6 Process System Calls

Processes are created, destroyed, and manipulated by user applications via the system call interface. Process system calls can be grouped into six classes (see Table 5.1).

System Call Groups	System Calls
Process Table Entries	*fork()*
	exit()
	wait()
Process Table Entry Fields	*getpid()*
	getpgrp()
	getppid()
	setpgrp()
	getuid()
	geteuid()
	getgid()
	getegid()
	setuid()
	setgid()
	setulimit()
	umask()
	nice()
Process Regions	*execve()*
	brk()
	shmat()
	shmdt()
	lock()
Signals	*kill()*
	signal()
	pause()
Time	*time()*
	times()
	stime()
	alarm()
Debugging	*profil()*
	ptrace()

Table 5.1: Process System Calls

The first class of system calls is responsible for the creation and termination of processes. These system calls are separated from the others because of their unique manipulation of the process state and of the kernel *proc table*. The second class of system calls consists of those calls that manipulate various fields in the process *proc table* entry. The third class of system calls performs various operations on the data regions used by processes. The fourth class of system calls deals with sending, receiving, and handling signals. The fifth class of system calls performs time-related operations, and the last class of system calls provides support for debugging and tracing process execution.

5.6.1   Process Table Entries

Three system calls manipulate process states and the kernel process data structures in a unique way. While all system calls result in a change of the process state from **User Running** to **Kernel Running** and back again, two of these system calls, *fork()* and *exit()*, cause a unique state to be entered, while the third call, *wait()*, is responsible for freeing a previously allocated *proc table* entry.

The *fork()* system call begins by attempting to locate a free slot in the process table that can be assigned to the process that is being created (forked). Once a slot has been found, the newly created process is assigned a unique process identification number (PID), and its state is marked as **Being Created**. This unique state prevents the kernel from attempting to run the process prematurely. Following that, a logical copy of the parent process context is created in the newly allocated slot. Since the child process inherits access to files that were part of the parent's environment, all file and inode table counters held by the parent process are incremented, to ensure the consistency of the file system. An initial context layer is pushed into the child's context stack, in such a way as to allow the child process to recognize itself and begin its execution when scheduled. The child's timing fields in the *u area* are initialized and the child process returns from the system call with a value of 0. The process state of the child is then marked as **Ready To Run**, and the PID of the child process is returned to the parent process.

The *exit()* system call receives the exit status as an argument. This status will be reported to the parent process upon demand. The first action by *exit()* is to disable all further signals to the exiting process. This ensures that further signals to the process do not restart the *exit()* system call. If the process is the leader of a process group and possesses an active control terminal, all members of the leader's process group receive a "hangup" signal, **SIGHUP**. All open files and directories are appropriately released or closed. Memory regions that were used by the process are freed using the kernel routine *freereg()*. At this stage, the process state is marked as **Zombie**, following which, the parent process field in the proc-table entries of all child processes is modified to show that they are now children of *init()*. A death-of-child signal is sent to the process' parent. Finally, a context switch is performed and the system call terminates.

Finally, the *wait()*, system call allows processes to synchronize their execution with the termination of a child process. *Wait()* receives the address of an integer variable in which the exit status of the exiting child process is to be returned. It returns the PID of the child process that exited and its exit status. When invoked, *wait()* first verifies that the parent does indeed have at least one child, thus preventing the parent process from sleeping forever. The system call then searches for a zombie child process. If found, the zombie child process' resource consumption is added to that of the parent, its *proc table* slot is released, its exit code is written into the address argument supplied by the user, and *wait()* returns the child's PID to the user. In the event that no zombie children exist, *wait()* sleeps, until one of its children dies and the above procedure takes place.

5.6.2   Process Table Entry Fields

A number of system calls either query or modify fields in the process' *proc table* entry. The system calls *getpid()*, *getpgrp()* and *getppid()* return the PID of the calling process, its process group and the PID of the calling process' parent respectively. that of *getpid()*. Each call returns the value stored in a single field within the invoking process' process table entry.

The *setpgrp()* system call lets a process become a process-group leader, i.e. its process-group (and hence of its children) will become identical to its PID.

As in the case of PIDs, a number of system calls map onto a single system call entry. The *getuid()*, *geteuid()*, *getgid()* and *getegid()* system calls return the real UID of the calling process, the effective UID of the calling process, the real group identification number (GID) of the calling process, and the effective GID of the calling process respectively. These identification numbers may be set by the *setuid()* and *setgid()* system calls, both of which receive as arguments the new identification number requested by the user. The *setuid()* system call sets the real and the effective user ID of the process invoking the system call according to one of three instances:

1. If the effective UID of the calling process is root, then both the real and effective UIDs are set.

2. If the process real UID is equal to *uid*, the argument supplied by the user, then the process effective UID is also set to *uid*.

3. If the process effective UID is equal to *uid*, then the process real UID is also set to *uid*.

The *setgid()* system call works in a similar manner, modifying both real and effective GIDs.

The system call *ulimit()* allows processes to set limits on their system resource consumption. This system call changes the relevant fields stored in the process' *u area*. *Ulimit()* receives two arguments. The first argument is one of three commands that describe the limit that the user wishes to check or modify. The second argument is the new limit that the user wishes to set. Three such commands exist:

1. To return the maximum file size, in 512-byte blocks, that the process may write.

2. To set the maximum file size to a user-defined limit.

3. To return the highest possible break value; that is, the highest possible address in the data region.

When setting a new limit, the kernel first ensures that the limit requested is within the bounds of the limits allowed to the user invoking the system call.

The system call *umask()* receives an integer as its calling argument. This system call modifies the value of the file mode creation mask found in the process' *u area* and return the previous value to the user.

The last system call in this group is *nice()*. This system call allows the user to redefine the user-defined nice value used to affect the scheduling of the process. It receives as its argument an integer and after verifying that the integer is within the bounds allowed to the user, it resets the process' nice field in the process table.

5.6.3   Process Regions

There are two system calls that may require either the allocation, deallocation, or modification of regions belonging to an invoking process—*execve()* and *brk()*. A third system call, *lock()*, is used to manipulate the status of process regions. Two other system calls, *shmat()* and *shmdt()*, attach and detach shared memory regions respectively.

The *execve()* system call receives three arguments. The first is the name of the program file to be executed, the second is an array of character string arguments to be passed to the program, and the third is an array of character strings representing the environment of the new program. *Execve()* first retrieves the inode of the filename argument, verifies that the user has permission to execute the requested file, and makes sure that the file module can be loaded. The system call then copies its arguments from the address space of the calling process to the system space. All the regions attached to the process are detached, and for every region specified in the load module of the invoked program, a new region is allocated, attached, and loaded if necessary. At this stage the *execve()* arguments that were stored in the system space are copied into the new user stack region. The user register save area is initialized, the inode of the executable file is unlocked and control is passed back to the new user-mode program.

The *brk()* system call is used by a process to either increase or decrease the size of its data region. This system call is quite simple, receiving a new break value as an argument, and returning the old break value as output. When invoked, *brk()* first locks the process data region. If the size of the data region is being increased, then the new size must fall within the bounds allowed, otherwise the data region is unlocked and *brk()* returns an error. The region size is changed by invoking the kernel routine *growreg()* and all addresses in the new data space are zeroed out. The data region is then unlocked and the system call returns the old region size.

Super-user processes may lock or unlock process regions residing in system memory by invoking the *lock()* system call. Locking regions prevents them from swapping and is often useful when a process wishes to neutralize the actions of the swapper upon itself. This system call receives as its argument an integer representing the operation requested by the user. There are four types of operations available to the user:

1. Locking all the data regions of the calling process in memory

2. Locking only the text region of the calling process in memory

3. Locking only the data region of the calling process in memory

4. Unlocking all the locked regions of the calling process

5.6.4 Signals

There are two system calls for handling transmission and reception of signals in UNIX: *kill()* and *signal()*. Another system calls, *pause()* is used to synchronize process execution with signals.

The *kill()* system call is used to send signals to a process or group of processes. This system call receives two arguments; the first is the target or targets selected to receive the signal, and the second is the signal to be sent. *Kill()* first verifies that the signal being sent is a valid signal. It then ascertains that the calling process is either root or that either its real or effective UIDs match those of the target or targets requested. The targets may be defined by the integer value supplied as an argument, henceforth referred to as *target*.

- If *target* is a positive integer, it represents a single process as the target.

- If *target* equals zero then the targets are all of the processes in the sender's process group.

- If *target* equals −1 then the targets are all processes whose real or effective UID equals the effective UID of the process invoking *kill()*, unless the call was made by the super-user, in which case all processes become targets (but note that process No. 1 - *init* cannot be killed).

- If *target* is less than −1 then the targets are all processes in the process group with the absolute value of *target*.

Once the target's process table entry has been located, the appropriate bit representing the signal in the signal vector is set. When the process next returns to user mode, the signal will be detected and handled.

Signals may be caught and handled using the *signal()* system call. This system call receives two arguments; the signal to be caught, and the the action

to be taken upon receipt of the signal. This system call first ensures that the
signal whose handling is requested is a valid signal and not one of the few signals
that cannot be caught, such as **SIGKILL**. The action to be taken is installed in
the signal response vector. located in the process' *u area*. The action may be
one of three requests: to ignore the signal, to handle the signal according to
the standard system default action, or a request for a user-defined function to
be invoked. Special handling is required for the case in which the signal being
handled is **SIGCLD** and zombie children already exist. In this case, the kernel
routine *psignal()* is invoked by the process on its own behalf and the **SIGCLD**
signal is sent to the process.

The *pause()* system call is used to suspend a process execution pending the
receipt of a signal of any kind.

5.6.5   Processes and Time

Although UNIX was not intended to serve as a realtime system, a number of
system calls allow the UNIX process to take advantage of the system clock.
These system calls can be categorized into three classes: calls that request time
and timing information, calls that set time and timing information, and calls
that either take or refrain from taking actions until specific times.

The system calls belonging to the first class are *time()* and *times()*, which
respectively return the system time in seconds since 0:00.00 January 1, 1970
GMT, and the accounting time for the process.

The *time()* system call is quite straightforward; it merely reads the system
clock and returns its value to the user. The *times()* system call is slightly more
complex; it reads several fields from the process *proc table* entry. The information
returned in the *tms* data structure consists of four times:

1. The CPU time spent by the process in user mode

2. The CPU time spent by the process in kernel mode

3. The sum of the CPU times spent by the process and its children in user
   mode

4. The sum of the CPU times spent by the process and its children in kernel
   mode

The accounting information regarding the child process resource consumption
is updated in the *wait()* system call.

The second group, responsible for setting times, consists of only one system
call in UNIX System V Release 2, *stime()*. This call receives a pointer to a
variable of the type **long**. The call sets the system time to the given time after
ascertaining that the call is being invoked by the super-user.

The last group currently consists of only a single system call, *alarm()*. The
alarm() system call is used to trigger the realtime reception of a signal, **SIGALRM**,
by the calling process. It receives an unsigned integer argument specifying the

number of seconds to pass before the signal is sent. The system call first raises the kernel priority in order to block any clock interrupts and their resultant handling, the appropriate field in the process' *proc table* entry is then set to the specified value, following which the previous kernel priority is restored and the previous alarm value is returned.

5.6.6 Debugging

Two system calls provide support for debugging and tracing processes—*profil()* and *ptrace()*. The *profil()* system call receives four arguments. The first argument is the address of an array in user space, the second argument is the size of the array, the third argument is the virtual address of the first user subroutine that should be profiled, and the last argument consists of a factor that is used to scale the profile into an appropriate slot in the buffer array. The system call merely copies the values of the arguments supplied into the appropriate fields in the *u area* profile structure field. Once copied, the actual profiling is performed during the process execution.

The *ptrace()* system call is used to control the execution of a process that the user wishes to trace. The system call receives a command, a PID, a virtual address, and a data value. The command denotes the action to be taken and can have one of the following values:

1. If *command* equals 0 then the process is marked as being traced by the parent (and all the subsequent arguments to the system call are ignored). This is the only request that can be made by a process on its own behalf. All other requests can only be made by the parent process and the PID argument determines the process on whose behalf the action is to be taken.

2. If *command* equals either 1 or 2, then the data found at address *address* is returned.

3. If *command* equals 3 then a word of data is returned from the address *address* when taken as an offset in the traced process' *u area*.

4. If *command* equals either 4 or 5, then a data word *data* is written into the virtual address *address* in the traced process.

5. If *command* equals 6, then the data word supplied is written into the offset address *address* in the traced process' *u area*.

6. If *command* equals 7, then the traced process is allowed to resume its execution, optionally emulating a received signal.

7. If *command* equals 8, then the traced process is caused to exit.

8. If *command* equals 9, then a bit is set in the PSW register signifying that the process is to be executed in single stepping mode.

5.7   Summary

This chapter described traditional UNIX processes. It presented the organization
of system memory into regions, and described how the regions are manipulated.
It then described the organization of the process, including data structures such
as the process table and *u area*. Then process context was described, and how
it is affected by interrupts and system calls. Process states were then discussed,
followed by a description of process scheduling. Finally, several system calls
related to processes were described.

Chapter 6

The MOSIX Process

Processes in MOSIX have the same structure as UNIX processes – the only difference is that they can migrate and run on other processors. This has a few implications, which are the subject of this chapter. The main affected areas are remote paging, locating other processes, and interprocess communication. Other aspects such as region management, scheduling, and context switching remain unchanged.

6.1 Remote Paging

The organization of the system memory in MOSIX follows that of UNIX System V Release 2. MOSIX kernels contain regions and region tables, in accordance with the schema described in Chapter 5.

Text and data regions, which contained an inode pointer in UNIX, now contain a universal inode structure instead. The inode text reference is updated accordingly when a text region is allocated or freed, using Scalls. Holding the text file's universal inode structure allows handling local and remote paging in the same way.

Remote paging uses a very similar mechanism to Scall. A page must be brought in from the original demand-paged file, whether on the same processor or not. The upper-kernel page-fault routines do not make this distinction. The reason for using an extra mechanism and not just an Scall is that a page fault may occur while already performing an Scall when Funnel data to/from absent pages must be brought from another (possibly a third) processor. Otherwise, the mechanism is very similar to Scalls and the communication overhead statistics are collected in the same manner as Scalls.

Picking a page from a file (or swap) is a slow process and is usually avoided if the page can still be found anywhere in memory (from previous use), thus the whole portion of the unused memory is used as a cache. When a file (inode) is modified/removed, all the pages in core are marked as obsolete (i.e., removed from the cache). With remote files, however, it is not known whether they were modified or not – unless a text reference count is kept (but then they are marked as "text-busy" and modification attempts will fail). The text reference counts are kept as long as there are local processes actually running the program from that file. In MOSIX there is an extra code which ensures that the cache for remote text files is flushed when the last process using that text terminates or migrates away (but not before).

6.2   MOSIX Process Structure

Processes in MOSIX retain the same basic structure as in UNIX. Each MOSIX process has an entry in the process table of its current machine. All the tables required for running a process, such as the process *pregion table* and the *u area* are located in the same machine, allowing the process to be treated as a complete and distinct object. When the process is demand-paged, only the pages that were actually in use or modified are present on the process' machine, while the other pages remain in the original executable file, possibly on another machine. After a process migrates, none of its tables and memory pages remain on the sending processor.

In order to support dynamic process migration, additional fields were added to the process table and the *u area*. Otherwise, the standard UNIX fields remain mostly unchanged.

6.2.1   Process Table Extensions

As in the standard UNIX process table, previously described in Section 5.2, the MOSIX *proc table* data structure is composed of a fixed number of process table entries. Each process table entry contains all the information found in the process table entries described in Figure 5.2, as well as additional fields required by MOSIX to support distributed kernel operations between processors. The augmented MOSIX process table entry is shown in Figure 6.1.

Following are the main extensions to the process-table:

ZOMBIE BITMAP As mentioned in Section 5.4, exiting process are in the zombie state and their process table entries must be cleared by their parent. This is a relatively simple matter in a single machine environment. In a distributed environment such as MOSIX, however, the task of locating all the child processes that may have migrated requires some a priori knowledge if the extensive use of broadcasts is to be avoided. Zombie processes do not normally migrate (unless their machine is about to be turned off or disconnected) and may hence be considered static objects. An exiting process informs its parent process by setting the bit that corresponds to the node where it dies in the parent's zombie bitmap. The parent process clears that bit when all the zombie child *proc table* entries at the specific node are cleared.

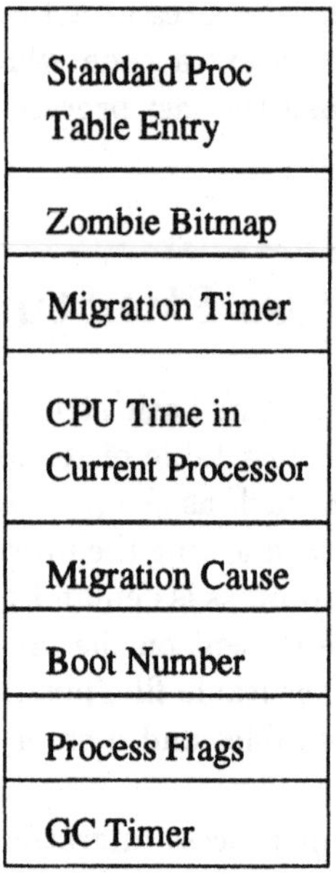

Standard Proc Table Entry
Zombie Bitmap
Migration Timer
CPU Time in Current Processor
Migration Cause
Boot Number
Process Flags
GC Timer

Figure 6.1: MOSIX Process Table Entry

MIGRATION TIMER This field accumulates the CPU usage since the last attempt to migrate the process away from the local machine to a remote one. This field is used for load balancing purposes by the kernel procedure *choose()*, shown in Procedure 8.6 in Chapter 8.

CPU TIME IN CURRENT PROCESSOR For migration considerations it is necessary to record the process' accumulated CPU usage on the current processor, either since it started or since it migrated to the processor.

MIGRATION CAUSE This serves as an indicator of the urgency or reason for the migration. Migration can be caused by:

- Explicit request, generated by the *migrate()* system call
- Load balancing mechanisms, which select the process as a candidate for migration
- Intensive remote I/O, which will result in a migration to reduce the I/O overhead
- Excessive forking, which will result in the probable migration of the parent process

- System shutdown, which will attempt to expel all foreign processes to either their home machines, or any other machine known to be available

BOOT NUMBER One of MOSIX's advantages is the ability to have nodes leave and join the network. In order to avoid the inconsistency generated by processors that have recently rejoined the network and are unaware of active processes created by a prior kernel session, each process is tagged with a boot number. The boot number, which is read from the local disk and immediately updated at boot time, provides a unique process identification.

PROCESS FLAGS The following process flags have also been added in MOSIX:

- **SAMB**, signifying that the process is an ambassador process
- **SMOVE**, signifying that the process is currently undergoing migration and cannot accept signals
- **SHERE** for processes that cannot migrate from the current processor
- **SMARK**, set periodically as part of the garbage collection mechanism, so that if the process is stuck halfway through migration (due to a crash on the sending site), or if it becomes a zombie and the parent process node crashes before executing a *wait()* call for it, then the process entry can be reclaimed
- **SDOGC**, indicating to the process that it is time to reclaim all its resources.

Note that each of the flags can be set or cleared independently by the appropriate kernel procedures.

GC TIMER Counts down the time until the next garbage collection. When this counter reaches zero, the **SDOGC** flag is set, the process reclaims its resources to prevent the garbage collector from discarding these resources as garbage, and the counter is reset for the next cycle.

6.2.2   The U Area Extensions

In addition to the standard UNIX *u area* fields, previously described in Subsection 5.2.2, the MOSIX *u area*, shown in Figure 6.2, includes the following main extensions:

IPC DEFAULTS The identity of the node, or a specific processor in multiprocessor workstation, to be used for establishing connections for the three types of interprocess communication (IPC) – shared memory, messages, and semaphores (see Section 6.5).

CHILD COUNT AND RECENT FORKS This field keeps track of the number of child processes and whether any were created recently. This is needed to make the *wait()* system call more reliable, for garbage collection, and for deciding to migrate the process if it performs excessive forks.

PROCESSOR OF CONTROLLING TERMINAL The controlling terminal is no longer determined by the device number alone, so the processor where that device is, must be recorded as well.

COMMUNICATION STATISTICS The accumulated amount of communication to different machines is recorded, for migration purposes.

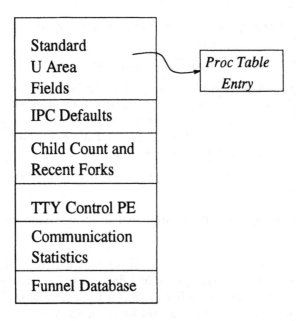

Figure 6.2: MOSIX U Area

6.3   MOSIX Process System Calls

MOSIX preserves the UNIX system call interface, but doing that in a distributed environment requires extra considerations. The system calls that are most affected are those requiring communication between two or more processes, which can be anywhere, or even in the midst of a migration. These system calls are *exit()*, *wait()*, *kill()*, and *ptrace()*.

In addition to the system calls that are listed in Table 5.1, MOSIX supports the following system calls:

sysps(), to locate a process and return the information required for *ps*

readkernel(), which has an option used to locate a process and read (parts of) its *u area*

migrate(), where a process requests an explicit migration and/or to remain locked in a processor or remove that lock

distsys() used also to allow/block process migration to/from particular processors as well as expelling all foreign processes (e.g., when entering single-user mode)

Other system calls are only slightly or subtly affected; for example, the *plock()* system call, which locks a process (or any of its regions) in memory, also implies locking the process on its current processor. Another example is the *getppid()* system call, which must locate the parent process just to see whether it is still alive.

6.3.1 Locating Processes

Most of the abovementioned system calls, as well as the ongoing garbage collection activity, require the ability to locate another process, such as the parent process, a child process, or any other process specified by the *kill()* system call. This is not a trivial task in an environment where processes can migrate at any time.

The primary means for locating a process is its *home* structure, located in the *home table* in one of the processors, usually the processor where the process was created.

Figure 6.3 depicts the fields of the *home* structure. The first field is the process identifier (PID). A simple function maps the process ID to the processor number where its home structure can be found. A process always updates its home structure when it migrates and when it terminates. This, however, does not ensure that the process will actually be found where it's supposed to be according to the home structure, because it might have migrated. Thus, if the process is not found, a few retries are necessary. If the process is still not found at the location pointed out by the home structure, then it is assumed to have crashed along with some processor. In this case, the garbage collection mechanism will clear the home structure.

The home structure also maintains a count of processes that have the process (whose home it is) as their process group leader, shown in Figure 6.3 as the Pgroup Count. This ensures that if the leader exits before the rest of its group, no other process will get the same process ID as that group, to avoid the (rare) possibility of merging signals from two distinct process groups. Another field in the home structure is a flag telling the process that it still has child processes. This flag is set by child processes and cleared by the garbage collection mechanism, so a parent will not wait forever if its child processes are gone (e.g., crashed with a processor).

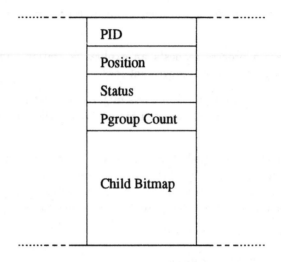

Figure 6.3: The Home Structure

6.3.2 MOSIX Process Creation and Termination

When a process forks, its child process is initially located on the same processor as its parent. This means that there is no remote forking in MOSIX. Note that migration may be considered just before forking; for example, when failing to fork, and thus trying somewhere else. In any case, the final result is that initially the parent and the child process are located on the same machine. The MOSIX *fork()* system call is shown in Procedure 6.1.

Special notes about *fork()*:

- A home structure is allocated for each child process. The child's process ID is determined by the processor where its home is allocated.

- The child's garbage collection timer is initialized. All the resources that the child process use are "touched" during the fork, so the child needs to reference them only in the next garbage collection cycle. This means that short-lived processes are not burdened with garbage collections.

- The child inherits the **SHERE** flag, so if the parent asked to avoid automatic migrations, then the child will also avoid automatic migrations, by default.

- Unlike a single-processor UNIX, incrementing file/directory universal pointers may fail due to a remote processor (or communication) failure.

```
fork ()

/* Upper Kernel fork() – on calling process' machine */

{
    if ((the machine is heavily loaded or
            the process already has a recent history of forking)
        and (this fork didn't already fail on 3 different machines
        after trying to migrate and find a place for its child))
            consider migration;                    /* forkmigrate() */
    allocate a new PID, preferably from this machine
            (but may be from another);
    invokes tellhome to register PID;              /* Scall */
    switch (create new process) {                  /* newproc() */
        case 1:
            initialize the child's process table entry;
            update parent process;
            return;
        case 0:
            increment number of child processes;
            break;
        default:
            if (no more than 3 migrations already
                attempted by this call)
            migrate the parent;                    /* forkmigrate() */
    }
}
```

Procedure 6.1: Fork System Call

When this happens, all other files/directories on the same (failed) processor must be discarded and the already-incremented files/inodes must be re-decremented.

The MOSIX *exit()* system call is shown in Procedure 6.2.
Special notes about *exit()*:

- An exiting process is not a candidate for migration.

- The process may be holding semaphore-undo-on-exit structures in several processors. They must all be respected.

- Short-lived child processes on the same processor are attached to their grandparent (or great-grand parent, etc.) for the purpose of fork-migration.

```
    exit (val)

    {
            disable process tracing and migration;
            mark process as exiting, ignoring all signals;
            detach all regions;                              /* detachreg() */
            Spgrpref to decrement the process-group size;    /* Scall */
            Stellhome to notify the home machine;            /* Scall */
            for (each open file)
                    Sclosef to close the file at the file's node;   /* Scall */
            Sidec to close the current and root directories; /* Scall */
            for (each node where the process holds semaphors)
                    Ssemexit to release any semaphores held;  /* Scall */
            clear all zombies;                                /* zclear() */
            connect dependent child processes to parent;
    loop:   if (tries < 10)
                    Sposition to locate position of parent;   /* Scall */
            else set error;
            switch (error) {
                    case no error:
                            if (parent located)
                                    break;
                    case parent already died:
    suicide:                if (parent found this process [by luck]) goto zomb;
                            mark process status as if migrated away;
                            goto nortrn;
                    default: Slocate to locate parent;        /* Scall */
                            clear error;
            }
            Sdie to send parent signal;                       /* Scall */
            if (error) {
                    if (tries > max or parent is already exiting)
                            goto suicide;
                    goto loop;
            }
    zomb:   set status to ZOMBIE;
            update proc table resource usage;
    nortrn: wake up parent if waiting for zombie;
            decrement running processes;
            relinquish the CPU by performing a final
                    context switch;                           /* swtch() */
    }
```

Procedure 6.2: Exit System Call

- The parent process needs to be located, so it is informed of the process' death.

- Zombie child structures may be spread across different processors and need to be cleared wherever they are.

- There are intricate race conditions when the exiting child tries to locate its parent while the parent tries to locate it at the same time, especially when there are communication problems with the parent's *home*.

The MOSIX *wait()* system call is shown in Procedure 6.3.

```
    wait ()

    {
loop:      while (a zombie child exists)
                  if (ignoring death of child)
                       clear all zombies;                    /* zclear() */
                  else
                       if (successfully collected zombie status)
                            return;
              if (a stopped child process exists)
                  return (pid of stopped child and the signal causing it to stop);
              if (positive child counter and
                  (recently forking or child processes registered at home)) {
                  if (no zombies exist and process isn't stopped)
sleep:            sleep;
                  goto loop;
              }
              if (positive child counter) {
                  log "child processes lost";
                  clear child counter;
              }
              return(error);
    }
```

Procedure 6.3: Wait System Call

A special note about *wait()*:

- If no zombie children are found and no recent *fork()* was made, the garbage collection mechanism of the *home* processor is consulted to find whether there are still any children. Note that if there are recent children, they probably did not report to the home machine garbage collection mechanism yet.

6.4 Process Migration

This section describes the mechanism of process migration once a decision to migrate is made. Further information about migration considerations is given in Chapter 8. Note that a user program may also decide to migrate via the *migrate()* system call.

6.4.1 The Migrate System Call

A user program can request to migrate via the *migrate()* system call. *Migrate()* receives two arguments: the destination processor, where to migrate; and whether to stay locked (avoid automatic migration) on the new processor. Two special cases of the processor number argument are possible: the first allows the process to stay on the current processor (but change the lock, allowing/disallowing automatic migrations); the second case indicates a request for a migration consideration by the kernel (which can allow a "controlled" automatic migration at certain times). The second argument is **lock**. This argument has 4 possible values: unlock, lock, keep the current lock state, and make sure the process is not locked (and if it is, return an error).

The *migrate()* system call, shown in Procedure 6.4, starts by checking the validity of its arguments. If the process is locked in memory (by the *lock()* system call or because it attached a shared memory region), the system call usually fails.

If migration is required, the "already migrated" indicator is set (it is passed to the new processor as part of the *u area*) and a migration is attempted. If the migration fails, the "already migrated" indicator is cleared and an error is returned, unless the request was for kernel consideration, in which case it is not an error to remain on the current processor.

6.4.2 The Actual Migration

When a decision to migrate is made, the process calls the *passto()* routine to perform the actual migration. The arguments to *passto()* are: where to migrate; whether this is a user request (which allows migration to less resourceful processors); whether this is due to load-balancing considerations; and if so, a threshold for the load of the remote machine, used to avoid migration if its load is increased in the meantime.

The migration routine *passto()* is shown in Procedure 6.5. The first step of *passto()* is to check that the process is allowed to migrate and that it is allowed to migrate processes to the destination processor. Then the remote *Smakeproc()* routine is called to allocate a process frame on the destination processor and initialize the process' memory regions. The process' *u area* is also passed to *Smakeproc()* via an output Funnel. Note that *makeproc()* may fail if the destination processor is not willing to accept processes from the sending processor, or if it has no space or sufficient free memory for the migrating process.

If the process is being migrated for load balancing purposes, then load balancing has been disabled up to this stage. Once the remote process is created

```
        migrate (whereto, lock)

        {
                validate lock value;
                if ((lock == migrate-only-if-unlocked) and process locked)
                        return(error);
                validate whereto value;
                if (process is locked in memory) {
                        if (whereto < 0)
                                whereto = 0;
                        if (whereto > 0 and whereto is not the local processor)
                                return(error);
                }
                if (whereto is local or already migrated successfully) {
local:                  if (migrated successfully)
                                relock the process if previously locked;
                        if (lock is a lock request)
                                disable migration for the process;
                        if (lock is an unlock' request)
                                enable migration for the process;
                        return(processor number);
                }
                mark that migration was considered;
                if (migration is disabled and (lock == 0))
                        mark that the process has migrated and needs relocking;
                else
                        mark that the process has migrated;
                set process' migration target to whereto;
                store migration status;
                allow migration temporarily, even if process is locked;
                attempt migration;                              /* consider() */
                clear the "has migrated" state;
                if (migration target is for the kernel to consider)
                        goto local;
                return(error);
        }
```

Procedure 6.4: Migrate System Call

```
    passto (to, usrreq, for_loadbalancing, maxload)

{
        if (to cannot be reached or migration is disabled or
            process is init or process uses shared memory)
            return;
        save user's floating-point registers;              /* savfp() */
        increase the process' priority for the migration;
        Smakeproc to invoke makeproc() on processor;       /* Scall */
        if (errors occurred) {
            goto nodeal;
        }
        if (process is being migrated due to high load)
            consider sending other processes;              /* load_balance() */
        pass the process' memory regions;
        if (errors occurred)
            goto nodeal;
        temporarily block traced children from sending their stop-status;
        Spassproc to pass the process table entry;         /* Scall */
        if (errors occurred)
            goto nodeal;
        Stellhome to update process' home site;            /* Scall */
        Sactivate to run the process at the new site;      /* Scall */
        clear the local process table entry;
        detach the process' local regions;
        release the CPU;                                   /* swtch() */
nodeal: clear error;
        restore priority;
}
```

Procedure 6.5: Migration Routine

and the local load reduced as if this process had already migrated, the load balancing is re-enabled, so that other processes may migrate simultaneously if the local load is still high.

The next step is passing the actual process data. Only modified memory pages need to be passed - *makeproc()* marked all the other pages either as demand-paged from the process executable file or as zero filled.

The next step, calling *Spassproc()*, is the commit point. If it succeeds, signals can arrive at the new site. Another function of *passproc()* is to set several *proc table* fields at the new site, which were left undefined until this stage. Once the successful, committing reply from the remote processor is received, the process informs its home about its location, then the remote site is informed that it can

```
    makeproc (pid, pgrp, tinm, touched, dinm, dpgsz, spgsz, usrreq,
              caps, from, wrote, maxload)

    {
          if (migration disabled or (export-load > maxload))
                return(error);
          if (not usrreq)
                ensure process' access to remote resources;
          copy the u area in;                          /* fun2mem() */
          verify that the process ID is not already in use;
          if (creating a new process returns an error)   /* newproc() */
                return(error);
          else
                ambassador return(success); and new process continues;
          allocate text, data, and stack regions;
          set status to ready;
          sleep on status;
          if (status is abort)
                goto fail;
          final memory management housekeeping;
          initialize communication statistics;
          restart process;                             /* prestart() */
    fail: for (each attached region)
                lock and detach the region;            /* detachreg() */
          set process' status to PASSED;
          relinquish the CPU;                          /* swtch() */
    }
```

Procedure 6.6: Process Allocation Routine

start running (*Sactivate*), passing to it any signals and zombie child information received while migrating, as well as the alarm time left (from an *alarm()* system call) and the "time-left to the next garbage collection cycle" timer. Finally, the local process and its memory are cleared.

While *passto()* is activated on the sending site, another procedure, *makeproc()*, shown in Procedure 6.6, is activated on the destination processor. *Makeproc()* is activated by an ambassador process. First, it makes sure that it is allowed to accept processes from the sending processor and that the local load still justifies process migration. Unless the migration was explicitly requested by the user (*migrate()*), *makeproc()* also ensures that the process maintains its ability to communicate with other processors, with whom it could communicate previously. The next step is to bring in the process *u area* from the Funnel. Just before creating the new process frame, it is verified that the migrating process

PID is not already in use (a rare possibility) due to a node crash or a communication failure. In this case, an error is returned and the migration is aborted. The ambassador then creates a new process, which inherits the upper kernel parts of the *u area* from the migrating process. The ambassador then returns the success/failure of creating the new process.

The new process frame continues by setting up its memory regions according to the *makeproc()* arguments, marks itself as "ready to accept data" and remains passive while new Scalls fill in its memory contents and *proc* fields. Eventually, it will be awakened for one of two reasons: a successful *activate()* or a request to abort the migration (due to failure in filling the process' data, extreme shortage of memory and swap space on the new processor, or by the garbage collection mechanism). If a request to abort is received, the new process frees its memory and itself. Otherwise the process performs some final housekeeping tasks, initialize its communication statistics and resumes running where the sending site left off.

6.5   Interprocess Communication

Five basic types of *interprocess communication (IPC)* are available in UNIX System V Release 2 [2], and therefore in MOSIX. They are:

- Messages

- Shared memory

- Semaphores

- Pipes

- Signals

A comprehensive explanation of all the mechanisms involved can be found in [3].

6.5.1   IPC Mechanisms in MOSIX

MOSIX supports almost the exact IPC interface between processes that run on different machines as the UNIX interface on a single machine. The following slight differences should, however, be noted:

- Shared memory is not allowed between processes on different nodes. This would have required the shared memory itself to migrate whenever a process needs it. Instead, a process that attaches a shared memory segment is migrated to the processor where the segment is, and is locked there for as long as it uses that segment. In the VME532 version of MOSIX a special (non-standard) form of shared memory is also available for processes on different processors within the same (multiprocessor) workstation. In this case, processes that use shared memory may migrate between the processors of the same workstation.

- The standard UNIX System V Release 2 interface uses *keys* (e.g., message keys, semaphore keys and shared memory keys) to identify global IPC objects. Since processors are autonomous and may run independent versions of the same programs, a fundamental problem is raised: software packages usually use unique constants as IPC keys. Such keys could now be associated with more than one object and the crucial uniqueness would be lost. The solution in MOSIX is that all keys are interpreted on the process' root processor by default. Distributed applications, however, may change those defaults (for each of the three types of keys respectively) at any time, so they can access any IPC object in the system.

- A new signal, SIGLOST, was added. This signal informs the process that one or more of the open files it was using, or its current directory (or even the root directory, when not any machine's root) is no longer accessible, due to a remote node crash or communication failure. Clearly, this cannot happen in standard UNIX, because when a machine crashes, all processes, files and directories crash along with it and there are no process left to receive such a signal.

6.6 Summary

This chapter described the MOSIX extensions that were necessary to allow UNIX processes to migrate, while retaining the standard interaction between them. It described the remote paging mechanism, extensions to the process structure, the process-related system calls and interprocess communication and the process migration mechanism.

Chapter 7

The MOSIX Linker

The role of the Linker in the MOSIX system architecture is to couple the processor-independent upper kernel to the site-dependent lower kernel. The upper kernel and lower kernel that are being linked may be on the same machine; or they may be on different machines, in which case, two Linkers—one on each machine—are involved. The Linker is composed of the following three layers: the kernel interface layer, the transport layer, and the network layer (see Figure 7.1).

The **kernel interface layer**, the highest layer of the Linker, provides the kernel with three abstract mechanisms: remote kernel procedure calls, data Funnels, and ambassador processes. The name used internally by MOSIX and in this chapter for a remote kernel procedure call is **Scall** (pronounced **ess call**), short for "span and call," since the mechanism allows kernel procedure calls to span interprocessor boundaries.

The Scall mechanism provides the MOSIX kernel with remote procedure call functionality. Each routine of the upper kernel that access a site-specific object (e.g., a certain file or inode structure) does so by calling its lower kernel counterpart via the Scall mechanism. If the object resides on the local site, the Linker calls the appropriate local routine directly. Otherwise, the Linker routes the call over the network to the object's host processor.

Funnels are one-way, reliable communications data channels between the upper and lower portions of the kernel. All data that is pushed into one end of a Funnel is read out of the other end in the correct order. Each MOSIX process can have an associated Funnel through which data is moved into or out of the lower kernel. For example, when a lower kernel routine reads a file from the disk, an input Funnel is used to transfer the file data to the upper kernel. If the file resides on a local disk, the Linker uses a local Funnel to transfer the data. If the file resides on a remote processor, a remote input Funnel is used to transfer the data over the network.

The third high-layer mechanism used by the MOSIX kernel is the **ambassador process**. Ambassador processes are light-weight kernel daemon processes that are created at boot time and used to handle remote Scalls. On the object's

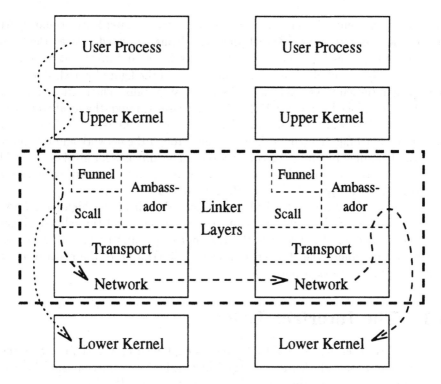

Figure 7.1: The MOSIX Linker

host processor, the Linker assigns an ambassador process the task of calling a routine on behalf of a requesting process. After the remote call completes, the ambassador process returns the result of the routine over the network and then awaits the next request.

The **transport layer** of the MOSIX kernel provides reliable, sequential network communications to the kernel interface mechanisms. The transport layer **port** mechanism is the logical endpoint for all actual network transactions. A port is assigned to each instance of an Scall by the transport layer. and used throughout the life of the call for all network communications by each of the higher level mechanisms.

The lowest layer of the Linker, the **network layer**, is composed of the network devices and their software drivers. Since this layer of the Linker is intrinsically implementation dependent, the chapter describes only those routines called directly by the transport layer.

Figure 7.1 traces the path that a system call takes while passing through the Linker. The figure shows the layers involved at two nodes—the local node on the left and the remote node on the right. The Linker layers are shown in the dashed box. A locally executed system call follows the path shown by the dotted arrow. A user process issuing a system call traps into the upper kernel procedure that executes the system call. The upper kernel activates its lower kernel counterpart via an Scall. Since the lower kernel procedure being activated is local, the Scall mechanism bypasses the transport and network layers and invokes it directly.

A remotely executed system call, represented in the figure by dashed arrows, is invoked in the same way as locally executed system calls. Then, since the lower kernel being invoked is not local, the request passes through the local transport and network layers and is transmitted via the LAN to the remote machine. At the remote machine, the request is passed up through the network and transport layers and handled by an ambassador process. The ambassador invokes the local lower kernel procedure on behalf of the remote user process. Return value(s) are passed back to the upper kernel via the reverse route.

Section 7.1 presents a detailed description of each of the high-level Linker mechanisms—Scalls, ambassador processes, Funnels, and the related Linker procedures. Section 7.2 describes the transport layer and its various routines. Section 7.3 concludes the chapter with a brief description of the network layer routines used by the transport layer.

7.1 The Interface Layer

The interface layer of the MOSIX Linker, as explained previously, contains the routines that present the kernel with the following high-level mechanisms: kernel-level remote procedure calls, ambassador processes, and data Funnels.

7.1.1 Kernel Remote Procedure Calls

The MOSIX Scall is a kernel-level Remote Procedure Call (RPC). Together with the Funnel mechanism and an ambassador process, a MOSIX Scall provides the upper kernel with the convenience of using the same calling sequence to invoke remote and local kernel procedures.

A typical MOSIX system call is a little more than a wrapper that does initial verification of the user's access rights and arguments before invoking the appropriate Scall to carry out the bulk of the work. If data needs to be transferred between processors during the call, the Scall mechanism uses the process' associated **Funnel** to handle the transfer (see Subsection 7.1.3).

Procedure 7.1 describes in detail the implementation of the Scall mechanism. *Scall()* is invoked with the following arguments:

processor: the number of the target processor on which to carry out the remote procedure call

args: a pointer to the argument list of the procedure

retval: a pointer to the structure in which to store the result of the Scall (for Scalls that return a non-scalar results)

callnum: the index of this call into the table of kernel remote procedures.

```
    Scall (processor, args, retval, callnum)

    {
        collect remote communication statistics;
        if (local call) {
            perform call locally;
            close the funnel;
            return(result);
        }
        allocate a port;                        /* portalloc() */
        send an Scall request to target processor;
        process funnel data;                    /* Procedure 7.3 */
        if (error) {
            if (local error)
                notify remote ambassador;       /* send() */
            close the funnel;
            return(error);
        }
        add Scall remote execution time to process time;
        clean up any leftover data in the process' funnel;
        close funnel;
        if (error detected)
            set u area error code;
        return(value or structure);
    }
```

Procedure 7.1: The MOSIX Span and Call (Scall) Procedure

The *processor* argument is used by the Linker to determine if this call is a local call and if not, where the call should be executed. For system calls that deal with files, the *processor* argument passed to the *Scall()* routine is the processor address from the universal inode structure of the file being manipulated.

Since the Scall mechanism is available only in the kernel, the list of legitimate kernel remote procedures is determined statically. The *callnum* is an index into an array of structures that specify which routine should be called, the size and type of the arguments and its return value.

As shown in Procedure 7.1, *Scall()* starts by collecting statistics that are used by the load balancing information tools described in Chapter 8. If the target processor is the local processor, then the appropriate routine is invoked directly. Note that even local calls make use of the Funnel mechanism and must close the Funnel before returning.

Remote calls must first allocate a port (see Subsection 7.2.1) before beginning the remote procedure call. After an Scall message is sent to the target processor to begin the call, *Scall()* sleeps until the remote processor acknowledges the call. If there is data that needs to be transferred via a remote Funnel, *Scall()* handles the local end of the connection as needed. *Scall()* then invokes Procedure 7.3, which will be discussed fully in Subsection 7.1.3, to process the Funnel data. Before returning, *Scall()* closes the process' Funnel and sets the appropriate error code in the *u area*, if required.

7.1.2 Ambassador Processes

Ambassador processes are (light-weight) kernel daemon processes that represent a remotely executing process for the duration of an Scall that is performed on the ambassador's local processor. During kernel initialization, a predetermined number of ambassador kernel processes are created. Each of these processes handles incoming requests as long as the system is running, as shown in Procedure 7.2. Whenever an ambassador port gets an incoming message, the next available ambassador process wakes up and processes the event. During calls that involve data transfer via the Funnel mechanism, the ambassador also services its end of the Funnel.

```
ambassador ()

{
    Forever {
        find task that needs to be served;
        if (task is an Scall)
            handle request;                 /* serve() */
        else                                /* must be a page fault */
            handle page fault;
        call task completion routine;
    }
}
```

Procedure 7.2: The Ambassador Routine

Ambassadors handle two types of events: Scalls, which are described in the previous section, and requests for pages of memory that are produced whenever a process page faults on a page that does not reside on that process' local disk. Ambassadors handle a page fault request by bringing the requested page into memory (if it is not already in the cache) and then sending it to the requesting processor.

When handling an Scall request, the ambassador process mimics the requesting process by setting various fields in its own *u area* to those of the process that it is servicing. In this way, the ambassador process is granted access only to objects that the requesting process itself could access. The appropriate procedure call is then made on the ambassador's processor. Note that the lower kernel routines are responsible for handling Funnel data.

7.1.3   Funnels

Funnels are one-way channels used to move data between the upper and lower kernel. The naming convention used for MOSIX Funnels indicates the direction of the data flow from the point of view of the initiating process: an **input Funnel** transfers data to the calling processor's upper kernel from the (possibly remote) lower kernel, while an **output Funnel** transfers data from the calling processor's upper kernel to the (possibly remote) lower kernel.

In standard UNIX, the kernel maintains most of its process-related information in a data structure called the *u area*, described in Chapter 5. Since each MOSIX process has no more than one active Funnel, MOSIX also uses the *u area* to hold Funnel information.

The MOSIX *u area* contains fields that describe two Funnels for each process: the **active Funnel** and the **backup Funnel**. The active Funnel information describes the Funnel that is currently being used to transfer data. A second, temporary Funnel is set up to handle the local data transfer. For example, the lower-kernel counterpart of the *mount()* system call, *mountl()*, needs to read the mounted superblock into memory, using *readi()*, which in turn calls *mem2fun()* to bring the data in. This must not be confused as a Funnel to the calling processor, so the previous Funnel (if any) is backed-up and a temporary Funnel is created. No process ever needs more than one active and one backup Funnel at a time.

The Funnel-related *u area* fields include:

- A flag indicating whether the Funnel is an input or an output Funnel

- The base address for input and output operations

- The number of bytes currently in the Funnel

- A flag indicating which memory segment the Funnel is using

- A pointer to the communications port associated with the Funnel

The Linker deals with four types of Funnels, which are depicted in Figure 7.2:

- Remote input Funnels, shown as the gray Funnel labeled "1," are used to transfer data from the lower kernel of Processor B to a process running in the upper kernel of Processor A.

- Remote output Funnels, shown as the gray Funnel labeled "2," are used to transfer data from a process running in the upper kernel of Processor A to the lower kernel of Processor B.

- Local input Funnels, shown as the white Funnel labeled "3," transfer data from Processor A's lower kernel to a process running in the upper kernel of the same processor. This is eventually done via a call to the standard UNIX *copyout()* function.

- Local output Funnels, shown as the white Funnel labeled "4," transfer data from a process running in Processor A's upper kernel to the same processor's lower kernel. This is eventually done via a call to the standard UNIX *copyin()* function.

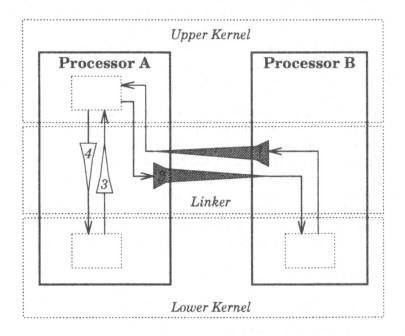

Figure 7.2: MOSIX Funnels

7.1.4 Funnel Kernel Procedures

The MOSIX kernel uses a small set of procedures that manipulate the various types of Funnels. The procedures *setinf()* and *setoutf()* are used to create new input and output Funnels respectively. The two routines start by verifying the access rights of the caller to the area of memory in the upper kernel. If the requested operation is legitimate, both routines finish by initializing the previously mentioned Funnel fields in the *u area*.

The routines that are used to transfer data via the Funnel mechanism, are called by the remote ambassador process or local lower kernel. For example, the *read()* system call sets up an input Funnel by calling the *setinf()* procedure and

```
active_loop (port, remote processor number)

{
    while (port is active) {
        switch (funnel type) {
        case input funnel:
            if (new data arrived) {
                copy from port cache to the process' address space;
                if (error)
                    return(error);
                continue;
            }
            if (more data to receive) {
                wake up remote ambassador;        /* send() */
                continue;
            }
            break;
        case output funnel:
            if (data to send and room in port cache) {
                compute amount to send;
                copy from the process' address space to port cache;
                if (error)
                    return(error);
                send data from port cache;        /* send() */
                continue;
            }
            break;
        }
        sleep until packet received on port;
    }
}
```

Procedure 7.3: The Active Funnel Procedure

then invokes the *Scall()* routine. *Scall()*, after initiating the transfer as described in Procedure 7.1, calls Procedure 7.3 to read the data out of the input Funnel into the process' address space.

The routine *mem2fun()*, described in Procedure 7.4, is used by a lower kernel routine, either locally or when called by the remote ambassador on the remote processor, to place the requested data into the input Funnel. If the file resides on a remote disk then the routine *rmem2fun()*, is used by an ambassador process on the remote processor to transfer the remote data into the input Funnel.

Similarly, data is pulled from output Funnels by *fun2mem()* and *rfun2mem()*, which take data from a remote output Funnel when called by an ambassador.

```
mem2fun (memory address, amount)

{
    if (no input funnel exists)
        return(error);
    if (called by ambassador) {
        invoke remote memory to funnel copy; /* rmem2fun() */
        return(status);
    }
    if (amount > number of bytes in funnel)
        return(error);
    if (amount is zero)
        return(0);
    copy data from memory address
        to user base;                    /* copyout() or bcopy() */
    adjust data counters;
}

rmem2fun (data address, amount)

{
    if (no input funnel exists or accessive amount requested)
        return(error);
    while (port is active and no errors detected) {
        if (port cache not full) {
            copy new data into port cache;   /* bcopy() */
            update count of number of bytes processed;
        }
        send all data in port cache;
    }
    return(port status);
}
```

Procedure 7.4: Copy from Lower Kernel to Input Funnel

7.2   The Transport Layer

The transport layer of the Linker provides reliable, sequential communication for the mechanisms mentioned in Section 7.1. Due to performance considerations, the transport layer uses a nonstandard protocol. In principle, however, the interface layer can be implemented on top of any standard protocol (e.g., TCP/IP). This section describes the high-level routines that interact directly with the Linker's interface level and the procedures used internally by the transport layer in implementing reliable network communications.

7.2.1   The Port Mechanism

The major mechanism of the transport layer is the **port**. Ports serve as the logical endpoint for network communications. Any Linker interface-level mechanism associated with a particular process sends and receives messages via the process' uniquely assigned port.

The port structure contains the following information:

- Status flags to indicate the port's status (connected, active, etc.)

- The processor address of the remote processor

- A timer field that terminates the connection if not reset frequently enough by incoming or outgoing requests

- A structure that stores incoming Scall requests and another to hold the exit status of completed Scalls

- A unique session identification number, used to detect failures of one of the processors involved in the transaction

- A data cache for data in transit to or from the network device's data buffers

- A field that indicates how much space is left in the remote port's data cache during a transaction

- Sequence numbers of packets received and sent

The MOSIX kernel is configured with two pools of ports: ambassador ports and Scall ports. The number of ambassador ports is equal to the number of ambassador processes. Ambassador ports are allocated by the transport layer's *received()* routine, shown in Procedure 7.7, when it receives a packet that requires handling by an ambassador process. An ambassador process sleeps until some activity is detected on one of the ambassador ports. After locating the newly activated port, the port's status is set to active and the ambassador handles the specific request.

Scall ports are created during the *Scall()* procedure by invoking the *portalloc()* routine, shown in Procedure 7.5. *Portalloc()* searches for an idle Scall port. If no ports are available, the routine sleeps until a port is freed. After finding a

```
    portalloc ()

    {
        while (no free port) {
            if (any port is idle) {
                mark port as allocated;
                set port session to next session; /* Mod max session */
                zero timeout, sequence, data transfer, and status fields;
                setup port fields;
                set funnel type to process funnel type;
                store process id and stage in system call fields;
                store pointer to port structure in u area;
                return;
            }
            sleep until a port is free;
        }
    }
```

Procedure 7.5: The Port Allocation Routine

free port, the port's session number is incremented in order to avoid any possible confusion with packets directed to a previous session. Then, the port's timeout and data count fields are zeroed and the port's identifier fields are set to those of the calling process.

The number of ports allocated to Scalls relative to the number of ambassador processes has an important effect on system performance. For example, the current configuration limits the number of Scall ports to the number of ambassador processes in order to prevent a single processor from swamping the network with remote requests. By increasing the number of Scall ports, the number of network operations performed in parallel is increased while possibly loading each processor with more requests.

7.2.2   The Transport-Level Send Routine

The kernel interface mechanisms interact with two high-level transport routines, *send()* and *received()*, shown in Procedure 7.6 and Procedure 7.7 respectively. As the names imply, *send()* is used to send a packet over a port, and *received()* is invoked by the network layer to carry out the actions required for a received packet.

The *send()* routine accepts a packet to be transmitted over the network. *Send()*'s arguments are the initiating and target processors' identification num-

```
send (from, to, type, port session, sequence number, data)

{
        compute absolute address of network header;
        set network packet header fields to arguments;
        if (network not configured)
                return(error);
        add package to send queue for target processor; /* send_on_queue() */
}
```

Procedure 7.6: The Send Routine

bers, the type of packet, the port's session number, the sequence number of the
current packet, pointers to the various packet segments, and their sizes. The
port's identifier is held in the *u area* of the initiating process. The procedure
starts by determining if the send is a multicast or a broadcast. If no network
device is configured and the target processor is not local, an error code is returned.

Send() finishes by invoking *send_on_queue()*, shown in Procedure 7.8, which
handles transmissions between processors. The transport layer of the Linker
maintains a separate **send queue** for each of the processors on the network. The
send queue data structure contains an identifier for the packet that is currently
being sent from this queue and for the next packet on the queue. In addition,
the transport layer maintains a linked list of send queues that are waiting for
access to the network. The send queue sequence number is used to identify
retransmission of the same packet. The other fields in the data structure hold
pointers to the various segments of the packet, a retry counter and some network-
specific fields for holding low-level information required by particular network
devices.

Send_on_queue(), shown in Procedure 7.8, continues where *send()* leaves off.
In addition to the send queue associated with each processor, the transport
layer maintains several arrays, which contain sequence numbers per processor
for both broadcast and regular transmissions. The *send_on_queue()* routine also
maintains a *pwake_on_sent* array that has an entry for each processor. The entry
contains a pointer to the process structure of the process currently sending a
packet, in order to wake it up after the packet is transmitted.

Based on the packet's processor of origin, the port session number, and the
sequence identifier of the transmission on the current port, the routine computes a system-wide unique packet identification number. At this point, the
relay_packet() routine, shown in Procedure 7.9, is invoked. *Relay_packet()*'s return status is examined to see if the packet was accepted or rejected. If the

```
received (from, to, type, id, seq, header, data, hdsz, dtsz)

{
      verify site, packet address;
      find active port associated with packet;
      switch (packet type) {
          case SCALL:
              if (no idle port)
                  return;
              allocate an ambassador port and initialize all its fields;
              allocate an ambassador;
              if (duplicate Scall request)
                  release ambassador process and return;
              return;
          case Returning Scall:
              check sequence number;
              if (there is also packet data) {
                  copy data into the port cache field;
                  wake up process that made Scall;
              }
              return;
          case INDATA or OUTDATA:
              fill the port's data-cache and wake up
              process that made Scall or ambassador;
              return;
          case INWIN or OUTWIN:
              mark that the other party is ready to receive more data;
              wake Scall process or ambassador to send more data;
              verify packet sequence number;
              return;
          case ALIVE:
              reset timeout;
              return;
          case RWAKE:
              find process;
              set process to run;
              return;
          default:
              return(error);
      }
}
```

Procedure 7.7: The Receive Packet Routine

---

send_on_queue (segment addresses, segment lengths)

{
    while (transmission in progress to target processor)
        sleep until transmission finishes;
    mark "send in progress" to target processor;
    map the local packet id onto a system-wide id;
    request to send a packet from send queue;   /* relay_packet() */
    if (packet sent or send failed)
        return(status);
    if (packet not sent)
        store in pending queue;
    if (another packet was ahead of current packet in queue)
        place packet at end of queue;
    sleep until packet has been sent or send fails;
    return(status);
}

Procedure 7.8: The Send on Queue Routine

return status indicates that the packet was accepted for transmission or an error code was returned, *send_on_queue()* cleans up and returns.

If *relay_packet()* returns the identification number of another packet, *send_on_queue()* waits until its packet reaches the head of the queue, resets the status flags of the packet, and sleeps until its packet has been sent by the network layer. After transmission of the packet completes, the status of the transmission is returned.

Relay_packet(), shown in Procedure 7.9, sends the packet out of the inter-processor queues. It must either accept the packet for delayed transmission, send it, or refuse it completely. If the targeted processor is local, the transport layer's *received()* routine is immediately invoked to process the packet since no transmission is required. At this point, the packet being sent should already be in the appropriate send queue. If the network is down, the procedure returns an error code.

If a transmission is currently underway, a flag is set to indicate that a process is waiting for network access, the send queue of the target processor is added to the linked list of waiting send queues, and the identification number of the packet currently being sent is returned.

The real work of *relay_packet()* starts by filling in the send queue structure with the packet's own information. The number of active send queues is incremented and the network driver routine is called to physically transmit the packet. Before exiting, the *nettimeout()* routine is added to the timeout queue (if not

```
    relay_packet (id, header info, segments, segments' lengths)

    {
            if (packet is addressed to local site ) {
                    call local receive packet routine;              /* receive() */
                    return;
            }
            if (no network or target's send queue empty)
                    return(error);
            if (network busy) {
                    set flag to indicate waiting for network;
                    add target's send queue to list of queues waiting for network;
                    return(packet id);
            }
            increment number of active queues;
            zero entry's number of tries;
            initialize network header to appropriate values;
            call driver send routine;                              /* phys_send() */
            if (net retry routine not in timeout queue) {
                    set flag to show retry is in timeout queue;
                    put net retry routine in timeout queue;       /* timeout() */
            }
            return(packet id);
    }
```

Procedure 7.9: The Relay Packet Routine

already scheduled), so that retransmission of the packet can occur if the current transmission fails. The routine finishes by returning the packet identification number.

The transport layer releases a packet from the send queue only after an acknowledgment packet has been received or the packet has been retransmitted the maximum number of times. The procedure used to retransmit an unacknowledged packet is *nettimeout()*, shown in Procedure 7.10. *Nettimeout()* is called every clock tick by the standard UNIX timeout mechanism to schedule packet retransmissions for all active send queues.

The various processors' send queues are handled in a round robin fashion; after checking to ensure that some send queue is active, the routine chooses a new send queue as the default. If there are no packets in this queue waiting to be retransmitted, then the other queues are searched for a waiting packet. If the number of retries has exceeded the maximum allowed, the packet is marked as failed. All other packets waiting for transmission to the packet's target processor

```
nettimeout (clock flag)

{
      if (no active send queues) {
            do not reschedule nettimeout routine;
            return;
      }
      set default send queue to next processor's queue;
      if (network already busy)
            return and reschedule this routine;        /* timeout */
      if (packet in selected queue to be sent)
            select it for retransmission;
      else
            select first packet waiting in another send queue;
      select next send-queue on a round-robin fashion;
      if (network already busy)
            return and reschedule this routine;        /* timeout */
      for (all active send-queues) {
            if (first packet was sent more than the maximal times) {
                  mark processor as down;
                  remove and mark all packets in this queue as failed;
                  decrement number of active queues;
            }
            if (time for (re)sending the first packet on queue) {
                  call network send routine;           /*phys_send() */
                  select next send queue for next nettimeout;
                  return and reschedule this routine;   /* timeout() */
            }
      }
}
```

Procedure 7.10: The Transport Layer Timeout Routine

are also removed from the send queue and marked with an error code. The target host is marked as down and the transport layer decrements the number of active send queues.

As the number of times that a packet has been retransmitted increases, the probability that *nettimeout()* will actually transmit the packet decreases. This allows very busy target processors to recover and send an acknowledgment without flooding them with retransmissions. The *phys_send()* procedure is invoked to actually resend the packet. *Nettimeout()* finishes by calling *timeout()* to reschedule itself (if necessary).

7.2.3   The Transport-Level Receive Routine

When receiving a packet, the flow of control begins with the network driver
routines, and works its way through the transport layer, finally reaching the
Linker interface level. When a packet arrives at a processor, the interrupt routine
for the network hardware, described in Section 7.3, is called first.

```
    system_packet (nethead in, len, broadcast)


    {
            if (packet is positive or negative acknowledgment) {
                    set flag to show that sending processor is up;
                    if (negative acknowledgement)
                            mark first packet in send queue "failed" and remove it;
                    else
                            mark first packet in send queue as "OK" and remove it;
                    return;
            }
            verify correct packet size;
            if (not broadcast) {
                    send positive acknowledgement;
                    if (packet has been received before)
                            return;
            }
            if (local processor is target)
                    invoke port receive packet routine;      /* receive() */
    }
```

Procedure 7.11: The Transport Layer Receive Packet Routine

The network driver invokes the transport-layer procedure *system_packet()*,
shown in Procedure 7.11. *System_packet()* is responsible for low-level handling
of the packet, including sending an acknowledgment, checking the size, and
passing the handling on to a higher transport-layer routine. By examining the
network header structure's fields, the routine extracts the low-level packet type,
the source of the packet, and the packet size.

All packets sent to a particular processor (but not broadcast packets) need
to be acknowledged by the receiving processor. No new packets will be sent to
that processor until the previous packet is acknowledged. The acknowledgmen-
t can be normal (positive) or negative, indicating refusal to receive. Packets
with errors (such as checksum errors) are not acknowledged at all until retransmitted without errors. Once an acknowledgment is received, the sent packet is
dequeued.

Receipt of a regular packet does not mean that the remote processor is accessible: MOSIX allows processors to selectively disable remote services in such a way that a processor may initiate remote transactions while refusing to handle remote transactions initiated by other processors. The *send_on_queue()* routine (described previously) is actually waiting for the acknowledgment packet, so in this sense, the first part of the *system_packet()* routine is also the final stage of the packet transmission process. If the size of a packet is incorrect, the message is discarded.

Next, the *system_packet()* routine checks that the packet is addressed to a legal processor and that the packet is not a duplicate. In the former case, a negative acknowledgment is sent to inform the sending processor that its packet is undeliverable. In the latter case, it is possible that a previous acknowledgment packet was lost so a new acknowledgment is sent. If the packet is targeted to the local processor, the transport-layer *received()* routine, shown in Procedure 7.7, is invoked to handle the port-layer processing of the packet. The routine's main purpose is to carry out the actions required by the high-level packet type; for example, an Scall request, a Funnel data packet, or a remote page fault.

7.3   The Network Layer

Network layer software tends to change frequently to adapt to increasing speed and reliability of communication hardware devices. The most recent MOSIX implementation, for example, can be configured with either an Ethernet or a token ring driver as the Linker's network layer. In both cases, the transport layer of the Linker implements the MOSIX protocols.

7.3.1   Network Driver Routines

Network transactions in MOSIX are interrupt driven. The three main routines provided by each network driver are the routine that physically sends a packet on the network media and the two routines that are called when handling interrupts from incoming packets or upon completion of a packet transmission.

Standard packets that are transmitted by the network driver contain up to three segments: the network and transport-layer headers are packed into one segment; control-data, such as the Linker's Scall and replies constitute the second segment; and actual data being transferred via the Funnel constitute the third segment. The last two segments are optional. Acknowledgment (or refusal) packets comprise of a single segment. Acknowledgment packets are held in a separate packet queue and are sent at a higher priority than normal packets.

The network header contains information required by the network hardware, such as the physical network addresses of the target and initiating processors. The transport header contains the message-type, a sequence number and all the information necessary to handle and/or place the received packet in a *port* structure (either a process' or an ambassador's port).

The routine that sends the packets over the network hardware, *phys_send()*, is implementation-specific and is not discussed here in detail. *Phys_send()* does not manipulate the transport layer message queue in any way. After making its arguments conform to those required by the network device, the routine simply sets the appropriate device registers to point to the fields of the packet waiting to be sent, initiates a DMA transfer and return. To ensure the consistency of the communication structure, no communication interrupts are allowed while already processing a previous interrupt, or during *phys_send()*.

The three transport layer routines that call the driver-specific *phys_send()* routine are *acknowledge()*, *relay_packet()* and *nettimeout()*, all compiled with the call to the specific driver routine; they do not attempt to change media dynamically in the event of network failure.

```
prxint ()

{
        check that the interrupt was not stray;
        check the status register of the network device;
        if (network not functional) {
                reinitialize the network;
                return;
        }
        if (acknowledge is pending){
                set status flag of acknowledge packet to "in transit";
                send head packet of acknowledge queue;
                return;
        }
        if (error) {
                wait for status register to show network ready;
                retransmit packet;
                return;
        }
        set net status to "not busy";
        Call the transport layer to check whether the network
                is required by other queues;
}
```

Procedure 7.12: The Network Transmission Interrupt Routine

Most of the work at this level is done by the two interrupt handlers *prxint()*, shown in Procedures 7.12 and *prrint()* (not shown). Note that these are ProNET token-ring routines and that similar routines exist for the Ethernet LAN.

When the asynchronous transmission of the packet finishes, the kernel receives an interrupt and activates the appropriate interrupt handler, in this case *prxint()*. *Prxint()*, after ensuring that it was invoked by a valid interrupt, checks the status registers associated with the network hardware. In the case of network failure (for example, the loss of the token in a token ring like ProNET), the network is reinitialized and the routine returns.

At this point, *prxint()* takes the opportunity to send a pending acknowledgment, if any, and returns. Such an acknowledgment is enqueued when the transport layer sends an acknowledgment while a transmission is in progress. If the hardware indicates a transmission error, then the last packet is retransmitted, otherwise, the network status flag is marked as idle and may be used for other queues (to other processors). The successful transmission of a packet is determined after its destination returns an acknowledgment packet. Until such an acknowledgment has been received, the kernel does not transmit any new packets to that destination (excluding the acknowledgment of arriving packets). Note that broadcast-messages do not require an acknowledgment.

The interrupt handler routine that handles incoming packets is *prrint()*. This routine first verifies the hardware operation, then, as early as possible, it assigns a new input buffer to enable new incoming messages. Only then is the packet checked and the *system_packet()* transport layer routine is called to analyze it.

The network hardware driver provides several other routines, not described here, for initializing the network interface, checking the status of the ring, and so on.

7.4   Summary

This chapter described the three layer of the MOSIX Linker: the kernel interface layer, the transport layer and the network layer. First, the kernel interface layer mechanisms were presented. Then the transport layer and the network layer, which are implementation-dependent, were discussed only where they impact on the higher level mechanisms. The main goal of the Linker is to provide efficient and reliable communication between the other parts of the kernel. The implementation of the Linker is a critical parameter in providing good system performance. The performance of some of the MOSIX Linker mechanisms is given in Chapter 10.

Chapter 8

Load Balancing

This chapter deals with load balancing issues in distributed computing environments and presents the MOSIX load balancing policy. In distributed environments, situations can arise in which one processor in the system uses a system resource to its utmost potential while that same resource at another processor in the system is idle. Load balancing attempts to allocate tasks among the processors of a system to achieve maximal system throughput and minimal system response time. A comprehensive load balancing policy must consider many different factors, ranging from the architecture of the sites composing the system to the characteristics of the tasks themselves. The factors that influence the selection of a load balancing policy and its performance are presented in Section 8.1.

There are many types of load balancing policies, each based on different factors. Policies tend to incorporate common features, making classification difficult. There are three basic types of load balancing policies: static, dynamic, and pre-emptive.

Static load balancing policies, presented in Section 8.2, rely on predefined algorithms for the allocation of tasks to processors. This type of policy is the simplest to implement and has almost no overhead. Static load balancing policies, however, are generally ineffective in systems in which there is no prior knowledge of which tasks will be run or their execution times.

Dynamic load balancing policies, presented in Section 8.3, monitor the workload of the system's processors and allocate tasks among the processors accordingly. These policies are more effective than static load balancing policies, but are more difficult to implement successfully because they require sophisticated algorithms and tools in order to provide an effective measure of load balancing at a minimal overhead.

Pre-emptive load balancing policies, presented in Section 8.4, are the most effective policies developed to date. These policies can be thought of as adaptive, dynamic load balancing. Unlike the other policies, in which task distribution among the processors is done only when the tasks are created, in a pre-emptive load balancing system the distributed system may choose to dynamically assign and suspend, or reassign and resume tasks at various sites. In many senses, these functions are equivalent to those of the process scheduler of the system. The main drawbacks of pre-emptive load balancing policies are the cost of this flexibility and the increased complexity of the implementation.

MOSIX load balancing has a pre-emptive policy. It was first described in [7]. Improvements to this policy were later described in [8]. An overview of the policy and the algorithms that comprise this policy are presented in Section 8.5. Section 8.6 presents the load calculation algorithms that are used by each processor to determine its local load. Section 8.7 describes the information dissemination algorithms for the exchange of load information among the processors. The algorithms that are used for migration consideration are presented in Section 8.8.

8.1 Foundations of Load Balancing

The goal of a load balancing policy is to equalize the system workload among all the participating processors of a multicomputer system. Load balancing is influenced by three factors: the environment in which one wishes to balance the load, the load balancing tools available, and the nature of the load itself. Each factor is influenced by at least one of the other factors. For example, the availability of a specific load balancing tool is often a direct function of the environment's support or lack of support for that specific tool.

8.1.1 Environmental Factors

For the purposes of this chapter, the environment of a distributed system is defined to include the following factors: the architecture of the processors that belong to the system, the type of resources that are to be shared among the processors, and the form and type of connections between the processors. The architecture of each of the processors in a distributed system defines to a large degree what kinds of objects can be shared. If the processor architecture varies among nodes, then processes cannot generally be balanced among non-homogeneous subsets of the processors, although disk resources can be accessed without restriction. The type of connection between the processors also plays a vital role: in a tightly-coupled system with shared memory available to the processors, maintaining global shared information becomes trivial. On the other hand, shared-memory systems are usually not dynamic in nature and their load balancing algorithms are usually carefully crafted to handle specific system configurations.

The varied nature of distributed system environments requires a discussion of the prevalent strategies for the various environments. Such a discussion is not intended to address the multitude of hybrid strategies. However, the presentation of the mainstream strategies does allow the reader to judge the degree that hybrid strategies are influenced by the nature of their computing environments.

It is possible to identify three primary architectural criteria that can serve as the basis for such a classification:

1. Heterogeneous vs. homogeneous systems

2. Resource allocation

3. Data transfer facilities

In a homogeneous environment, all of the processors in the system are **binary compatible**; that is, a program compiled at one site in the system does not require recompilation to be executed at another site in the system. A heterogeneous environment, in the context of a distributed system, is limited to the use of remote procedure calls when attempting any form of load balancing among its processors.

Resource allocation is a subtle aspect of the environmental criteria. While a system may consist of homogeneous sites under the previous definition, a disproportionate allocation of resources among sites may result in a skew in the load balance. For example, such a situation might arise when all of the disk devices are connected to the same processor of a system. In such a case, even when the tasks are evenly distributed among the processors of the system, tasks running on the server processor will have the best response time for I/O operations while suffering computationally whenever the remote disk accesses are being processed.

A distributed system must often transfer data between sites. The data transfer facilities between sites have a higher overhead than those within a site. This overhead is a function of both the size of the data transfer (i.e., the number of packets sent over the network) and the amount of time spent in transit between the transmitting site and the receiving site. If the connections between sites are asymmetrical, then even though the system is otherwise homogeneous (or even identical), the response time of the different sites will vary.

8.1.2 Load Balancing Tools

Load balancing tools are procedures or programs that facilitate load balancing. To a large extent, the availability of specific tools is predetermined by the hardware of the system and is further constrained by the support provided by the operating system. Two classes of tools exist—information tools and process tools.

Information tools enable sites to determine the optimal placement of a task. These tools are responsible for the collection of information regarding the availability of various resources at other sites. In a master/slave environment, where one master site is responsible for determining the allocation of tasks to sites, an information tool would be responsible for updating a centrally located load table. In a symmetrical environment, an information tool might be invoked by any site and be responsible for updating the load table held at any other site. Obviously, information tools are dependent on the environment. While a shared-memory system can trivially maintain a central load table, a message passing system may tend to use local load tables.

Distributed process tools transfer processes between processors in a distributed environment and provide access to the various resources of the distributed system. In a standard UNIX environment, the only process tool is the UNIX kernel itself. The kernel parcels out system resources in response to the demands made by various local processes.

One of the most basic distributed process tools allows the system to execute a process at a predetermined site just as a remote procedure call mechanism allows a programmer to remotely execute a specific subroutine at a predetermined site. A more complex tool might permit local sites to suspend the execution of a remotely executing task, temporarily freeing resources for another remote task with a higher priority. An even more comprehensive tool would allow the transfer of a task currently executing at one site to another site where it could continue its execution.

8.1.3 The Workload

An optimal allocation of resources to tasks is dependent on the resources needed by the tasks to be run. In general, tasks tend to be classified as either I/O-bound, CPU-bound, or as mixed tasks. This simple model sufficed in a uniprocessor environment since the system resources were invariant. In a distributed environment this model needs to be updated to reflect the varied nature of the distributed system resources at each node. A more precise classification must specify which resources will be needed and to what extent.

In some cases, a system is dedicated to performing one specific task or set of tasks, such as a "batch" system. In these cases, the question of which resources will be needed can be predicted with great accuracy. The resulting load balancing policy should be simple, yet precise. The more general case, in which no *a priori* knowledge exists as to the exact nature of the resources that will be demanded by a task, is more interesting. To function correctly, the load balancing policy must be able to give a close approximation of the resources needed by a task without excessively consuming system resources in doing so. A poor approximation would result in the placement of a task at a site lacking the necessary amount of a certain resource.

The problem of predicting a task's resource consumption is not restricted to distributed systems. In uniprocessor systems, forecasts are statistically based on the benchmark results of a variety of tasks. These forecasts serve as the basis for initial resource demands. Once a task begins its execution, this forecast is replaced with the actual resource demands and is continually updated to provide an accurate profile of the resources recently used and those still in current use. In a distributed environment, the same basic inability to accurately forecast resource demands remains, but it is still possible to construct a resource profile. It is the task of the information tools, mentioned in the previous subsection, to provide this data to a site in an acceptable format. Based on this information, the load balancing policy decides which site is eligible for the execution of a task and invokes the proper process tool to execute the task at that site.

8.2   Static Load Balancing

Static load balancing policies attempt to attain some of the advantages of load balancing with as negligible overhead as possible. These policies are based on the *a priori* allocation of tasks to processors. Once allocated, a task uses resources at its allotted site until the task's completion. It is possible to view the matter as a task scheduling problem in which tasks are scheduled to be executed at specific sites. From this viewpoint, the selection of a site depends solely on a predetermined allocation algorithm. The selection of a site may be based on a random distribution algorithm or according to some cyclic distribution.

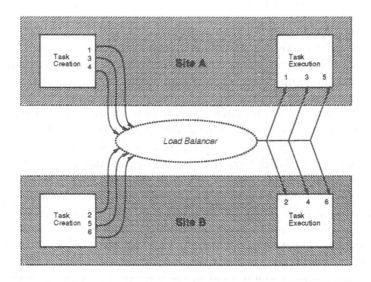

Figure 8.1: A Static Load Balancing Policy

An example of a cyclic algorithm is a **round robin** load balancing policy wherein consecutive tasks are sent to be executed at consecutive sites in the order in which they are created. Figure 8.1 depicts a round robin load balancing policy implemented in an environment consisting of Sites A and B. Each site is divided logically into a unit that creates tasks and a unit that executes them. A third logical unit, the load balancer, serves as a multisite task scheduler. The tasks are globally numbered in the order that they are received by the load balancer. Once scheduled, the tasks are marked by solid arrowheads.

The load balancer, under the round robin load balancing policy, receives the tasks and allocates each consecutive task to an alternate site. Thus, although Tasks 1, 3, and 4 were created at Site A, Task 4 was executed at Site B. For similar reasons, Task 5 was executed at Site A.

While static load balancing policies incur a low overhead, they are extremely limited in their usefulness. In the above example, if Tasks 1 and 5 had each required more resources than those required by any three of the remaining tasks (Tasks 2, 3, 4, or 6), this policy would have had a detrimental effect on the system throughput. Through the use of mathematical modeling and statistical measurements of a typical load, it is possible to construct a comprehensive static load balancing algorithm that is less susceptible to short term imbalances. However, these imbalances cannot be eliminated completely without foreknowledge of the future load of the system.

8.3 Dynamic Load Balancing

Dynamic load balancing policies can be viewed as static load balancing policies with enhanced capabilities. In addition to the static algorithm that distributes tasks among the sites, dynamic load balancing policies make use of information tools to collect current resource usage data from the sites in the system. Once the data has been collected, a profile of the current resource usage at the sites can be formed. This profile enables the load balancer to select the best site at which a newly arrived task should be run. Since the profile reflects short term imbalances that arise due to diverse task workloads, the load balancer is able to react dynamically to the system loads, hence the title **dynamic load balancing**.

There are two predominant methods by which dynamic load balancing algorithms are implemented:

1. Centralized task control strategies, in which one specific processor is responsible for collecting, correlating, and distributing information gathered from other processors

2. Distributed task control strategies, in which processors independently contact candidate processors and exchange load information with them

Centralized task control strategies are based on a single delegated site responsible for calculating a global load average. This global load average serves as the primary criterion for load balancing. Processors with an above-average load can select a processor with a below-average load as a target for process assignment. The overhead associated with this approach is quite high, since each processor must first send local load information to the delegated processor and later receive the loads of all the active processors.

One popular algorithm that lends itself readily to a central implementation is the **bidding algorithm**. In bidding algorithms [33, 44], each site announces its resource availability upon request. Usually, this would occur when a task is received by the load balancer and is awaiting its site allocation. While some implementations use a token passing mechanism to allow each site to act as a master, these implementations are still considered to be centralized.

Distributed task control strategies do not require a site to construct a global resource usage profile. These strategies attempt to eliminate the overhead incurred by the invocation of a global information tool by constructing a partial resource usage profile consisting of a select number of sites. Only these sites are considered by the load balancer when a task requires site allocation.

The decentralized approach reduces the difference between the loads of each processor that initiates a contact and the processor that it contacts. The drawback inherent in this method is the larger number of process assignments that may be required until a system-wide balanced load is achieved.

A **diffusive** load balancing algorithm is easily implemented in a decentralized manner. Diffusive algorithms allow each site to consider only a specific subset of the available remote sites as candidates for site selection. Allowing sites to belong to more than one subset enables the site load to "diffuse" outward. This policy is effective in environments with varying communications costs between sites.

The two-site system introduced in Figure 8.1 is presented once more in Figure 8.2 using a dynamic load balancing policy based on bidding. In Figure 8.2, the load balancer is replaced by the two distinct tools that compose it—the process tool and the information tool. Both Site A and Site B have identical information tools that can direct the actions of the process tool. The process tools are logically located in the system's global environment, although they actually reside at individual sites. When a task is created at a site, that site constructs a resource usage profile via the information tools. Once the profile is complete, the process tool decides on a target site for the task's execution. If the workload is homogeneous in both the number of tasks created, and their resource needs, then the task assignment is reduced to a static load balancing policy implementation. Given tasks that are numbered in the order of their creation, where Tasks 1 and 5 each require greater resources than the combined resources required by any three of the remaining tasks, the following occurs:

Task 1 when created is the first task at either site. It is therefore executed locally.

Task 2 is created at Site B. After querying Site A and comparing the resource usage at Site A to the zero local usage, it executes Task 2 locally.

Task 3 is created at Site A. Since both of the previous tasks are still executing, it is executed remotely at Site B.

Task 4 is treated in a manner similar to Task 3.

At this point, Task 1 completes its execution, followed by Task 2.

Task 5 is created at Site B, which compares the resource usage incurred by Task 3 and Task 4 to that of Site A, which is currently inactive. Therefore, Task 5 is allocated to Site A.

Task 6 is created at Site B and, due to the current resource usage (Task 5 at Site A as opposed to Task 3 and Task 4 at Site B), is executed locally.

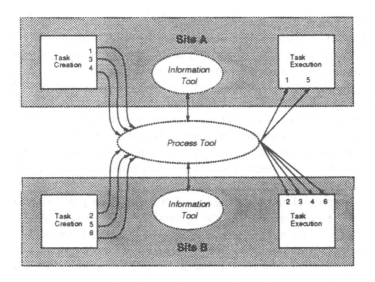

Figure 8.2: A Dynamic Load Balancing Policy

8.4   Pre-emptive Load Balancing

Though dynamic load balancing policies offer a higher degree of adaptability to fluctuations in the workload than static load balancing policies, they still suffer from imbalances. This is due to their inherent quality of **static site assignment**. Once a task is assigned by the load balancing mechanism to execute at a site, this assignment is static and will not change throughout the life of the task. The load balancing policy is therefore dependent on the unceasing creation of new tasks if it is to balance the load.

To illustrate this point, consider a state of balance in a two-site system in which each site is host to an equal number of tasks with equivalent resource demands. If the tasks at one of the sites, for example Site A, complete their execution prior to any of the tasks at Site B, then an imbalance in the load will occur. This imbalance cannot be rectified until the occurrence of at least one of two possible events:

1. The completion of an equivalent number of tasks at Site B

2. The creation of new tasks that will be assigned to Site A

Under a pre-emptive load balancing policy, a task may begin its execution at its originally assigned site and, due to a fluctuation in the system load, be reassigned to another site. This reassignment is accomplished by a process migration mechanism. In the previous example, some of the tasks at Site B would be reassigned to Site A, enabling the imbalance to be corrected within a reasonable period of time. One drawback of process migration is that it causes system overhead. If not carefully managed, it may decrease system throughput by slowing down the migrating processes and other non-related system activities.

Pre-emptive load balancing policies consume greater amounts of system resources and are more difficult to implement than either static or dynamic policies. They require complex process tools capable of allowing tasks executing at remote sites to be suspended and reassigned to other sites. These policies are susceptible to some of the problems that plague dynamic load balancing policies. A prime example is the problem of accurate assessment of resource demands with minimum overhead. A dynamic policy with central control is required to construct a resource load profile every time a task is created. The pre-emptive load balancing policy must, in addition to the above requirement, reconstruct the resource load profile often enough to ascertain that no imbalance has arisen due to task termination. This introduces some overhead and requires efficient information passing tools.

8.5 The MOSIX Load Balancing Policy

This section describes the goals, algorithms, and procedures of the MOSIX distributed pre-emptive load balancing policy. The main goal of this policy is to balance the loads of all the participating processors. This is accomplished by continuous attempts to reduce the load differences between pairs of processors, and by dynamically migrating processes from processors with a higher load to processors with a lower load [7]. This policy is symmetrical and distributed in the sense that all of the processors execute the same algorithms and that the reduction of the load differences is performed independently by any pair of processors. Other goals of the MOSIX load balancing policy are to respond to changes in the loads of the processors, the runtime characteristics of the process-es, and the number of processors. This policy also attempts to reduce the overall communication overhead by migrating processes "nearer" to the resources that they require.

The MOSIX load balancing policy is designed to respond quickly to fluctu-ations in the processor' loads and other events that may cause uneven resource use. At the same time, the policy uses several threshold functions to stabilize the load by avoiding excessive migration and useless swinging of processes from one processor to another. One mechanism for imposing the required stability is the **residency rule** for each process. According to this rule, each process must establish a minimum execution time (residency) on the current processor. This rule applies to both newly created processes and processes that have just migrated from another processor. One advantage of this requirement is that short-lived processes are not migrated. As with any rule, there are some special circumstances in which the residency rule is waved. One exception is the case in which a parent process creates many child processes in a relatively short period of time. In this case, if possible, the "chronic" forker is continuously migrated among the processors, in an attempt to avoid overuse of certain critical resources in one processor (e.g., process-table entries) and at the same time distribute the initial load evenly. Another exception to the residency rule is when a new pro-cess is created and the current processor does not have sufficient free memory for the process. In this case, using information that is already available in each processor, the system attempts to create the new process on a different proces-sor that has sufficient free memory. Note that if a processor with sufficient free memory is not found, then the new process is created locally and subsequently swapped out.

An important parameter of the load balancing policy is the duration of the residency period. The goal is to avoid useless migrations by migrating a process only if it results in substantial performance gain (e.g., a reduction of the process execution time). No method can guarantee that performance will be actually gained, or even that it will not suffer from the migration, because the remaining execution time of a process is unknown, but it is generally assumed that the process will exhibit a "past-repeat" execution pattern; that is, the process is expected to continue its execution for a period of time that is at least equal to the time it has executed so far. Based on this probabilistic assumption, and since the migration itself is time-, CPU-, and communication-consuming, the residency period in MOSIX is determined by a **competitive algorithm**. Briefly, a competitive algorithm allows a process to migrate only after it executes for a period of time that equals the predicted migration time. Note that this duration depends on the speed of the two processors, the current load of the network and the processors, and other local parameters. In spite of these, a migration policy that is based on a competitive algorithm is simple to implement, provides an adequate method for imposing the residency requirement, and adapts well to the current state of the participating processors. From a more theoretical point of view, it can be shown that a migration policy that is based on a competitive algorithm guarantees that the total execution time of the process is at most twice the optimal execution time. See [41, 11, 24] for studies on the use of competitive algorithms in various computational problems. Note that this worst case scenario occurs only when the process finishes its execution immediately after the migration. The combined effect of the past-repeat assumption and the competitive migration algorithm results in a stable policy that tends not only to balance the load, but also to optimize the execution times of many processes that are running on different processors.

There are other considerations that are used in MOSIX to stabilize the fluctuations in processor loads. One such parameter, called the **viscosity**, imposes a time delay between successive migrations to or from a processor. The duration of this delay is called the **viscosity degree**. In MOSIX the viscosity degree is a function of the current processor load, the amount of free memory, and the availability of other system resources. When the load is increased abruptly, the viscosity degree is lowered for outgoing processes and at the same time new processes are not allowed to migrate to this processor. This algorithm is also used if the amount of free memory is decreased, or when one of the system resources is almost used up. Another method that is used in MOSIX to stabilize the load is to smooth the decrease of the load function. Whenever there is a sudden decrease in the value of the local load, this value is smoothed by averaging it with the previous known load for this processor.

In addition to the above considerations, the strategic decision of when to migrate a process depends on the execution profile of each process, its use of resources, and the overall system load. The profile of a process is a general characterization that classifies the process as CPU-bound, I/O-bound, or communication-bound, with further subclassification according to the target location of the I/O operations, if any. The goal of the appropriate load balancing algorithm is to identify a process that performs many remote operations to a specific target machine, then based on the circumstances (e.g., that there are no other processes with similar needs), the process is migrated to the target machine. Another parameter that influences the load balancing policy is the overall load of the system. When this load increases, then the load balancing activities are slowed down.

Other decisions that are made by the load balancing policy include which process to migrate and where to migrate it. In MOSIX these decisions are based on three different algorithms. These algorithms intermesh hierarchically, where each algorithm serves as the foundation for the next level algorithm of the policy. The **load calculation algorithm** serves as the basis for the policy. Usually, the load values that are calculated by this algorithm are sent by the **information dissemination algorithm**. This information is used by the **migration consideration algorithm**, the apex of the policy, to select a target processor when attempting to balance the load via process migration.

The next three sections present these three algorithms and give some details about the MOSIX procedures that implement them. These algorithms, which constitute the policy, support the following set of assumptions:

1. The number of processors in the multicomputer system is arbitrarily large.

2. All the processors in the system use the same algorithms.

3. Each processor executes its algorithms independently of the others.

4. Nodes may join and processors or nodes may leave the network at any time.

5. There is no synchronization between the processors.

6. All the processors use the same unit of time.

7. The processors may have different speeds.

8. There is no *a priori* knowledge about the execution times of the processes.

9. Each processor maintains a small load vector consisting of its local load and the processor number and load values of some other processors.

10. Each node has a direct communication link to every other node through which load vectors may be exchanged.

11. Due to scaling considerations, no broadcasts are allowed as common procedures.

12. A node failure should not effect the other nodes.

13. Once a process migrates successfully, it is not affected by the failure of its original processor.

8.5.1   The Load Balancing Procedures

The fundamental data structure manipulated by the load balancing routines is the *loadinfo* structure, shown in Figure 8.3. The structure is an array of records containing four fields:

1. The processor number

2. The processor speed

3. The known processor load

4. The amount of the processor's free memory

Each entry in this array represents one processor of the system. The size of the array is determined by probabilistic considerations, as will be discussed later in this chapter. The first entry in the array is used for the local processor. The remaining entries represent a subset of the other processors that have recently communicated with this processor.

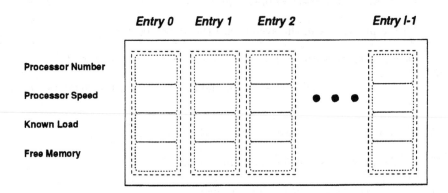

Figure 8.3: The *Loadinfo* Vector

8.6   The Load Calculation Algorithms

The calculation of local loads (i.e., the resource load) at each single processor is a prerequisite for successful load balancing. The algorithm given in this section is executed independently by each processor when estimating its local load. These load values are the primary source of information for the other algorithms of the load balancing policy.

A simple measure for the instantaneous load of a processor, as defined in [7], could be based on the number of processes that are ready to run and are waiting for the CPU; that is, the length of the *ready-to-run* process queue at that processor. This value must be correlated with the processor use at the instant that the queue length is measured. Measurements show rapid fluctuations in the loads when measured at several points in a relatively short time span. These fluctuations could cause transmission of misleading load information, resulting in potentially non-productive migrations. For example, Processor A may momentarily record a low load value because at the instant the load was measured, all the processes at that processor were waiting for the completion of some I/O operations. A short time later, a process residing on Processor B might decide to migrate to Processor A. On arrival, it could discover that while the migration was taking place, the pending I/O operations had been completed and the load at Processor A is now higher than that of Processor B. The above example implies that the load value cannot be based on a single measurement. The following section presents the algorithm used in MOSIX.

8.6.1   The Local Load Algorithm

In MOSIX, the local load is measured by each processor every atomic unit of time, t, called a **quantum**. In practice, a quantum depends on the (realtime) clock rate since the probing is done at the clock interrupt time. The measured load values are accumulated and then averaged every period of time T, where T is a unit of time for load balancing considerations, to be further discussed shortly. For simplicity, assume that T is an integer product of t, $T = \mu \times t$, where μ is a constant. Let W_i denote the number of processes that are ready for execution at a given processor during the time interval $(t_{i-1}, t_i), i = 1, 2, \ldots, \mu$. Then an initial approximation for the local load of this processor, L_T, during each unit of time T, is given by:

$$L_T = \sum_{i=1}^{\mu} W_i. \tag{8.1}$$

In a configuration with processors of different speeds, L_T must be divided by the relative speed of the processor, defined as the ratio between the speed of the specific processor (CPU_{sp}) and the speed of the processors with the maximal possible speed (CPU_{mx}). This normalization provides a common basis by which the local loads of different speed processors can be compared. In these cases, the local load at time T is given by:

$$LLoad_T = \frac{L_T \times CPU_{mx}}{CPU_{sp}}. \tag{8.2}$$

For example, if the system has two processors, one with the maximal speed and one with half that speed, then the load of the latter will be twice as high as the load of the first processor when they are running the same set of processes.

Implementation Notes

The local load that was defined previously is obviously only an estimate for the actual load. Several factors may cause the load value to function inadequately:

1. The load is measured over the period T. If T is too long then the load value may change substantially during T and information regarding this resource availability would be obsolete.

2. There are many fluctuations in the value of the local load due to processes that require very small services. For example, some processes are triggered on a regular basis to test for a simple condition. If the condition has not been met, the processes resume sleeping. These fluctuations must not influence the load balancing. If T is too small, the reflected load may rise disproportionately to the real load. This in turn may place an unnecessarily heavy burden on the load balancing policy by causing processes to migrate too often.

In MOSIX, these two problems were solved by defining $T = 1$ second, the order of time required to migrate an average-sized process; and $\mu = 30$, the (realtime) clock interrupt rate. Another measure taken is to age previous loads when receiving new ones.

Each processor uses the maximal speed (CPU_{mx}) to determine its relative speed. This value is independently computed and set at kernel initialization time by each processor.

8.6.2 The Export Load Algorithm

While the above algorithm provides a good approximation of the local load of each processor, it is not sufficient to balance the load of the system. This section presents some of the difficulties encountered and how they were solved in MOSIX.

Assume that Processor A has a lower load than Processor B. Processor B could then decide to migrate one or more processes to Processor A, resulting in an increased load at Processor A. If the load of Processor A is increased beyond that of Processor B, then Processor A may decide to migrate some processes back to Processor B. For example, Processor B may initially have one process and Processor A may be idle. This scenario could result in the process oscillating back and forth between the two processors, or **swinging**, without any improvement to the actual execution time of the process. This example shows that the local load of one processor cannot be naively compared to the local load of another processor.

The solution to this problem, first presented in [8], is to use two load measures for each processor. The first is the local load, as defined in Equation 8.2. It reflects the actual (internal) measured load of the processor. The second measure is the external load, called the **export load**. This value is the load other processors are informed of. It is important to note that the difference between these two loads is the key to achieving stability within the system.

The expression for the export load at time T is given by:

$$ELoad_T = LLoad_T + C_{Export},\qquad(8.3)$$

where C_{Export} is a constant given by:

$$C_{Export} = \frac{CPU_{mx} \times (\mu + \epsilon)}{CPU_{sp}},\qquad(8.4)$$

where ϵ is a small constant. Note that the value of C_{Export} is slightly larger than the load of a single, purely CPU-bound process.

Each processor also monitors its utilization, CPU_{ut}, which is defined as the percentage of time that the processor is available for task execution. Under normal operating conditions (i.e., the processor is not thrashing), $CPU_{ut} = \mu$, which represents 100% utilization. When the CPU is thrashing, the utilization is decreased by the amount of time that the processor cannot execute ready processes. Assume that ω out of the μ possible quanta that this processor can provide during T, were not available to any process because all runable processes, though some exist, were waiting for memory (e.g., had a page fault). Then the utilization is defined as:

$$CPU_{ut} = \mu - \omega.$$

In this case the export load is multiplied by a factor of μ/CPU_{ut} while the local load remains unchanged. Note that by raising the value of the export load, incoming migrations are discouraged. This gives the thrashing processor time to resolve its local problems without having to deal with incoming processes from other processors.

Implementation Notes

The following considerations are used for tuning the export load in order to optimize its performance and further stabilize the system:

1. When the local load comes down, the export load is decreased more slowly than the local load to lessen the effect of short-lived load fluctuations.

2. The export load is increased by an amount equal to a CPU-bound process for each arriving process as soon as the decision to accept the process is made. This measure is necessary because newly arrived processes have not had a chance to affect the local load yet. Similarly, the local load is reduced by the portion of the load caused by a migrating process as soon as the migration decision is made. If the migration fails, the load information is restored accordingly.

3. The export load is increased whenever any system resource (e.g., the process table) is near its full capacity.

8.6.3   Load Measurement Procedures

The calculation of the local and export loads is embedded within the clock routine. Each time the routine is invoked following a clock interrupt, the variable *load_adder*, which serves as an accumulator of the "normalized running load," is calculated by adding the number of running processes. This provides the basis for the code shown in Procedure 8.1, which describes the operations taken by the routine every unit of time T.

The first step taken by the routine is to normalize the *load_adder* with regard to the relative CPU speed as shown in Equation 8.2. Both the relative local and export loads can then be recalculated. The accumulated load, stored in *acc_load*, is calculated from the *load_adder* by decaying the old accumulated load, and then adding the new value of the *load_adder*. The decay of the previously accumulated load allows the new load value to have a greater influence than that of the previous load. This load is then multiplied by a positive factor, which serves to avoid integer rounding problems.

The variable *upper_load* behaves as a upper estimate for stabilizing the value of the local load. This threshold function is used to calculate the export load. If the local load rises above its previous value then the value is increased to the current local load.

```
clock()

{

    /* Calculate new local and export loads */

    load_adder = load_adder * maxcpuspeed / cpuspeed;
    acc_load = acc_load * DECAY + load_adder * NEWDATA;
    local_load = acc_load;
    if (load_adder ≥ upper_load)
        upper_load = load_adder;
    else
        upper_load = (upper_load * x + load_adder) / y;
    acpuse = (acpuse * z + cpuse + z) / (z + 1);
    export_load = upper_load + stable_export
                + arriving * (μ * maxcpuspeed)
                / (acpuse * cpuspeed) + ptax[nproc];
    arriving = arriving * DECAY + incoming * NEWDATA;
    if (local_load < outgoing)
        local_load = 0;
    else
        local_load -= outgoing;
    outgoing *= DECAY;
    cpuse = load_adder = 0;

}
```

Procedure 8.1: Load Calculation

If, however, the local load drops below the current threshold value, then the variable *upper_load* is decayed gradually, at the rate of only $x/y < 1$ in each unit of time.

The CPU's utilization, previously described in Section 8.6.2, is stored in the variable *cpuse*. The variable *acpuse* is used to prevent panics in the event that the system has been thrashing for only one second, by smoothing out the value of *cpuse*.

The next step is the calculation of the export load, stored in the variable *export_load*. The export load is composed of the above threshold value *upper_load*, a stabilizing machine-dependent factor *stable_export*, and the load generated by any processes that might have recently migrated to the local processor. This load is then multiplied by μ and divided by *acpuse*, thus introducing a measure of the CPU's utilization into the exported load. Finally, the export load is increased by an additional penalty if the local process table is full or nearly full.

This penalty helps prevent processors that are considering migration of processes from selecting this processor.

Once the loads have been calculated, the local load is reduced by the load of any processes that might have left the local processor, stored in the variable *outgoing*. The incoming and outgoing loads decay at the same rate as the standard load. After these actions both *cpuse* and *load_adder* are reset, ready for the next cycle.

8.7   The Information Dissemination Algorithms

The information dissemination algorithms are responsible for a continuous exchange of load information among the processors, so that each processor has sufficient information about other processors. This algorithm is decentralized; no single processor has global knowledge of the loads of all of the processors at any given time. Instead, each processor sends its load to a randomly selected processor, and at the same time, each processor maintains information about the most recently obtained loads of a limited subset of processors. The algorithm is probabilistic in the sense that the choice of the processor to be informed of the local load is selected on a random basis from the set of all processors. Another property of this algorithm is that it supports dynamic configuration; processors can be added and removed.

8.7.1   A Simple Load Exchange Algorithm

This section presents a simple load exchange algorithm. This algorithm was used in the system described in [6].

Let T denote a unit of time for load balancing considerations, as discussed in the previous section. Assume that the processors are numbered $1, 2, \ldots, n$, where n denotes the number of processors, not all of which are necessarily active. Let *Load[j]* denote the jth entry in the load vector, $0 \leq j \leq (l-1)$, where l is the size of the load vector maintained at each processor.

Then Algorithm 8.1 is executed asynchronously, every unit of time T, by each processor. The algorithm interleaves the newly received load value entries with those previously held in the load vector, retaining only the latest load values, as shown in Figure 8.4.

In this figure, the load vectors are arranged in order of the load's age. Each load vector shown here is of the size $l = 4$, where each entry represents the processor number, its relative speed and its load; that is, the first three items of each entry in the *Loadinfo* vector. Since the local load is the only load value that has not been adjusted by the export load constant, it is considered "reliable," and is stored in the first slot. In Figure 8.4, Processor 2 has randomly chosen Processor 1 as a receiver of information. Following Step 3 of Algorithm 8.1, it sends the first half of its load vector to Processor 1.

Upon receiving the load vector from Processor 2, Processor 1 performs Step 4 of the algorithm. The local load value that was recalculated in Step 1 of

Step 1: Update the local load value,

Step 2: Choose a random integer i, $1 \leq i \leq n$,

Step 3: Send the first half of the load vector entries to processor i.

When receiving a portion of a load vector, each processor performs:

Step 4: Merge the information into the local load vector, using the mapping:

$$Load[i] \mapsto Load[2 \times i], \qquad\qquad 1 \leq i \leq l/2 - 1,$$

and

$$Load_R[i] \mapsto Load[(2 \times i) + 1], \qquad\qquad 0 \leq i \leq l/2 - 1,$$

where $Load_R[i]$ are the components of the received vector.

Algorithm 8.1: A Simple Load Exchange Algorithm

the algorithm remains in the first slot. The first two load values received from Processor 2 are placed in the second and fourth slots, and the contents of the second slot are moved to the third slot. On conclusion of Step 4, the values in the newly generated load vector remain sorted by their age.

In Algorithm 8.1 the number of operations required to handle each load vector is $O(l)$. The total number of messages that are passed through the network in each unit of time T is n. Note that this algorithm allows duplication, i.e., a load vector may contain more than one load value for a specific processor.

8.7.2   An Improved Load Exchange Algorithm

Based on experience with older versions of MOSIX, the simple information exchange presented in the previous section was improved in the latest version of MOSIX to speed up the rate of information dissemination and to reduce the overhead needed to integrate the old load vector with the newly received load values. Unlike Algorithm 8.1, which uses both direct and indirect load information that is sent to a single destination, the improved Algorithm 8.2 transmits only direct information (i.e., the processor's export load) to several receivers.

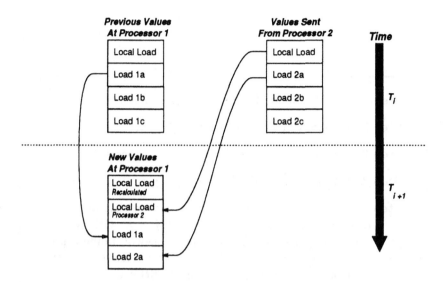

Figure 8.4: Integrating Load Information

In order to ensure that the information is distributed in a more comprehensive manner, and to overcome partial machine failures, Algorithm 8.2 distinguishes between three types of target processors:

1. A randomly selected processor i,

2. A randomly selected processor j, previously known to be active,

and, in the case of a multiprocessor workstation:

3. A randomly selected processor k, in the same node.

The first type is intended to incorporate new processors that have just joined the system into the load exchange ritual. Note that new processors send their own load messages, so they will be counted as soon as they send the first load exchange message. The second type is intended to give some priority to processors that are already known to be active. This is particularly important in a sparse system, where the number of active processors is small. The third type is used to give priority for migrations within multiprocessors, in order to take advantage of high speed connections (i.e., a bus) between two or more processors in the same node.

Let T denote a unit of time for load balancing considerations. Let n denote the number of processors. Let $Load\ [j]$ denote the jth component of the load vector, $0 \leq j \leq (l - 1)$, where l is the size of the load vector maintained at each processor. Then the following steps, taken asynchronously every unit of time T

Step 1: Update the local and export load values.

Step 2: Choose a random integer i, $1 \leq i \leq n$.

Step 3: Send the local *loadinfo* structure to processor i.

Step 4: Choose a random integer j, $1 \leq j \leq n$.

Step 5: Verify that j is among the processors that are previously known to be active and that $j \neq i$. Otherwise if the configuration is sparse, select a new j, random processor from those currently known to be active, or if the configuration is not sparse, return to **Step 4**.

Step 6: Send the local *loadinfo* structure to processor j.

In a multiprocessor node:

Step 7: Choose a random processor k in the same node.

Step 8: Send the local *loadinfo* structure to processor k.

When receiving a load value, each processor will:

Step 9: Acknowledge the received information by sending its own export load.

Step 10: Incorporate the received load value into the next cyclic slot in its load vector.

Step 11: Clear any duplicate slots held by the same processor.

Algorithm 8.2: Information Exchange Algorithm

by each processor, guarantee that newly arrived load information will be stored in the vector such that only the latest load values will be maintained.

Note that in Algorithm 8.2, the number of operations required to handle each load value remains $O(l)$ due to the need to eliminate redundant values. The total number of information exchange messages now passing through the network has doubled. Also note that at each moment, only a limited number of processors have information about the load of any specific processor. This property will further be discussed in the following section. Finally, note that the exchange algorithm employs rapid information dissemination. Further details on the rate of the information dissemination can be found in [1, 16]

Determining the Size of the Load Vector

One of the critical factors in determining the performance of the load exchange algorithm is selecting a value for l, the size of the "window" of each processor to the other processors. On the one hand, l must be sufficiently large to facilitate meaningful load information exchange and rapid information dissemination. On the other hand, too much information may lead to migration decisions that are based on outdated load information. A related problem is flooding, which may result from a rapid scattering of certain load information resulting in simultaneous attempts by many processors to overload a single lightly loaded processor; for example, a processor that has just joined the network. The last considerations imply that l must be small and the rate of information exchange should not be too high. An optimal value for l is therefore difficult to define and must be tuned to a given system.

In MOSIX, l is chosen as a small constant, $l = 8$. It is estimated that with this value the system can function adequately with up to 512 processors. As for the rate of the load message exchanges, MOSIX uses a unit of time $T = 1$ second, the amount of time required to migrate an average-sized process, as discussed in Section 8.6.1.

The following paragraphs examine the rate of replacement of the components in the load vector, assuming that each processor sends only one message per unit of time. Note that if each processor sends more than one message per unit of time then this rate is even increased.

Let $\mathcal{P}(X, k)$ denote the probability that k different processors select Processor X in the next step. Since the probability that any processor will select Processor X is $p = 1/n$, it is easily verifiable that:

$$\mathcal{P}(X, k) = \binom{n}{k} p^k (1-p)^{n-k} \approx \frac{1}{ek!}.$$

For large values of n, the probability that Processor X will not be selected in the next step by any processor is therefore given by:

$$\mathcal{P}(X, 0) = (1 - \frac{1}{n})^n \approx \frac{1}{e}.$$

By using these results, it is possible to calculate the probability that any load value is not updated during the last N seconds, for any values of N and l, as shown in [7]. One outcome of this study is that for a given value of N, the probability that any load value is not replaced decreases with increasing values of l. For this reason, it was earlier recommended that the value of l be sufficiently small.

8.7.3   Information Dissemination Procedures

The kernel process *idaemon()*, described in Procedure 8.2, is responsible for disseminating load information among the active processors. This process is created at boot time. The routine documented here supports the improved load exchange algorithm, previously described in Section 8.7.2.

```
idaemon ()

{
    while (1) {
        sleep for one second;                          /* delay() */
        select a random processor;                     /* randpe() */
        inform the selected processor;                 /* do_inform() */
        select a random processor;                     /* randpe() */
        if (the processor is not up and some processors are up)
            if (the processors are not sparse)
                while (not up)
                    select a random processor;  /* randpe() */
            else
                select a random processor;       /* sparse() */
        if (this processor has not been previously selected)
            inform it;                                 /* do_inform() */
    }
}
```

Procedure 8.2: Information Dissemination Daemon

After a preliminary initialization, the information daemon enters an infinite loop in which the essential part of the algorithm is performed. The first command in the loop is a *delay()*, which ensures that the *idaemon()* is run once per unit of time. This corresponds to the period T, the rate of the algorithm execution. At this point the *idaemon()* can proceed with the actual distribution of the information.

The kernel routine *randpe()* is invoked. It returns the number of a random processor that is within the range of all the processor numbers in the system.

This corresponds to the performance of Step 2 of the algorithm. *Idaemon()* invokes the kernel routine *do_inform()* to automatically attempt to pass the information to the processor number returned by *randpe()*, implementing Step 3 of the algorithm.

Then the kernel routine *randpe()* is invoked again, and the result is compared to the data vector of all the previously known active processors. If the target processor is marked inactive, this step is performed again, until an active processor is found. This step corresponds to the performance of Steps 4 and 5 of the algorithm. Then the kernel routine *do_inform()* is invoked as before, and the target processor is given the export load data, implementing Step 6 of the algorithm.

```
do_inform (to)

/* Upper Kernel do_inform() - on calling process' machine */

{
        copy the export load into an information structure;
        Sinform to invoke inform on target machine;        /* Scall */
        if (error)
                mark target machine down;
        else {
                if (target machine marked as down)
                        mark target machine up;
                update local load vector with target's returned values;
        }
}
```

Procedure 8.3: Send Information

The actual distribution of the load information is performed by the kernel routine *do_inform()*, described in Procedure 8.3. The only argument used by *do_inform()* is the number of the target processor. The routine is divided into two parts, the upper kernel section, which is executed locally, and the lower kernel section, which is executed on the target processor. The upper kernel section is responsible for sending the export load structure to the lower kernel of the target processor. The kernel uses this opportunity also for sending it's time, for clock-synchronization. If the Scall returns an error, the target processor is marked as inactive. If the call completes successfully, it is verified that the target processor is marked active and the local load vector is updated to include the export load values that were returned by the target processor. This last action corresponds to Step 9 of Algorithm 8.2.

The lower kernel portion of *do_inform()* is performed by the *inform()* routine,

```
inform (info, time, knows)

/* Lower Kernel inform() – on remote machine */

{
        if (remote processor was marked down)
                mark it as up;
        pick the next cyclic slot in the load vector;
        place the info in the new load vector slot;
        for (every entry in the load vector)
                if (entry ≠ slot and it is an entry for the remote processor)
                        clear entry;
                        break;
        should process consider migration based on the new information;
        if (a recent stime() system call occured)
                return
        if ((remote processor knows the date and local processor doesn't)
                or ((given date – local date > 2 seconds)
                and (remote processor knows the date
                or local processor doesn't)))
                reset local clock;                    /* stime1() */
        set myload.load to export load;
        set myload.speed to export speed;
        return (myload);
}
```

Procedure 8.4: Receive Information

described in Procedure 8.4. Its primary function is to accept load information from other processors and incorporate it within the local load table, implementing Step 10 of Algorithm 8.2.

After verifying that the sending processor is marked as active in the active processors vector, *inform()* places the export load received from the remote processor into the next cyclic slot in the *loadinfo* array. Then it removes any duplicate entries for the sending processor, to ensure consistency. After that, the kernel routine *load_balance()* is called to perform load balancing if necessary.

At this point the routine *inform()* switches to its second duty, the performance of clock synchronization. Unless a recent *stime()* system call was performed, the routine uses the arguments *time* and *knows*, which correspond to the latest clock time of the sending processors, and the validity of this information as claimed by the remote processor, to reset the local clock.

The last action taken by *inform()* is to return the local export load to the remote, calling processor.

8.8   The Migration Consideration Algorithms

This section presents the migration consideration algorithms, which include an algorithm for choosing a good candidate process for migration and a target processor to migrate to. The goal of these algorithms is to determine whether the migration of the candidate process to the target processor will result in an improvement to the load balance of the system. Another goal is to improve, if possible, the execution performance of a process by migrating it to a better execution environment. The migration consideration algorithms are completely distributed. They are executed independently by each processor, without any central control. Furthermore, even within processors, there is no central decision-making in MOSIX, and each process performs its own migration considerations.

In order to reach a decision to migrate a process, MOSIX measures the execution profile of each process. These measurements are performed during the lifetime of each process or since its last migration, and the profile is updated continuously. The profile reflects the resources requested by the process at various processors, and its CPU consumption. When considering migration it is assumed that the process will maintain the same profile as it had during its stay at the current processor. Ideally, the target processor selected for that process is the processor at which the cost of execution would be minimal.

Various factors influence the successful migration of a candidate process to a targeted processor. Below are the main considerations that are used in MOSIX.

Response Time

The primary motivation for load balancing migration is the improved response time that the migrating process may receive at a given host. The response time is inversely proportional to the load at that host. Accordingly, it is more desirable to migrate to a lightly loaded processor than to a heavily loaded processor.

Communication Overhead

MOSIX does not distribute files between processors. If a process wishes to perform a remote I/O operation on a device that resides at a remote processor, then the actual I/O operations and the relevant (lower) kernel operations are performed at the remote processor, regardless of the location of the requesting process.

The use of remote operations increases the communication overhead because remote operations require that both the local and remote CPUs execute the communication protocols. This overhead can be eliminated if the requesting process is migrated to the remote processor. The selection of a target processor should be influenced by the resulting change in the communication overhead.

In MOSIX, each process records the amount of communication overhead it has caused since it arrived at the processor (or since it was created, if it was never migrated). This is accomplished by maintaining communication-overhead estimates for a set of processors with whom the process often communicates.

The same communication overheads are also kept for all calls to the local lower-kernel, in order to estimate what **would** be the communication overheads to the current processor if the process migrated. Whenever the Linker is called (except for broadcasts), these overheads are updated: local estimates are simply added to the local record. Otherwise, if the called processor is already in the set, the local and remote communication overhead estimates are added to the appropriate records. If, however, the called processor is not in the set and the (fixed-size) set is already full, then the same communication-overheads are subtracted from the records of the processor with the lowest records within the set. If, as a result, those records reach zero or below, then they are cleared and the called processor joins the set instead.

Migration Time

The duration of the migration is itself significant in the decision making. The migration time is a linear function of the size of the process.

Descendant Processes

In MOSIX, as in any UNIX system, a process can create child processes via the *fork()* system call. These in turn can create further child processes and so on. Often the parent process sole activity consists of creating child processes and awaiting their termination. If each child consumes minute amounts of system resources there will be no justification for their migration. The total resource consumption of all the descendant processes might, however, be significant e-nough to justify migration of the parent process.

Process Table Capacity

If the process table is nearly full, and a process wishes to create a child process (using *fork()*), migration will be almost mandatory. In such a case, almost any available processor may be selected for migration.

Amount of Free Memory

If there is not enough free memory to allow the creation of a new process, then an attempt will be made to create the new process on another processor that has sufficient free memory.

Combining the Considerations

When a process detects a migration flag, which indicates the necessity to consider migration, it arrives at the routine *migrate()*. The task of *migrate()* is to integrate all the migration considerations and decide whether to migrate to any of the processors for which the current load is available. Since the load of processors in the *often-communicated-to* set are generally not available at the current site, and if the amount of communication to those processors is significant enough, then the load of those processors is explicitly requested.

The last three considerations—the descendant processes, the nearly full process table, and the lack of memory—become more important when a process executes the *fork()* system call. This is especially true for distributed programs that use the *fork()* system call intensively.

In these cases, when a process that executes *fork()* already has child processes, it is often desirable to create new child processes elsewhere, so that different child processes will run on different processors. The best time for migration is just before the *fork()* is performed, since then, only the parent will migrate, whereas if the parent intends to create more processes afterwards, both the parent and the child processes will have to migrate.

Similarly, when the process table is full or nearly full, it is best to migrate the parent process just before it requests another slot in the process table. Moreover, the UNIX interface implies that if there is an empty process slot anywhere in the system, a *fork()* system call should not fail. Although it seems difficult to ensure this last property, since it requires knowledge of some global information, MOSIX attempts to reduce the probability that full process tables at some processors will cause unnecessary failures of *fork()* when it could succeed on other processors. Therefore, it attempts to migrate the parent process even when the process table is only nearly full. Accordingly, if a process starts executing the *fork()* system call and detects either that it already has other child processes, or that the local process table is nearly full, it calls the routine *forkmigrate()*, which considers migration more favorably.

During the actual transfer from one processor to another, the process ceases its execution. Furthermore, since the two processors must support the migration and dedicate both CPU, network, and memory resources to the migration, the effective overhead is felt on both the target processor and the processor of origin. A process with a life span in the order of magnitude as required for its migration would therefore be a poor candidate for migration, regardless of the contribution of that process to the local load. In order to discourage short-lived processes from migration, MOSIX uses a dynamic competitive algorithm, as described in Section 8.5.

8.8.1   Selecting a Candidate Process

Selecting a candidate process for possible migration requires the traversal of all the processes in the process table. For each user process, the algorithm compares the relevant migration parameters (e.g., execution time or residency period) in order to find the best candidate process. The algorithm employs several predetermined threshold values to optimize the selection. The implementation of the algorithm, including further considerations and details, is described in the next section. Note that this algorithm is responsible only for marking candidate processes and does not initiate actual migrations.

8.8.2 Selecting a Target Processor

Let i denote the current processor's identifying number, $1 \leq i \leq n$. Let $Load[j]$ denote the jth entry of the load vector at processor i, where $0 \leq j \leq (l-1)$. Let $C[j]$ denote the cost of executing a candidate process at the processor whose information is stored in $Load[j]$. Recall that $Load[0]$ is used for the load of the local processor. Let k be the index of the best target processor for load balancing considerations. Let COM_{Lk} and COM_{Rk} denote the local and remote communication overhead incurred by the candidate process by communication with the kth processor from the load vector. Let t denote the amount of CPU time consumed by the candidate process at the current processor, and let t_m denote the time required for the migration itself.

Then Algorithm 8.3 calculates the different costs $C[j]$, and thus enables the selection of the best target processor k, which has the minimum cost $C[k]$:

Step 1: Find

$$t \times Load[j] \rightarrow C[j], \quad 0 \leq j \leq l-1.$$

Step 2: Update the communication overhead for $0 \leq j < l-1$:

$$C[j] + \sum_{k=0}^{l-1}[COM_{Lk} \times Load[j]] + COM_{Rk} \rightarrow C[j],$$

Step 3: Add cost of migration to another processor

$$C[j] + t_m \rightarrow C[j], \quad 1 \leq j \leq l-1.$$

Step 4: Select the preferred processor k by finding

$$index[min(C[j])] \rightarrow k.$$

Algorithm 8.3: Selecting a Target Processor

The first step of Algorithm 8.3 initializes the costs of process execution at each processor. The values are determined by multiplying the load at the candidate processor by the CPU time consumed by the process. In Step 2 of the algorithm, the communication overhead that would be caused by migrating the process to each possible target processor is calculated. Next, Step 3 of the algorithm adds the approximate cost of the migration itself to each remote processor. The selection of the preferred processor is accomplished in Step 4.

Once the costs have been calculated, a candidate process will attempt to migrate to the processor with the lowest cost, processor k.

8.8.3   Migration Consideration Procedures

The first kernel routine invoked to transfer a process for load balancing purposes
is *load_balance()*, described in Procedure 8.5. This routine is called whenever new
load information arrives (by *inform()*) and when a process which was previously
selected to migrate for load-balancing purposes, decides to migrate and update
the remote load-information accordingly. Note that processes consider migration
for load-balancing purposes only one at a time. First, the *load_balance()* routine
searches the load vector for a processor that has a load value lower than the
local load. Note that a threshold value is used to prevent process swinging. If a
processor with a lower value is found, then the kernel routine *choose()* is invoked
to select a candidate process for possible migration.

```
load_balance ()

{
        set load variable to local load;
        for (each processor in the load vector)
            if (valid entry and the load is lower than the local one){
                choose a candidate process for migration;    /* choose() */
                return;
            }
}
```

Procedure 8.5: Scan Loads

The kernel routine *choose()*, depicted in Procedure 8.6, selects a candidate
process and requests it to consider migration to another processor. The criteria used for the selection of a candidate for process migration are based on
the elapsed process runtime, measured from the time that the process was last
examined as a possible candidate. The sole limitations imposed at this level
of selection are those that render the candidate totally unacceptable (e.g., the
candidate has a shared-memory region).

After setting a threshold value for the best process priority, the routine begins
the selection by scanning the process table on a per process basis. If any process
is found to be already marked as a candidate for load balancing, the routine
returns immediately. if the process cannot migrate because it is either sharing
a memory resource with other processes, If the process cannot migrate because
it is either sharing a memory resource with other processes, is being created, is
currently being transferred, or is locked in the local processor, *choose()* moves on

```
choose ()

{
      for (each user process)
            if (process is not being (moved or created or locked)) {
                  if (process is already a candidate for load balancing)
                        return;
                  if (process has a shared memory region/* findpreg() */
                        or process is already marked for migration
                        or process did not accumulated a minimal
                        amount of CPU time on this processor)
                        continue;
                  set priority based on the CPU time elapsed since last
                  try and the process' current contribution to the load;
                  if (priority > best_priority [found so far{
                        set best_priority to priority;
                        set candidate process pointer to current process;
                  }
            }
      if (no candidate found)
            return;
      mark candidate process;
      reset candidate's CPU time since last attempt to 0;
      if (candidate process is sleeping on a long-latency event
            or candidate process is stopped)
            set the process running;                    /* setrun() */
}
```

Procedure 8.6: Choose the Best Process for Migration

to the next process. Otherwise, a priority function, based mainly on the elapsed
CPU time since the last attempt to migrate this process and secondarily on the
process' current contribution to the local load, is compared to the best priority
found so far, so that the process with the best priority is located.

After the candidate is found, it is marked as such and its elapsed examination
time is reset to zero, so that different processes are selected the next time if, for
any reason, the selected process remains and does not migrate. If the process is
sleeping on a long latency event or it is stopped, then the process state is set to
"ready to run" and it is placed at the head of the run queue.

The purpose of *choose()* is to mark candidate processes. The next step
in the load balancing scheme is taken when one of the conditions for possible
migration, discussed previously in Section 8.8 is fulfilled. In each of those cases,
Procedure 8.7 is invoked by the process itself to consider whether and where to

```
consider ()

{

        if (process is locked in the local node or migration is disabled)
                return;
        if (a specific target has been requested)
                migrate the process to the target and return;      /* passto() */
        if (the migration is not desparate) {
                include the local processor in the calculation;
                if (forking and the process-table is nearly full)
                        penalize the local load;
        }
        include all remote nodes in the load vector in the calculation;
        for (each node which is heavily-communicated to) {
                if (not yet included)
                        Sgetload to get the target node's load;      /* Scall */
                        include that node in the calculation;
        }
        for (each entry considered)
                calculate the CPU time to be consumed at that node;
        for (each calculated cost) {
                increase this cost by the extrapolated communication costs;
                if (not the local node)
                        increase the calculated cost by the migration time;
        }

loop:for (each calculated cost)
                if (the cost < the lowest cost found so far)
                        set the best node to the current one;
        if (the best node is the local node)
                return;
        increase the target node's load by slightly more than one;
        mark process as being moved for load balancing purposes;
        attempt to migrate the process to the target;      /* passto() */
        if (migration failed)
                goto loop;
}
```

Procedure 8.7: Selecting the Best Target Processor

migrate and, if so, perform the actual migration.

The *consider()* routine is called to select a target processor, according to Algorithm 8.3, to which the candidate process may be migrated. First, it makes sure that the process is actually allowed to migrate at all: processes that use shared memory, processes that asked to be locked in the current processor or in memory and the *init* process are not allowed to migrate. Also, if the process is requested to migrate to a particular processor, the selection algorithm is by-passed and the process is migrated to the requested processor. The next action is to compute the execution costs of the process at each possible target processor using the loads of the processors currently in the local load vector. If the candidate process performed large amounts of communication with a processor that is not represented in the global load vector, then a specific request is made for that processor's load. This request is performed via an Scall to the remote processor, activating the lower kernel *getload()* routine, which retrieves the export load of that processor. At this stage, Step 1 through Step 4 of Algorithm 8.3 are performed.

Once these calculations have been completed, the processor possessing the minimum cost is selected as the target processor. If the target processor is the current processor, then no migration is performed. Otherwise, the target processor's load is increased by slightly more than one load unit. This prevents flooding by ensuring that the load at the target processor will now reflect the additional load generated by the migrating candidate. The process is then marked as "migrating" and a migration is attempted by calling *passto()*. If the migration fails, the routine continues to search for the next optimal target processor for the candidate process based on the previously calculated costs.

8.9 Summary

This chapter presented the load balancing algorithms of MOSIX. It began by describing three types of load balancing methods—static, dynamic, and preemptive. In each case the advantages and disadvantages of the method were discussed. Then the chapter described the main goal of the MOSIX pre-emptive, distributed load balancing policy, how it copes with stability problems, the method it uses to distribute information among the processors, how a process is chosen for migration, and how the destination processor is chosen.

One of the more interesting properties of the MOSIX load balancing policy is the use of probabilistic algorithms for information dissemination. The policy tends to distribute the load information evenly, and it works better as the size of the configuration is increased. Another advantage is the ability of the policy to support a dynamic configuration, to which processors and nodes may join or fail at any time.

The policy described in this chapter is implemented inside the MOSIX kernel and is transparent to users. The main routines that are employed by the policy were described. One goal of these routines is to distribute the load evenly among the processors. Another goal is to optimize the use of resources (e.g., lowering communication overhead) by an adaptive allocation of all the running processes. This is done by heuristic algorithms that obtain near-optimal allocation at a low overhead cost. The main implication is that the application programmer need not care about the distribution of processes and the way these processes use the resources. In particular, users are not informed about the number of processors available, and they need not change applications whenever the size of the configuration changes.

Despite its complexity, the above advantages when combined with the performance of distributed applications, as shown in Chapter 11, provide one of the most powerful tools of modern computing. On the one hand they allow efficient resource use and on the other hand they provide a method for building "supercomputers" based on a distributed system architecture, using only software components and standard hardware.

Chapter 9

Scaling Considerations

This chapter presents some of the MOSIX design considerations and algorithms that ensure that the system will run as well on large configurations as it does on small configurations. The chapter begins by identifying the difficulties in using existing distributed operating systems in configurations with a large number of processors. Then, based on the experience gained in the design of MOSIX, the chapter presents several principles that serve as guidelines for scaling. These principles include symmetry, client/server protocols, the use of partial knowledge, and randomness in the system control algorithms. A set of ten laws, some of which address scaling issues, were used in the design of the POOL distributed system [39].

The second part of the chapter explains how these principles were used in MOSIX, and the third part describes several algorithms in MOSIX that closely follow these guiding principles. The algorithms include the information dissemination algorithm of the load balancing scheme, the garbage collection algorithm for remnant objects due to processor failures, and the algorithm for locating processes in a large scale configuration.

9.1 Principles of Scaling

Future multicomputer systems are expected to consist of a large number of interconnected computers. To simplify the use of these systems, multicomputer operating systems must be developed to integrate a cluster of computers into a unified and coherent environment. Using existing multicomputer operating systems is inappropriate, since many commonly used techniques get clogged and lead to congestion once the system is enlarged over a certain size.

Ideally, the performance of the operating system, measured in terms of throughput, response time, and availability, should expand linearly with the increase in the number of processors. No existing operating system has achieved this goal. In fact, many systems will grind to a halt when required to handle even a hundred processors. Multicomputer systems that currently achieve a large size (in the number of processors) execute only special applications, like electronic mail systems [40], but do not operate as general-purpose computing facilities in a system-wide manner.

A close examination of the inability of existing operating systems to function properly in a large configuration reveals that the dominant cause is the use of inappropriate algorithms and control mechanisms. Primary examples are the bottlenecks created when systems are controlled in a centralized manner. Other prominent examples are communication and information dissemination schemes that use broadcasts. These become completely clogged when more than tens (possibly a hundred) of processors are used.

These two recurrent themes are both due to an elementary property of computer and communication hardware, that unfortunately is often overlooked when designing small systems: the functional capacity of any component in the system, be it a processing element, a communication channel or a whole computer, is bounded and does not grow when the system in which it is embedded is enlarged. Consequently, any algorithm that requires from a single component an amount of service proportional to the number of processors, is destined to become clogged once the system grows beyond a certain size [5].

The above and similar observations have lead to the definition of eight principles for scaling [5]:

- **Bounded Resources:** The service demand from any component of the system should be bounded by a constant. This constant is independent of the number of processors in the system.

- **Symmetry:** All nodes should have an equal capability to execute all the system's functions and each node should be able to execute every such function independently of the other nodes.

- **A Client/Server Protocol:** Each client/server interaction should involve a minimal number of processors, preferably only two processors.

- **Partiality:** Every decision should be based on information from a finite subset of the other processors.

- **Symmetry-Breaking Through Randomness:** The set of processors with which a processor interacts is chosen at random.

- **Limited Duration of Interaction:** Any interaction that involves more than one processor is limited to the duration of a single system operation.

- **Invariant Replication Degree:** The replication degree of any object, information, or activity should be invariant with respect to the number of processors in the system.

- **Isolation, Cooperation, and Information Hiding:** Isolation of the nodes from each other ensures that remote failures and illegal remote requests are screened appropriately. But in a distributed system the nodes must also cooperate to enable the resources of the nodes to be used efficiently. Information hiding ensures that the interfaces of the various components of the system are well defined.

The **Bounded Resources** principle recognizes that any shared physical component of a system has a finite capacity. For example, assume that a process migration algorithm requires each processor to update a centralized table before migrating a process. If the table information can be updated at most k times per second, then the performance of the system-wide process migration algorithm is restricted to at most k migrations per second.

To prevent this type of bottleneck from developing, the principle of **Symmetry** requires that each node be able to perform all functions independently of all other nodes. The example presented above clearly violates this principle, since no node can migrate a process without communication with the node that maintains the centralized table. Another ramification of the **Symmetry** principle is that no single mechanism's failure can cause system-wide failure.

Clearly, the first two principles promote the use of fully autonomous nodes. A naive implementation of the process migration algorithm described above might simply have all of the nodes use global synchronization in place of the centralized control. In the modified scheme, for example, each processor would maintain its own copy of the table mentioned above and broadcast updates to the table at the end of each migration cycle.

The **Client/Server Protocol** principle ensures that the processors have no need for global synchronization. In its extreme case, the principle states that each transaction should involve only two parties: the requesting processor and the servicing node. The process migration algorithm described above, using this new principle, must be modified so that the processor that initiates the migration of a process and the processor that accepts the incoming process are the only participants in a migration cycle.

One immediate result is that no processor can be required to know the state of an arbitrary number of others before acting. This leads to the **Partiality** principle. The MOSIX process migration algorithm's information tools, as explained in Chapter 8, conform to this principle by maintaining a fixed size load vector at each processor in the system. When making process migration decisions, each processor makes its decision based on information from a limited, predetermined number of other processors.

Experience with the MOSIX load balancing algorithm shows that the load average can suddenly swing wildly up and down on one processor or even a set of processors. Any scheme, even one that conforms to the partiality principle, that always uses the same partners when making decisions cannot adapt to such a dynamic environment. The **Symmetry-Breaking Through Randomness** and the **Limited Duration of Interaction** principles ensure that the information used in system operations changes frequently and that processors do not always interact with a fixed set of partners.

Another common goal of distributed systems is to increase the availability of resources (e.g., files) by some kind of replication mechanism. To prevent any conflict between the desire to replicate a resource and the preceding principles, the principle of **Invariant Replication Degree** requires that the number of copies of any object not be dependent on the number of nodes in the system.

The final principle, the principle of **Isolation, Cooperation, and Information Hiding**, ties all of the principles together by requiring nodes to maintain the correct balance between isolation and cooperation of the nodes and ensures that the resulting system "hides" the complexity of its system operation from its users.

9.2   Scaling Considerations in MOSIX

The design and algorithms of the MOSIX system include many considerations that ensure that the system will run well on a configuration with a large number of processors. These considerations include an efficient, two-party protocol, the decentralization of data and control, symmetry between nodes, node independence, and the use of probabilistic algorithms. This section explains these considerations and how they were implemented in MOSIX.

9.2.1   A Two-Party Protocol

Due to the design of the MOSIX kernel architecture, as described in Chapter 2, all the interactions between a process and its resources are performed either on the same machine or between exactly two machines—the requesting machine on which the process is executing, and the machine that has the requested resource. The ability of the MOSIX kernel to support this (at most) two-party interaction is due to the symmetry of its organization, the use of global (universal) naming, and the avoidance of specific servers for any type of service. Note that in many cases if a process requires an extensive amount of access to a remote resource, then the load balancing mechanisms attempt to migrate this process to the machine that has the resource, thus further reducing the amount of communication overhead.

The most important ramification of the two-party protocol is the decentralization of control in a symmetric manner. This means that since all nodes can have an equal role in the execution of every operation, each node becomes a locus of control. Protocols structured in a symmetric way lead to independence of nodes because no node relies on others for the execution of its operations. Thus, nodes may join the system and processors or nodes may leave the system at any time without affecting the others.

A naive implementation of a mechanism in a symmetric way may require global coordination of nodes, since no node controls other nodes. This requires from each node a coordination effort that is linear with the size of the system, a violation of the bounded resources principle. A more sophisticated form of symmetry that avoids this problem can be derived by observing the relationship between the kernels of two machines that participate in the execution of some joint operation. Suppose that the kernel of one machine requests a remote service by executing a remote procedure call, or equivalently, by sending a request message that activates a server process in another machine. A client/server relation is formed between the two machines. The duration of this relation is limited, and normally ends when the operation is completed.

The ability to perform system operations by forming pairs of clients and servers implies that a finer notion of symmetry, which prevents the need for global coordination, could be developed. In this scheme, all operations are short interactions between two parties, a requester and a server. To allow all nodes to possess equal functional capability, all remote operations are performed by this protocol. Thus each node functions as both a client and a server, depending on whether it has initiated a request or is responding to one. Since in a multiprocessing system many of these operations are performed concurrently, each node should be able to function simultaneously as both client and server in several operations. This design implies that the resulting control overhead for executing each operation is independent of the number of nodes.

The two-party interaction protocol that is implemented in MOSIX according to the client/server principle is a highly efficient mechanism for large scale configurations, because it incurs the minimal amount of internode coordination and communication. An immediate outcome of this principle is that no global operation or synchronization is attempted within the system. Rather, any such system-wide operation is the collective result of many separate local interactions.

9.2.2 Partiality and Randomness·

In order to improve the performance of MOSIX, decisions made by one processor are sometimes based on information about the state of other processors. Consider, for example, the decision to migrate a process from one processor to another, in order to reduce the workload of the first. These decisions and the associated information-gathering operations can be performed as a sequence of two-party interactions, as suggested in the last section. A decision based on information gathered from more than a single processor, however, allows a faster convergence to good performance (e.g., balanced load). On the one hand, it might seem that decisions based on information about the state of all the processors would achieve much better performance (e.g., response time) than the case in which a decision is based on information from only a subset of the other processors. This demands a large portion of the available resources, such as processing and communication bandwidth. However, experience with MOSIX shows that even for relatively small configurations, the use of partial information achieves performance which is as good as that obtained using complete information. The salient feature of this example is that each processor's decision-making should be based on information obtained from a limited subset of other processors. This idea is a further generalization of the principle of symmetry, in order to make it compatible with the bounded resources principle.

In order to implement the partiality principle, each processor chooses a bounded subset of other processors to interact with. Since all processors are equal, this requires each processor to break the symmetry between the other processors. Breaking the symmetry can be done in a variety of ways, the simplest of which is a static partitioning into subsets. This has two disadvantages, however, the more intuitive one being its inherent unreliability. A more subtle disadvantage is that dependence on a fixed subset may lead to performance deterioration due to the unpredictability of users' resource requirements. For example, in the load balancing scheme, since the length of process execution times is unknown beforehand, any static partitioning of processors into resource sharing groups may lead to uneven performance.

From these remarks it appears that a flexible scheme for breaking symmetry is required. A natural implementation is the use of randomness in choosing a subset of the other processors. Intuitively, a random choice of the subset of processors with which one processor interacts in an effort to share resources is better than interaction with a fixed subset of processors. Random choice has another important role: it breaks the symmetry between the processors requesting an interaction in a way that avoids congestion. This simply follows from the fact that the probability of many processors making a request to the same subset of processors is very low. In MOSIX, symmetry-breaking through randomness is used in the information dissemination algorithm of the load balancing scheme and in the algorithm to locate a process. In both cases the set of processors with which a processor interacts is chosen at random.

Actually, randomness is not enough, because a random choice made only once has all the disadvantages of a single, fixed choice. A limitation on the duration of interactions should supplement the random choice. This is done by using the limited duration of interaction principle, which is also applied to the execution of service operations in accordance with the client/server principle. For example, when allocating objects to remote processes, some mechanism must ensure that this allocation is terminated when the remote processor crash. One such mechanism is the garbage collection algorithm, described in the next section.

9.2.3 Modularity and Isolation

Another aspect of scaling is the increased complexity of the system's kernel and handling the more varied failure modes of the system. Simply stated, a large system can have many more types of failures than a small system. MOSIX attempts to limit the scope of these problems by structuring the system's kernel as a set of loosely-coupled modules with minimal and well-defined intermodule interfaces, and by using hierarchical kernel organization with a high degree of information hiding, as described in Chapter 2.

An effective measure for limiting the scope of failures is isolation. In MOSIX, each machine is suspicious of any incoming remote request. This means that each such request is first validated before it is served. A simple method that MOSIX uses for implementing isolation is a dynamically generated password for some remote interactions. For example, when a process running on one machine opens a file on another machine, the latter assigns a password to the file entry. Then any operation on the file is validated against this password. An important outcome of isolation is the avoidance of propagation of faults; that is, faults are also isolated. This means that when one MOSIX processor fails, then except for processes that were using that processor, the remaining parts of the system are unaffected.

9.3 Probabilistic Algorithms

This section describes several probabilistic algorithms that are used in MOSIX for internal management and control. These include the algorithm for information dissemination, the algorithm for locating processes, and the remnant (garbage) collection scheme.

9.3.1 Information Dissemination

To illustrate that one can indeed implement algorithms that embody all the principles discussed in the previous sections, consider an algorithm similar to the MOSIX algorithms for disseminating load information, as described in Chapter 8. In a configuration with n processors, assume that each processor arrives at its process migration decisions by considering the load of l other processors. Then the following algorithm can be used. Each processor starts by measuring its own load. Then, every unit of time, each processor sends all the load measurements it has collected so far to some randomly chosen processor. As shown in [5], after $1.7095 \log_2 l$ units of time, almost all the processors are expected to have l different load measurements. It is also shown in [16] that by using the same algorithm, the load of any specific processor can be scattered to almost all the other processors in $1.693 \log_2 n$ units of time. Note that an alternative algorithm for disseminating information without broadcasting was presented in [1].

The above algorithm is completely symmetrical and hence insensitive to the identity of the initial source of information. It uses random routing of messages in order to avoid blocking of information propagation due to failed processors. This robustness is due to the principles of symmetry-breaking through randomness and limited duration of interaction. In the algorithm the information is dispersed through routine transmission of one-way messages by each processor. This algorithm does not use polling or timeouts, to avoid delays when waiting for failed processors. The routine transmission of messages, instead, indirectly limits those delays.

9.3.2 Locating Processes

Processes in MOSIX are located via their **home** structure - see Section 6.3.1. If the home site crashes, the user may no longer be able to locate a process. To overcome this problem, The home structure approach can be extended so that each process has multiple, fixed number of home sites. These homes are established when the process is created and they are placed on different processors.

The number of home sites depends on the hardware reliability and the required degree of fault tolerance, and does not depend on the size of the system.

Algorithm 9.1 describes a scheme for creating a set of m homes for each new process. This is done by using a unique (global) process identification number (PID), obtained by concatenating the creation site number with a local unique process number, and by using a universal hash function, that is known to all the processors, to distribute the location of the homes among all the available sites in a uniform manner.

Step 1: For each new process, establish a home on the processor where it is created. Then send $m - 1$ "home creation" messages to processors whose numbers are given by a universal hash function.

Step 2: Every unit of time, each process sends an update message containing its present location to all of its homes.

Step 3: When a processor receives an update message and a home exists for the sending process, it registers the location of the process and the (local) time of the update. Otherwise, the processor checks (using the process number and the hash function) if it should have a home for that process. If true, then a home is created and updated, otherwise the message is ignored.

Step 4: If a home entry is not called by its process for several (a parameter) consecutive units of time, then it is removed.

Step 5: When a process is terminated, it removes all its home entries.

Algorithm 9.1: Maintaining Multiple Home Structures

Based on Algorithm 9.1, Algorithm 9.2 needs only to use the PID and the universal hash function to locate it. This algorithm is executed locally, at the site of the requesting process. Due to the structure of the PID, this algorithm can find the creating site instantly and the other sites by using the universal hash function.

Algorithm 9.2 can overcome a home site crash and recovery by re-establishing a home site entry after such a recovery. Note that the algorithm is completely transparent to the user since it is initiated and executed by the MOSIX kernel. In the actual implementation, if all the home sites of a process fail to respond, then MOSIX uses a broadcast message as a final resort to locate the process. Note that this is almost the only occasion in which broadcasts are used in MOSIX.

Step 1: Send an inquiry message to the creation site of the process. If there is no reply, then using the hash function, send inquiry messages to all the other homes of that process.

Step 2: If all the inquiry messages fail, then wait one unit of time and return to Step 1. After several (a parameter) retries, if the process is not found, then respond negatively to the calling process.

Step 3: When a processor receives a request for information about the location of a process, and the information is available, it promptly provides the information to the requesting process.

Step 4: When a processor receives an inquiry message about a process and it does not have a home entry for that process, it responds negatively.

Algorithm 9.2: Locating a Process using Home Pointers

9.3.3 Garbage Collection

In MOSIX, processes executing at one site may have allocated resources or objects at other sites. Examples of such resources include files, texts, inodes, file locks, semaphore exit structures, process groups, zombies and *home* structures. Since processors, nodes, and communication links are inherently unreliable, failures may disconnect a process from its objects. Crashed sites are seldom able to notify other sites of their failure, so these resources become orphans, and must be detected and reclaimed for reuse.

Garbage collection due to processor failures is a delicate situation. Intuitively, this is due to the fact that a remote process that is slow in accessing a resource (perhaps due to a lost message) is indistinguishable from a process at a crashed site. This problem is similar to the problem of detecting lost messages in communication protocols through the use of timeout. Thus, declaring an object as an orphan due to failures is inherently bound to err. On the other hand, by its very nature, garbage collection is an irreversible operation. Once done, a process is no longer allowed to access the reclaimed object. Any practical scheme for garbage collection must nevertheless be performed within a finite period. Hence, it can only strive to lower the probability for error, but cannot achieve complete certainty.

The following garbage collection scheme is implemented in MOSIX [5]: when an object is allocated, a timer is attached to it. Processes are responsible for resetting the timer of the objects they use. This is done whenever an object is accessed, or when it receives a special **keep-alive message**. A garbage collection process periodically scans all the objects, and releases those whose timers have expired.

The timers are implemented by tagging each object with a unique creation time, and using a fixed upper limit on objects' lifetimes. Resetting the timer is done by resetting the tag. Since the probability of a single machine failure is low, the garbage collection algorithm is run infrequently.

The special keep-alive messages are periodically transmitted by each process to all its objects. These messages are required to reduce the probability of erroneously reclaiming objects which are still needed. Note that the garbage collection method is a client/server protocol.

The frequency of the garbage collection algorithm of the latest version of MOSIX is 5 minutes for the keep-alive messages, and 12 minutes for removal of orphan objects.

9.4 Summary

This chapter presented scaling considerations taken in MOSIX in order to allow the system to function properly when used in a large multicomputer configuration. It identified some of the difficulties associated with using existing operating systems mechanisms, and then defined a set of principles for constructing algorithms for large scale multicomputers. These principles include symmetry, client/server protocols, partiality, and randomness.

To demonstrate the effectiveness of these principles, the chapter presented several probabilistic algorithms for collecting information on the state of the system, for use in management and control of resources. The interesting properties of these algorithms are their completely decentralized nature, their use of only partial information about the global state of the system, and their limited degree of node coordination. The performance of the algorithms in terms of the quality of results and overhead per processor is insensitive to the size of the system.

Alternative algorithms for disseminating information reliably without broadcasting in a LAN-based system are described in [1]. These algorithms use repeated forwarding and packaging of messages to disseminate information. In these algorithms, broadcast of a message to all the processors can be achieved quickly with only point-to-point messages.

Chapter 10

System Performance

This chapter presents measurements of MOSIX system performance. All of the measurements and results pertain to the VME532 version, described in Chapter 2. A diagram of the configuration used in most of the measurements is shown in Figure 10.1. It includes two identical workstations, also called node machines, that are connected by a ProNET-80 token ring. Each node machine includes up to four processing elements (PEs), which are based on the National Semiconductor NS32532 microprocessor running at 25 MHz (8 MIPS) with 4 MBytes of local memory. A 12-MByte expansion memory board was added to the first PE in each node. The PEs within a node machine communicate over a VME bus.

One way to measure the performance of the MOSIX system is to compare the performance of a set of system calls and user applications on a single MOSIX processor to their performance on the base version of UNIX from which MOSIX evolved on the same processor. In the case of the VME532 version of MOSIX, the performance of a single machine running MOSIX and the performance of the same machine running UNIX System V Release 2 was found to be identical. This phenomenon has been observed both with different machine architectures and with different base versions of UNIX. These similarities in performance are a result of the efficient implementation of the Linker module in the kernel, and the manner in which the Linker treats local system calls.

The first two sections of this chapter present the performance of the mechanisms used by the MOSIX Linker. In Section 10.1, several of the important system calls are measured. The timing of each call is presented when dealing with local objects, as opposed to remote objects (i.e., objects that reside on some other processor). The results reflect the performance of the **Scall** mechanism. Section 10.2 uses a similar technique to measure the performance of the **Funnel** mechanism. The efficiency of the MOSIX **load balancing** algorithms is measured in Section 10.3. These measurements compare the processor utilization achieved by the MOSIX migration algorithms to the optimal processor utilization achievable by a static processor assignment. Section 10.4 gives performance measurements for the DAEMON toolkit monitoring facility.

For performance measurements of distributed applications running on the

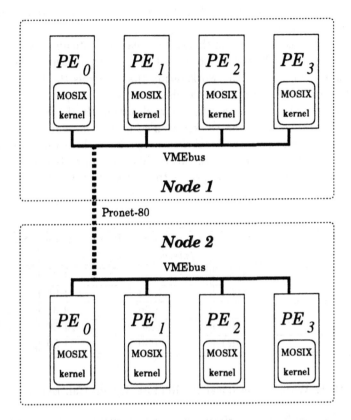

Figure 10.1: A 2-Node, 8-Processor MOSIX Configuration

MOSIX system, see Chapter 11.

10.1   Scall Performance

This section presents measurements of the time required to perform local and remote system calls, from which it is possible to show the overhead associated with the MOSIX **Scall** mechanism. Due to the architecture of the multiprocessor workstation, only one designated processor in each workstation actually controls the I/O devices belonging to that workstation. This processor is called the **master** processor of the workstation. The other processors in the workstation are referred to as **slave** processors. Slave processors perform I/O operations indirectly by communicating with the master processor over a VME bus. For example, a slave processor file system call that access a file on some remote workstation is first sent to the local master processor, and then routed to the remote workstation's master processor. Note that the architecture of the MOSIX kernel allows many system calls to be performed locally by each site without any slowdown penalty. System calls of this type include, but are not limited to: *getpid()*, *signal()* and *time()*.

The system calls presented in this section read or write universal inode structures as described in Chapter 4. Local system calls are measured while running on the master processor of the workstation that controls the file's device. Remote system calls are measured both when run on a slave processor of the same workstation and when run on a different workstation. In the first case, the data transfer is performed over the workstation's bus and is relatively fast. In the second case, the data uses the local area network, in this case a token ring, to communicate with the remote workstation. The system calls were measured by timing a set of benchmarking programs that execute each call on both remote and local objects 100,000 times.

System Call	(size)	Local Time (msec.)	Remote Time (msec.)	Slowdown Ratio
read	(1 KByte)	0.34	1.36	4.00
write	(1 KByte)	0.68	1.65	2.43
open & close		2.06	4.31	2.09
fork	(256 KByte)	7.80	21.60	2.77
exec	(256 KByte)	25.30	51.50	2.04

Table 10.1: Workstation Local vs. Remote System Call Execution Times

The times required to perform the most frequently used file system calls between processors in the same workstation are given in Table 10.1. All times given are in milliseconds. The system calls themselves appear in the first column, along with the size of the object that the system call operated on. The second column, entitled "Local Time," shows the time required for a process running on the master processor to access a local file. The third column, entitled "Remote Time," shows the time required for a process running on a slave processor to access the same file (via the workstation bus and that workstation's master processor). The fourth column shows the slowdown factor associated with remote system calls within the same workstation. It is computed as the "Remote Time" divided by the "Local Time."

A useful measure of the overall effect of remote access on a process is a **weighted average** of the slowdown factors. Using known frequencies of system calls, as presented in [15], the frequency of each call is multiplied by the slowdown factor associated with remote execution. The results show a weighted slowdown factor of 2.8 when comparing the times measured for a set of system calls executed by a slave to those measured for the same set of system calls executed by the master.

Table 10.2 lists the execution times of the same set of system calls when executed between two different workstations, from one master processor to another, over a local area network. In this case the weighted average of the slowdown

System Call	(*size*)	Local Time (*msec.*)	Remote Time (*msec.*)	Slowdown Ratio
read	(*1 KByte*)	0.34	1.93	5.67
write	(*1 KByte*)	0.68	2.33	3.42
open & close		2.06	5.19	2.52
fork	(*256 KByte*)	7.80	23.10	2.96
exec	(*256 KByte*)	25.30	53.80	2.12

Table 10.2: LAN Local vs. Remote System Call Execution Times

factors is 3.69. The comparison of the time required to perform system calls between a master and slave in the same workstation, using the workstation's bus, and the time required between two masters in different workstations, using the local area network, shows an additional slowdown of only 32%. Some of the slowdown can be directly attributed to the overhead of the network protocol, which could be significantly reduced by using more suitable hardware. The current network protocol, which uses a software generated Cyclic Redundancy Check (CRC) at both the sending and receiving processors, as well as an acknowledgment message, is an example of this reducible overhead.

10.2   Funnel & Process Migration Performance

This section presents measurements of the MOSIX Funnel's speed using the techniques of the previous section. Funnels, as explained in Chapter 7, are used by the MOSIX file system and the process migration mechanism to transfer data between processors.

As a reference point, the first two lines of Table 10.3 show the rate of a memory-to-memory copy using the Funnel mechanism between processes running on the same processor, and the rate of a similar copy from a process running on a master processor to a process running on a slave processor in the same workstation. The following lines display the speed of process migration among different types of processors, within the same workstation and among different workstations.

Table 10.3 shows that the speed of process migration between different workstations (e.g., from the local master processor to a remote master processor using the LAN) is about 35% slower than the speed of local migration from the master processor to a local slave processor. This difference in migration speeds is consistent with the slowdown rate of many systems calls, as presented in the previous section. This slowdown ratio is expected to diminish as faster LANs with higher reliability become available.

System Throughput	KBytes/*Sec.*
Funnel Copy Same Processor	11,299
Memory Copy Master to Local Slave	1,820
Process Migration Master to Local Slave	1,235
Process Migration Slave to Local Slave	1,254
Process Migration Master to Remote Master	794
Process Migration Master to Remote Slave	702
Process Migration Local Slave to Remote Slave	636

Table 10.3: System Data Throughput

10.3 Load Balancing Performance

This section presents the efficiency of the MOSIX automatic load balancing policy, using a configuration of two identical workstations, each with three processors. The program employed to carry out the measurements creates one parent process, which assigns equal computational tasks to several identical child processes. Upon completion of a task, each child process communicates with the parent process, and is then assigned a new task. The amount of computation performed by each child process in each iteration was increased from 0.1 seconds to 10 seconds, resulting in a decrease in the communication and management overhead of the parent process.

In each test, two different initial process assignment schemes were used. The first used MOSIX's automatic load balancing while the second used a static assignment, made by the parent process, of each child process to a processor. In the first case, due to residence requirements of the MOSIX load balancing scheme, each process was executed for at least 1/3 second at the processor in which it was created before it was allowed to migrate. In the case of static assignment, each child process immediately migrated to its designated processor. As a point of reference, the total execution time of the benchmark, when executed as a single process with no communication overhead, was exactly 60 minutes.

Table 10.4 shows the results of executing a parent process and six child processes. The first column of the table shows the granularity of the work; that is, the amount of work assigned to each child process by the parent process. The columns labeled "Elap." contain the elapsed execution time for the whole benchmark. The total overhead time, shown in the "Overh." columns, is defined as both the user and system times that were a result of the work distribution and the communication overhead. The "Speedup" columns shows the speedup, computed as the ratio between the total execution time of a single machine divided by the elapsed time using six processors. The utilization listed in the next column is defined as the ratio between the sum of the single machine execution time and the measured overhead, divided by the product of the elapsed time and the number of processes.

Work	Automatic Migration				Static (Optimal) Assignment			
Unit	Elap.	Overh.	Speed	Util.	Elap.	Overh.	Speed	Util.
(Sec.)	(Min.)	(Sec.)	up		(Min.)	(Sec.)	up	
0.1	11.83	2.890	5.07	85%	11.63	2.820	5.16	86%
0.2	11.00	1.457	5.45	91%	10.83	1.493	5.54	92%
0.4	10.67	0.773	5.62	94%	10.43	0.773	5.75	96%
0.5	10.50	0.627	5.71	95%	10.37	0.632	5.79	96%
1.0	10.33	0.328	5.81	97%	10.20	0.340	5.88	98%
2.0	10.23	0.237	5.87	98%	10.13	0.235	5.92	99%
3.0	10.23	0.190	5.87	98%	10.10	0.168	5.94	99%
5.0	10.27	0.165	5.84	97%	10.10	0.152	5.94	99%
10.0	10.28	0.106	5.84	97%	10.07	0.172	5.96	99%

Table 10.4: Automatic Process Migration vs. Optimal Static Assignment

Note that utilization refers to CPU utilization for all work done including overhead time, while speedup refers to the actual work done not including any overhead. The corresponding results for the optimal static process assignment are given in the right-hand side of the table, in congruent columns.

A comparison of the task granularity shows that even for small units of work, the speedup and utilization obtained are quite good—greater than 85%. Comparison of MOSIX load balancing and the optimal static assignment shows a maximal difference in the utilization of only 2%.

10.3.1   The Time Required to Balance the Load

Another way to measure the efficiency of the load balancing mechanism is by measuring the time it takes to balance the load on all the participating processors, using a different number of processes. Table 10.5 presents the results of executing an equal number of identical processes on an 8-processor MOSIX system. In this test, all the processes were created on one processor and then they migrated freely, until the load of all the processors became equal. The execution time of each process was set to exactly 1 minute. In the table, the first column lists the number of processes. The second column lists the measured time, in seconds, to balance the load. The "Elapsed" column lists the execution time of the last process to finish the execution. The last column gives the percent of the machine utilization, which is the ratio between the optimal execution time (assuming zero distribution time) and the measured elapsed time for this execution. In each case, the test was executed four times and the average of the results was taken.

Number of processes	Load Balancing Time (Sec.)	Elpased (Min.)	Efficiency (%)
1	0.0	1.00	100.0
2	0.4	1.02	98.0
4	0.8	1.04	96.2
8	10.2	1.06	94.3
16	21.3	2.06	97.1
24	30.2	3.05	98.4
32	31.1	4.03	99.3
40	25.2	5.05	99.0
48	29.0	6.04	99.3
64	35.1	8.03	99.6
80	40.0	10.07	99.3
128	65.0	16.08	99.5

Table 10.5: Time to Balance the Load

10.4 DAEMON Toolkit Performance

The MOSIX kernel was extended to provide support for the detection of realtime errors that occur in distributed programs. These extensions were undertaken as part of the Distributed Application Environment MONitor (DAEMON) project [19], a software implemented monitoring toolkit. The extensions provide kernel mechanisms for logging events and two new system calls that allow processes to alter their monitoring state and collect logged events. The DAEMON toolkit program is described in Chapter 11.

One of the goals of the DAEMON monitoring toolkit was non-intrusiveness. In order to measure the amount of overhead generated by the implementation of the DAEMON toolkit on the MOSIX system, three suites of the same benchmark were executed. The first suite was executed on the standard MOSIX kernel. The second suite was executed on an enhanced kernel supporting the DAEMON monitoring toolkit facilities, although the monitoring itself was not activated. The third and final suite was executed on an enhanced kernel supporting the DAEMON monitoring toolkit facilities while monitoring was activated.

All the benchmarks were run on the MOSIX system using one node containing 4 processors. No user processes, other than standard system daemon processes, were executed during the measurements. The results presented are the average of four runs, measured using the UNIX System V Release 2 **timex** utility. This utility provides three time measurements:

Real time — the total duration of the execution as compared to the system clock.

User time — the sum of the times spent by the process and any child processes it may have forked, executing in user mode.

System time — the sum of the times spent by the process and any child processes it may have forked, executing in kernel mode.

In the three tables that follow, the first column contains the number of slave processes used to execute the subtasks. The second column contains the elapsed time measured as returned by the **real time** of t imex, while the third and fourth columns respectively show the **user time** and **system time**.

Number of Processes	Elapsed Time (Sec.)	User Time (Sec.)	System Time (Sec.)	Speedup
1	829.20	825.87	1.73	1.00
2	421.95	827.70	1.73	1.97
3	281.90	828.57	1.59	2.94
4	215.43	827.37	2.15	3.85
5	213.80	828.30	2.90	3.88
6	216.10	827.73	2.21	3.84
7	213.20	828.42	2.38	3.89
8	214.20	828.38	2.17	3.87

Table 10.6: Application Performance on an Unextended Kernel

Table 10.6 presents the performance results for the execution of a sample benchmark using a MOSIX kernel without the DAEMON toolkit extensions. The execution times show a near-linear speedup proportional to the number of processes used up to the number of processors available. The speedup is defined as the ratio between the elapsed time using one process to the elapsed time using N processes. As the number of processes grows beyond the number of available processors, the elapsed time begins to vary, gradually increasing as more and more processes compete for CPU resources on the available processors. Because the load balancing mechanisms used are probabilistic, the speedup degradation is not linear.

The benchmark results shown in Table 10.7 were measured on the enhanced MOSIX kernel, supporting the DAEMON monitoring toolkit activities. During the executions, the monitoring facility was not employed, enabling this measurement to ascertain the overhead to unmonitored processes that might be caused by the DAEMON toolkit kernel enhancements. As seen from the results, the elapsed times tended to vary from those originally measured by less than 2%, while the total **user time** remained unaffected. A slight increase in the **system time** was noted as the relevant system calls now assumed additional responsibilities (e.g., triggering event report generations).

The third suite, shown in Table 10.8, was executed while being monitored by the DAEMON toolkit facilities. In order to provide an accurate assessment of the overhead generated by monitoring, a daemond process was run to gather the monitoring events. Although an increase in the elapsed time was noted, this

Number of Processes	Elapsed Time (Sec.)	User Time (Sec.)	System Time (Sec.)	Speedup
1	836.70	827.38	1.96	1.0
2	421.97	827.61	2.06	1.98
3	280.95	827.43	1.61	2.98
4	212.89	827.89	1.70	3.93
5	215.31	827.70	2.15	3.89
6	212.18	824.44	4.00	3.94
7	216.56	826.36	3.55	3.86
8	217.34	824.86	3.96	3.85

Table 10.7: Unmonitored Application Performance on an Enhanced Kernel

Number of Processes	Elapsed Time (Sec.)	User Time (Sec.)	System Time (Sec.)	Speedup
1	847.65	828.50	2.23	1.0
2	422.11	827.53	2.47	2.00
3	281.02	827.74	2.08	3.01
4	214.24	827.46	2.80	3.96
5	214.36	830.44	1.41	3.95
6	213.09	828.54	2.12	3.98
7	215.64	828.53	2.41	3.93
8	216.52	827.70	3.10	3.91

Table 10.8: Monitored Application Performance

increase was actually less than 2.25% when compared to the performance results shown in Table 10.6. A small increase was also observed in the **user time** and the **system time**.

10.5 Summary

This chapter presented the performance of several MOSIX kernel mechanisms. Among these are the Linker mechanisms (Scalls and Funnels), several system calls, the process migration mechanism, the load balancing mechanism, and the overhead incurred by the monitoring toolkit.

The results presented in this chapter demonstrate efficient utilization of the hardware by the MOSIX system. This is due to the architecture of the MOSIX kernel and the efficient implementation of the above mechanisms in the MOSIX kernel.

The performance of the MOSIX internal mechanisms shows that message passing systems are a viable alternative for the construction of large scale multicomputer systems. This is made possible because the overhead incurred in each of these mechanisms is relatively small, compared to the same mechanisms running on a single machine or a shared-memory multiprocessor. This is further demonstrated in Chapter 11, where the performance of some distributed application examples is given.

Chapter 11

Distributed Applications

Upon completion of the earlier versions of MOSIX, it became evident that MOSIX provides a sturdy platform for research in parallel and distributed applications. The purpose of this research is to develop methods to speed up the execution of programs at a rate that is proportional to the number of processors. Clearly, this is possible in applications that can be partitioned into many independent tasks, but it is more difficult in single-threaded or heavily I/O-bound and communication-bound programs. This is because MOSIX does not provide any means for "automatic" program partitioning or runtime parallelization beyond those available in UNIX. Thus, in the MOSIX environment, it is the responsibility of the application programmer to create programs that can benefit most from the multicomputer environment.

The execution of distributed applications requires a minimal understanding of the services provided by the MOSIX system. These services fall into two categories: operating system level services, which are provided by the MOSIX kernel, and user-level services, provided outside the MOSIX kernel. The kernel level services include the ability to create multiple processes, the means for interprocess communication (IPC), and support of (transparent) process distribution among the processors for better resource utilization.

Section 11.1 presents some of the user-level services that are currently available, including an extension of a high-level programming language to support concurrency. Section 11.2 presents examples and performance results of a range of applications that have been successfully enhanced on MOSIX. A description of the monitoring capabilities added to the kernel for measuring the execution and interaction of multiple processes is given in Section 11.3.

11.1 Writing Distributed Applications

This section presents two methods for writing applications that can benefit from the MOSIX environment. The first method uses standard UNIX mechanisms for the creation and execution of multiple processes, and for interprocess communi-

cation (IPC). The second method is a language-level extension for the support
of parallel programming, called the Multicomputer Programming Environment
(MPE), comprised of a preprocessor and a runtime library of routines.

The easiest way to write a program with multiple processes is to first partition
the program into logical parts that can run independently on different processes,
and then to use standard mechanisms such as *fork()* and *exec()* for process
creation and execution and IPC mechanisms for interprocess communication.
These mechanisms are available to the C-level programmer. For other high-level
languages, such as FORTRAN, it is possible to use a simple library of programs
that provides these services.

First, it is important to note that not every algorithm can run efficiently
on a distributed system. An example of an algorithm suitable for a distributed
system is an algorithm composed of one or more sequential computational phases. Each phase is characterized by a period of heavy computation which can
be partitioned into independent parts. Figure 11.1 depicts such a phase of an
algorithm programmed in a sequential manner.

At the onset of each phase, initialization and preprocessing take place. The
main section of the phase contains a CPU-bound procedure that is governed by
a DO LOOP control structure. Often, the loop control variable is either passed as
an argument to the procedure, or is used to calculate such an argument. Once
the computation has been completed, some postprocessing may be required.

Since each invocation of the computational procedure is independent, these
invocations may be performed in parallel. A degenerate example of such a
structure is a simulation program that must be run independently a number of
times using different parameters. A more general case would be a tree search
algorithm, in which the search can be partitioned into smaller sub-searches. For
example, consider the **n-queen problem** in which n chess queens are to be
placed on an $n \times n$ chessboard such that no two queens are on the same row,
column, or diagonal. The solution space, consisting of all the $n!$ permutations of
the n-tuple, can be organized as a tree. Each leaf vertex in the permutation tree
corresponds to one solution in the solution space. The solution space is defined
by all the possible paths from the root vertex to a leaf vertex. An algorithm for
solving the problem would search the tree to find a leaf representing a valid queen
placement. In the parallel algorithm, the tree is partitioned into 2^i subtrees,
where each vertex in the ith level is the root of a subtree. Then, each subtree
can be searched independently in parallel.

11.1.1   The MPE Model

The Multicomputer Programming Environment (MPE) [22] is a set of library
routines that enhance C and FORTRAN to support parallel programming for
a distributed memory multiprocessor, with coarse grain parallelism. In order
to ease the task of programming, these extensions are minimal, with a small
execution overhead. The conversion of a sequential program to a parallel version is achieved by reorganizing the program on the master/slave model (see
Figure 11.2). In this model, the master process distributes independent parts of

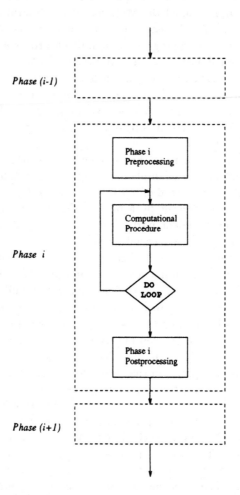

Figure 11.1: The Sequential Flow

the computation to the slave processes, which in turn perform the computations and return the results to the master process. The master may then do some postprocessing before continuing on to the next phase.

The main advantages of the master/slave scheme are ease of control and distribution of work. The first property allows the master process to control and synchronize the execution of the slave processes. Also, the requirement to distribute the computational tasks among several slave processes enforces parallelism in the flow control of the program. The main drawback of the master/slave model is that it does not support direct IPC among the slave processes, thus limiting the possibility of recursion in the generation of processes.

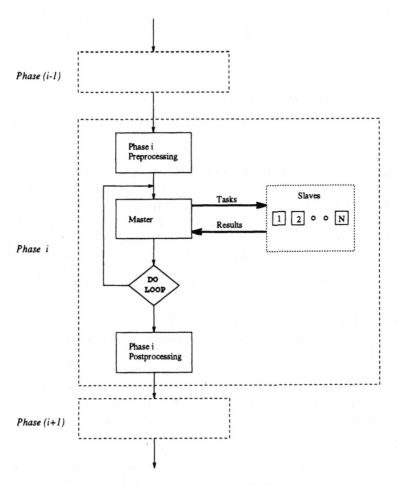

Figure 11.2: The MPE Master-Slave Execution Model

Note that the MPE master/slave programming model allows a master process to distribute disjoint tasks to slave processes. Thus it is possible to achieve an abstract, high-level programming environment that is not dependent on any specific computer architecture or topology.

MPE consists of two main parts, a parallelizing precompiler called *parpp*, and a runtime library. A program, written in C or FORTRAN, is first precompiled by *parpp*. The precompiler expands the macros, adding new functions, and includes the runtime library routine calls. The result is a program in C or FORTRAN that can be compiled by a standard compiler and linked to the runtime library.

11.1.2 The MPE Functions

The MPE macros and functions, which range from declarative statements to executional invocations, are **Pfunc**, **Pinit**, **Pcall**, **Pwait**, **Pexit**, **Pbroad** and **Pjoin**. This section presents a synopsis and a description for each of these functions in C-programs.

Pfunc – Declaring the distributed function

The **Pfunc** macro is a declaration statement describing the assignment to be enqueued by the master. This macro must appear in the declaration part of the master function that creates the assignments.

The main purpose of the **Pfunc** macro is to declare both the number and the length of the input and output arguments of each distributed assignment. Due to the lack of shared memory support, passing a memory address between processors is insufficient. Instead, the whole memory segment must be passed from the master to the slave or vice versa. The programmer is responsible for specifying the name and the type of each argument. Any variable definition statement that is valid in C is also valid as an argument declaration in the **Pfunc** macro. There is no need to specify the length of the arguments; this is done by the preprocessor.

The syntax of the **Pfunc** macro is as follows:

Pfunc (*distributed-function, input-arguments, output-arguments, collect-function*);

The number of assignments in a program is unlimited, although each one must have an appropriate **Pfunc** macro. The distributed function is a standard C function that is executed by each slave upon receiving that assignment's *input-arguments* and *output-arguments*, which serve as the input and output arguments of this function respectively.

The *collect-function* arguments is optional. The function it specifies is executed by the master and is designated for synchronizing the master with the completion of the slaves' assignments. Whenever a slave returns its results, the *collect-function* is called with the slave's outputs as argument. The programmer must verify that such a function, with argument declarations matching those of the **Pfunc** macro, actually exists in the program.

When the **Pfunc** macro is preprocessed, several functions, which are transparent to the programmer, are automatically created. These functions handle the argument passing from the master to the slaves, return the results to the master, and if required, activate the *collect-function*.

Pinit – Creating a slave

The master process creates slaves by invoking the **Pinit** function. The number of slaves may be explicitly declared by the user or chosen by the system. Each slave inherits the creating master's environment at the time of its creation. **Pinit**'s syntax is:

int **Pinit** (*n*);

where *n* is the number of slaves to be created. If *n* is zero, the number of slaves will default to the number of processors operating at that time. A negative value causes the slaves to be forcefully migrated and evenly dispersed among the available processors. Each slave is a UNIX process created by the *fork()* system call. Normally, the slave processes are (transparently) dispersed among the processors using the automatic load balancing mechanism of MOSIX. Upon completion, **Pinit** returns the number of slave processes that were actually created.

Pcall – Enqueuing assignments

The distribution of work to the slaves is done by calling the **Pcall** macro for each assignment. When a slave becomes available it takes an assignment from a common queue, which is created by the master process. Upon completion of its assignment, the slave returns the results to the master and requests the next assignment. Note that the distribution of assignments, as well as their computation, are completely asynchronous. This means that the master process does not have any knowledge of when the slaves start processing, and it cannot determine the order of the execution of the assignments. The syntax of **Pcall** is:

Pcall (*distributed-func*, (*input-args*), (*output-args*), *collect-func*);

This macro enqueues a task from the master to be executed by a slave. The slave executes the function *distributed-func* using the input arguments specified in *input-args*. It stores the results in *output-args*, which are then sent back to the master.

In general, **Pcall** can be viewed as an asynchronous Remote Procedure Call (RPC). This means that like RPC, **Pcall** is a transfer of control, but unlike RPC, the calling program resumes its execution immediately, without waiting for the completion of the computation or the arrival of its results. The only assumption the calling program may make is that the input arguments have been transferred and no changes that are made to these arguments will affect the task previously enqueued.

The *collect-function* argument is optional. If omitted, the results are asynchronously returned to the master. The master can then be informed upon the termination of all of the assignments by calling the **Pwait** synchronization call (see below). If, however, the master wishes to be informed of every assignment termination, a *collect-function* may be provided. This function is a standard C function that is executed by the master when it receives results from one of its slaves. The arguments of this function match the outputs of the slave.

The **Pcall** statement has a similar structure to the **Pfunc** macro. **Pfunc** serves as a declaration of the distributed function, describing the number of its arguments and their size, while the **Pcall** statement specifies pointers to memory locations where the arguments reside at the time of the call.

Pwait – Synchronization call

The master process can "wait" at some point in its execution for all of the assignments to be completed. It can also be notified when each assignment is completed. The **Pwait** call enables the master to know when all of the previously sent assignments have terminated. Its syntax is:

Pwait ();

Usually, **Pwait** appears after the loop containing the **Pcall** statement. Note, however, that it is not required to be contiguous to the loop itself.

Pexit – Killing the slaves

Pexit complements **Pinit**, which creates a slave process. **Pexit** will generally be preceded by a **Pwait** call to prevent it from terminating assignments that are being executed at the time of the call, or are still awaiting their execution. Its syntax is:

Pexit ();

Pbroad – Broadcasting to slaves

A broadcast operation enables the master to share new information with all of its slave processes. This is a synchronous operation in the sense that it guarantees that all of the slaves will receive the broadcasted information before they get any new assignments.

The slaves created by the **Pinit** operation inherit their master's environment. In some algorithms, it may become necessary for new information, that is revealed by some slave during the execution, to be shared with the others. This can be done by a sequence of **Pexit** and **Pinit** calls that are executed between two consecutive phases of the algorithm, when the slaves are idle. Alternatively, it can be done by calling **Pbroad**, which allows the master to interact with the slaves at any time. Its syntax is:

Pbroad (*v, size*);

The result of the **Pbroad** is a broadcast of the variable *v*, of *size* bytes, to all the slaves.

Pjoin – Collecting information from the slaves

This operation enables the master process to collect information from the slaves in a synchronous mode, just like broadcast.

The MPE model allows the master to send assignments to slaves for execution and in turn to receive their results. All the modifications that the slaves make to data that is not included in their output arguments remain local. The **Pjoin** call provides the only means for this information to be sent from each slave to the master. This cannot be done via the **Pcall** mechanism because the master does not know which slave executed a specific assignment. **Pjoin** guarantees that all of the slaves will send the requested data immediately to the master. The syntax of the **Pjoin** call is:

Pjoin (*address, length, join_func, slave_func*);

The first two arguments are the address and the length in bytes of the data item requested from the slaves' memory. Instead of transferring the data directly to memory locations supplied by the master, the data is passed as an argument to the function *join_func*. This function is activated within the master for each slave transfer. This allows the master to process the data in a convenient manner. The *slave_func* is an optional function that is activated within each slave just prior to the data transfer.

11.2   Examples of Distributed Applications

This section presents the performance of several applications that were written using MPE and executed on a configuration of two identical workstations, with a total of 8 processors. In each case, first the sequential algorithm is described, then the parallel algorithm, which includes the MPE constructs. Then the performance of the serial version is given, followed by the performance of the parallel program, using 1-12 processes. Due to the MOSIX load balancing, as long as there were up to 8 processes, each process had its own processor. In order to show the overhead of the internal mechanisms of MOSIX, the number of processes was increased to 12, so that more than one process executed on some processors.

11.2.1   The Traveling Salesman Problem

The first example is the Traveling Salesman Problem (TSP). This example is a classical case of an algorithm that can easily be partitioned (distributed) into several subtasks. The TSP problem is as follows: Given N cities and the costs of travel between any two cities, find a minimal cost tour visiting each of the N cities exactly once.

More formally, consider a complete graph $\mathcal{G} = (\mathcal{V}, \mathcal{E})$, where $\mathcal{V}$ is a set of n vertices and $\mathcal{E}$ is the set of edges between these vertices. If C_{ij} is the cost associated with edge $\mathcal{E}_{ij}$, then $|C_{ij}|$ is the cost matrix of the graph $\mathcal{G}$. The objective of the TSP algorithm is to find a minimal cost Hamiltonian circuit of $\mathcal{G}$. There are many ways to solve this problem. The method used here is a symmetric non-Euclidean approach, which gives a good approximation to the optimal solution.

The Sequential Algorithm

The sequential algorithm used to solve the TSP problem consists of $n-1$ stages, where the jth stage attempts to find the shortest path between $j+1$ cities. The starting point for each stage is a set of the m best paths found in the previous stage, where m is a parameter. In the first stage this set has only n elements, consisting of the initial set of cities. For each path in the set, a fixed depth search of 4 tours is performed and the next destination city is chosen. The resulting complexity of the algorithm is therefore $O(mn^5)$.

```
nress = nnodes;
for (stage = 1; stage ≤ nnodes - depth; stage++) {
        for (i = 0; i < nres; i++)
                search (i, stage, oldpath[i], newres);
        heap_sort (newres, npass);
        makepath (step, newres, oldpath);
        nress = npath;
}
```

Program 11.1: Sequential TSP Algorithm

The sequential algorithm, shown in Program 11.1, requires only *nnodes - depth* stages of computation. This is due to the positive value of the search depth, which returns the best complete path at stage n - 4. The variable *nres* represents the number of best paths passed from one stage to the next stage. Initially it equals *nnodes*, the number of starting vertices. Once past the first stage, its value is *npass*, which was previously defined as *m*.

At the onset of each stage, the array *oldpath* contains the *nress* best results from the previous stage. A search is conducted to find the next best vertex for each given path. The results of the search are accumulated in the heap structure *newres* by the function *search()*. Once all the *nres* searches have been completed, the heap is sorted. Then *makepath()* is invoked to create the paths for the next stage.

The Distributed Algorithm

In the distributed version of the algorithm, shown in Program 11.2, all the searches that are performed in a single stage are executed simultaneously. This is accomplished by having the master process create several slaves that execute search tasks via the **Pcall** mechanism.

As in the sequential algorithm, in the beginning of stage *j*, the array *oldpath* contains the best *nres* paths of length *j*. The master enqueues *nres/gran* tasks to be executed in parallel. Each task contains *gran* paths on which the slaves search for the best *j* + 1 city. This search is performed by the function *son_search()*, which consists of the sequential *search()* function, modified to handle the *gran* argument. Each slave accumulates the best *nres* results per stage in the buffer *resbuf*.

Prior to task creation, the master initializes the buffer *resbuf* in each slave using the **Pbroad** function. After the tasks have been enqueued by **Pcall**,

```
nress = nnodes;
for (stage = 1; stage ≤ nnodes - depth; stage++) {
      first = 1;
      for (i = 0; i < nres; i++)
            resbuf[i].length = 0;
      Pbroad (resbuf, npass * sizeof(struct result));
      for (i = 0; i < nres; i += GRAN) {
            gran = min(GRAN, nres - i);
            Pcall (son_search, (&i, &stage, &gran, oldpath[i]), (&dummy));
      }
      Pwait ();
      Pjoin (resbuf, npass * sizeof(struct result), merge, son_sort);
      nress = npass;
      makepath (stage, resbuf, oldpath);
}
```

Program 11.2: Distributed TSP Algorithm

with *son_search()* supplied as the function argument, the master awaits their completion via **Pwait**. Once the tasks have been completed, the results are collected by invoking the **Pjoin** function with arguments that cause each slave to select the *nres* best results and return them to the master. The master sorts the *nres* results gathered from each slave into a single list containing new paths of length $j + 1$. The *gran* argument determines the size of the task that each slave receives from the master. The task size is a direct function of the number of input paths that each task includes.

Performance Results

The MPE version of TSP for 50 cities was executed on an 8-processor MOSIX system. The execution times are shown in Table 11.1. The first line lists the measured times of the sequential program, with one process. In order to measure the performance of the parallel version of the program, the speedup and efficiency of the sequential execution are set to 1.00 and 100%, respectively. The remaining lines list the measurements for the parallel program with a varying number of slave processes, as follows: the first column lists the number of slave processes, *nproc*. The total CPU time, given in the second column, is defined as the total number of CPU seconds spent in user mode by both the master and the slave processes. The measured elapsed time consists of the actual execution time, in seconds, of the program. The next column shows the speedup, defined as the ratio between the elapsed execution time of the serial program, and the measured elapsed execution time with the current number of processes. The last column

gives the efficiency, defined as the percent of the machine utilization, which is
the ratio between the obtained speedup and the maximum number of processors
used for this execution.

Number of Slave Processes	CPU Time *(Sec.)*	Elapsed Time *(Sec.)*	Relative Speedup	Efficiency (%)
Sequential	23052	23058	1.000	100.0
1	23076	23136	0.997	99.7
2	23100	11634	1.982	99.1
3	23100	7770	2.968	98.9
4	23124	5838	3.950	98.7
5	23118	4734	4.871	97.4
6	23172	3930	5.867	97.8
7	23148	3414	6.754	96.5
8	**23214**	**3018**	**7.640**	**95.5**
9	23238	3024	7.625	95.3
10	23190	3054	7.550	94.4
11	23268	3162	7.292	91.2
12	23244	3558	6.481	81.0

Table 11.1: TSP Algorithm Performance

Observations

In the execution of the program, the number of slave processes was gradually
increased from one to 12, though only 8 processors were available. As expected,
the total CPU time for all the executions was approximately the same, regardless of the number of slaves. As long as there were up to 8 slave processes, the
speedup gain was near-linear. The best speedup result, obtained with 8 processors, is presented in boldface in Table 11.1. When the number of slaves was
increased from 9 to 12, the speedup decreased gradually, but remained close to
the maximum speedup obtained.

This decrease in the speedup can be attributed to the following facts:

- The behavior of the MOSIX automatic load balancing mechanism is nondeterministic. When more processes are created, it takes more time to
  balance the system.

- The total elapsed time depends on the system utilization during the execution of the last set of tasks. Since MPE does not impose execution
  synchronization, and due to the fact that the tasks of a parallel program
  are not distributed evenly among the processors, some processors become
  idle during the last phase of the execution, thus increasing the total execution time.

11.2.2 Graph Coloring

The **m–graph coloring problem** can be stated as follows: Given a graph G and m colors, assign colors to the vertices of G such that each vertex is assigned one color and no two adjacent vertices have the same color. It is well known that for $m \geq 3$, the graph coloring problem is NP-complete [25].

A heuristic algorithm for this problem can be stated as follows: Let the graph G be represented by its adjacency matrix $G[n][n]$, where $G[i][j] = 1$ if (i, j) is an edge of G, and $G[i][j] = 0$ otherwise. Let the different colors be represented by the integers $1, 2, \ldots, m$, and let the solutions be given by the n-tuple $(x[0], x[1], \ldots, x[n])$, where $x[i]$ is the color of vertex i.

The Sequential Algorithm

A general backtracking algorithm for solving the graph coloring problem is shown in Program 11.3. This method uses a state space tree of the mth degree and height $(n+1)$. Each vertex at level i of this tree has m successors, that correspond to the m possible color assignments of $x[i]$.

```
mcoloring (x, s, n, m, nres)
Color x[ ];
int m;
int *s;                        /* index of starting node */
int *nres;
{
        int i, k;

        k = *s;
        *nres = 0;
        while (k ≥ *s)
             if (nextcolor(x, k, m))
                  if (k == *n) {        /* have we reached a solution */
                       print (x, n);
                       (*nres)++;
                  }
                  else
                          k++;
             else
                  k--;
}
```

Program 11.3: Sequential Graph Coloring Algorithm

In the algorithm, the function *nextcolor()* assigns the next color to $x[n]$, assuming that such a color exists. The value of 1 is returned if a valid color for

n was found, otherwise 0 is returned. In order to find all the valid schemes for coloring the graph, *mcoloring* must be called with an initial value of $s = 0$.

The Distributed Algorithm

The problem can be distributed using the scheme shown in Program 11.4. The argument DEPTH determines the grain size of the solution. Increasing the value of DEPTH will cause a larger number of smaller tasks to be executed in parallel. For example, in the benchmark presented below, DEPTH was chosen to be 3, resulting in m^3 parallel calls to the function *mcoloring()*.

```
p_mcoloring (x, n, m, nres)
Color x[];
int n, m, *nres;
{
      int i = 0, d = DEPTH;

      Pfunc(mcoloring, {Color x[N]; int depth; int n; int m;},
            {int nres;});
      Pinit(0);
      while (i ≥ 0)
          if (nextcolor(x, i))
                if (i == DEPTH - 1)
                        Pcall(mcoloring, (x, &d, &n, &m), (nres));
                else
                        i++;
          else
                i--;
      Pwait();
      Pexit();
}
```

Program 11.4: Distributed Graph Coloring Algorithm

Performance Results

Table 11.2 presents the execution times, in seconds, of the distributed algorithm *p_mcoloring*, on an 8-processor MOSIX machine. The example shown is for a graph with $n = 25$ vertices and $m = 8$ colors. As can be seen from the table, the best result is obtained when 9 slave processes are used. Otherwise, both the format of the table and the resulting observations are similar to the TSP case. Note the small overhead and high efficiency of the execution when the number of slave processes is increased from 8 to 12.

Number of Slave Processes	CPU Time (Sec.)	Elapsed Time (Sec.)	Relative Speedup	Efficiency (%)
Sequential	8772	8814	1.00	100.0
1	8908	8914	0.99	98.9
2	8908	4461	1.98	98.8
3	8912	2978	2.96	98.7
4	8912	2262	3.90	97.4
5	8911	1831	4.81	96.3
6	8913	1523	5.79	96.5
7	8914	1290	6.83	97.6
8	8913	1143	7.71	96.4
9	**8917**	**1142**	**7.72**	**96.5**
10	8913	1145	7.70	96.2
11	8916	1145	7.70	96.2
12	8917	1146	7.69	96.1

Table 11.2: Graph Coloring Algorithm Performance

11.2.3   Molecular Dynamics Simulations

The Molecular Dynamics simulation computes the time-evolution of a collection of particles that individually obey the classical laws of motion. If the position and velocity of each particle (i.e., the phase space) at a given time and the interactions between the particles are known, then classical mechanics predicts the phase space of the system at any later time. To compute the time-evolution, Newton's equations of motion have to be solved for every particle in the system. Such a calculation is called a classical phase space trajectory.

More formally, consider a system of N particles in which Newton's Second Law is given by:

$$m_i \ddot{x}_i = -\sum_{j=1}^{N} \frac{\partial V(r_{ij})}{\partial x_i},$$

where:

$V(r_{ij})$ is the potential between particles i and j;
x_i is the x component of the i-th particle; and
m_i is the mass of the i-th particle.

For an N-atom system, there are 3N second-order conjugate differential equations to solve. It is useful to reduce this set to 6N first-order differential equations using the Hamilton formulation.

The Sequential Algorithm

The sequential algorithm is presented in Program 11.5. This algorithm is composed of an initialization phase, a **DO LOOP**, and a small number of postprocessing actions.

```
        open data files
        set parameters for interaction potentials
        do 10 k = 1, ntraj
              read input data from file
              call init(y, n, m, k)
              call energy(y, n, m, t1)
              call integral(y, n, m, k)
              call energy(y, n, m, t2)
    10    continue
        print results
```

Program 11.5: Sequential Molecular Dynamics Algorithm

In the first stage of the algorithm, all the files that are accessed by the application for data retrieval are opened. The parameters of the potential between particles, $V(r_{ij})$, are calculated for the various types of particle interactions. The number of differential equations to be solved and the number of particles are stored respectively in the integers n and m. The number of trajectories to be calculated is represented by the variable *ntraj*. A vector y of length n is used to store the results of the differential equation solver.

After the initial calculations have been completed, the **DO LOOP** starts. This loop is executed once for each trajectory, where each phase consists of five different operations. The first operation reads the particle data from the data file. After that, the initial state of the particle system is calculated. Then the initial energy level is computed and the result is stored in the variable *t1*. The problem is then integrated, after which the energy level of the state is recalculated and returned via the variable *t2*. The difference between the two energy levels is the desired result of the program.

The Distributed Algorithm

Distributing the algorithm using MPE was relatively easy, since each trajectory is calculated independently. The process partition point is the **DO LOOP**. Among the five operations in the loop performed by the sequential algorithm, the first (data retrieval) was not modified. The remaining four operations

```
      open data files
      set parameters for interaction potentials
      Pfunc (quad, (real y(n), integer n, integer m, integer k),
          (real t1, real t2))
      Pinit (nprocs)
      do 10 k = 1, ntraj
              read input data from file
              Pcall (quad, (y, n, m, k), (t1, t2))
   10    continue
         call Pwait()
         call Pexit()
         print results
```

Program 11.6: Distributed Molecular Dynamics Algorithm

were replaced by calls to subroutines. These calls were placed in a new sub-routine envelope, called *quad*, that facilitated their distribution using the MPE macros. This modification, albeit a minor one, was necessary because the macro **Pcall** can handle only one function or subroutine, while in the current case it is necessary to allocate tasks composed of four subroutines.

Number of Slave Processes	CPU Time *(Sec.)*	Elapsed Time *(Sec.)*	Relative Speedup	Efficiency (%)
Sequential	826	831	1.00	100.0
1	827	833	0.998	99.8
2	828	419	1.983	99.2
3	828	280	2.968	98.9
4	829	213	3.901	97.5
5	826	173	4.803	96.1
6	828	145	5.731	95.5
7	828	123	6.756	96.5
8	**828**	**110**	**7.555**	**94.4**
9	827	111	7.486	93.6
10	825	111	7.486	93.6
11	828	111	7.486	93.6
12	828	112	7.420	92.7

Table 11.3: Molecular Dynamics Algorithm Performance

All the initializations preceding the actual loop were left untouched, so were all the postprocessing I/O operations that handled the calculated results. The resulting parallel algorithm is presented in Program 11.6.

Performance Results

The MPE version of the Molecular Dynamics Problem solving 7 particles, using 43 differential equations, was executed on an 8-processor MOSIX system. The results of these executions are given in Table 11.3. In the table, each line represents the average execution times of four separate runs. The best result is obtained when 8 slave processes are used. Otherwise, both the format of the table and the resulting observations are similar to those of the TSP performance.

11.2.4 Matrix Multiplication

```
int A[N][N], B[N][N];              /* input matrices */
int C[N][N];                       /* output matrix */

matrix()
{
        int i, j;
        Pfunc (dot_prod, {int i;, int j;}, { int k;});

        Pinit (NPROC);
        for (i = 0; i < N; i++)
                for (j = 0; j < N; j++)
                        Pcall ((&i, &j), (&C[i][j]));
        Pwait();
        Pexit();
}


dot_prod (i, j, k);
int *i, *j, *k;
{
        int l;

        *k = 0;
        for (l = 0; l < N; l++)
                *k += A[*i][l] * B[l][*j];
}
```

Program 11.7: Distributed Matrix Multiplication

The last example, shown in Program 11.7, is for computing the product matrix $C = A \times B$.

Since each element of the product matrix C can be computed independently, the actual computation can be performed in parallel. The distribution of these parallel computations to the slaves is accomplished by means of a "distributed" call to the function *dot_prod*. This function multiplies the ith row of A with the jth column of B and returns the element $C[i][j]$. This distributed call is executed by the macro **Pcall**. The **Pfunc** macro is used to declare *dot_prod* as a distributed function. The **Pinit** function creates the slaves and initializes the system. The **Pexit** function kills the slaves and return. **Pwait** is a synchronization function, in which the master awaits the termination of all the computations. Note that the C-language nature of the original program is preserved.

Performance Results

The execution performance of Program 11.7 for two 512×512 matrices using 8 processors is given in Table 11.4. Note that due to the relatively small granularity (amount of work) that is done by each slave process in each execution, the IPC overhead becomes quite significant. This leads to a reduced speedup gain and lower efficiency. One way to improve the results obtained in the matrix multiplication example is by reducing the IPC overhead. This can be done by allocating several lines in each invocation of the slave processes. Otherwise, the format of the table and the resulting observations are similar to those of the TSP case.

Number of Slave Processes	CPU Time *(Sec.)*	Elapsed Time *(Sec.)*	Relative Speedup	Efficiency (%)
Sequential	401	401	1.00	100.0
1	534	538	0.75	74.5
2	534	273	1.47	73.4
3	534	186	2.16	71.9
4	534	144	2.79	69.6
5	534	115	3.49	69.7
6	534	101	3.97	66.2
7	534	86	4.66	66.6
8	**534**	**78**	**5.14**	**64.3**
9	534	78	5.14	64.3
10	534	80	5.01	62.7
11	534	82	4.89	61.1
12	534	90	4.46	55.7

Table 11.4: Matrix Multiplication Algorithm Performance

11.3 Monitoring Distributed Applications

The DAEMON toolkit [19] supports monitoring of applications and sites in the MOSIX distributed operating system. DAEMON was designed as a monitor, not a debugger; it detects and reports on events rather than providing the more detailed operations of setting breakpoints and examining data structures that are typical of a debugger.

This section gives the design goals of DAEMON, followed by a description of its use in detecting, collecting, accessing, and correlating events. The DAEMON design is based on the following objectives:

Meaningful Views An application tracefile can contain a large amount of information, describing events of various types occurring in a number of processes. In order to be useful, a monitoring system must be able to provide access to all events, but must also allow the user to select relevant information.

Ease Of Use A monitoring facility should require little or no modification of existing application source code, and should have an interface that is user-friendly to both novice users and system designers.

Portability DAEMON's event detection mechanisms are implemented at the level of the system platform. It is portable in the sense that it provides users with the same monitoring capabilities for all programming languages. On the other hand, it loses some degree of portability, since it has become part of the system platform.

Transparency Monitoring facilities should interfere with the application's execution as little as possible; one of DAEMON's design goals was therefore that the system-resident portion of the package not incur high overhead.

11.3.1 Events and Their Detection

Events are composed of two pieces of data. The first indicates the nature of the event; the second provides information about the environment in which the event occurred, enabling the correlation of various events. Information about the environment includes a unique identifier of the task that generated the event, a **timestamp**. and an identifier of the node at which the event occurred.

A distributed environment has no global clock; different nodes in the system may have different ideas of what the current time is. DAEMON is currently implemented on MOSIX, in which processors may have realtime clocks that are approximately the same, drifting within a certain limit $- b$. Therefore, for each pair of events occurring locally, it is possible to determine with absolute certainty the order of occurrence. On two different nodes, N_1 and N_2, however, two events, E_1 and E_2, occurring at their respective nodes in that order might receive the timestamps t_1 and t_2 in which t_1 might be either greater, less than, or equal to t_2.

DAEMON distinguishes between two classes of events—System-Generated Events (SGEs) and User-Generated Events (UGEs).

Event	Cause
BORN	Creation of a child process
KILL	Process termination
STOP	Process inactivity
EXEC	Process activity
DPRT	Process migration from the current node
ARRV	Process migration to the current node
SSGE	SGE monitoring enabled
QSGE	SGE monitoring disabled

Table 11.5: System-Generated Events (SGEs)

SGEs, shown in Table 11.5, are caused by processes being manipulated as objects by the system. This can result from direct requests made by the application via system calls, but they operate on the process as a whole. Note that the single action of process migration from one node to another is composed of two distinct events. Having two separate events, each occurring at a single node, avoids the issue of locality but preserves a causal relationship between the two nodes.

Event	Cause
SEND	Message enqueued
RCVE	Message dequeued
INIT	Message queue allocated
CTRL	Message queue removed
SBLK	Process blocked waiting to enqueue message
RBLK	Process blocked waiting to dequeue message
SUGE	UGE monitoring enabled
QUGE	UGE monitoring disabled

Table 11.6: UGE Events

UGEs, shown in Table 11.6, are directly caused by an application's IPC resource utilization. These events do not directly influence the process as an object, since they manipulate the message resources on the system. (Two events that are categorized as UGEs, SBLK and RBLK, do not fall strictly under these guidelines, but are classified as UGEs because they are the direct results of attempts to use the message resources on the system.)

The basic mechanism for enabling or disabling monitoring is the *daemon(pid, status)* system call. It receives two arguments, a target *pid* and a status *flag*. The target is used to specify the process, or group of processes, that is to be affected. The flag specifies how they will be affected.

11.3.2 Collecting Events

Detected events cause the generation of event records. These event records are collected and made accessible to the user. If every record was made accessible separately, the resulting overhead would lead to a degradation in system performance. It is therefore necessary to store event records in core and collect groups of records.

The in-core mechanism is implemented as a specialized FIFO kernel buffer, with no blocking options. This results in the oldest events being lost if they are not transferred before the buffer is filled; new events will simply overwrite existing ones. Each time the *daemon()* system call is invoked to enable both SGE and UGE monitoring (by oring the flags), the buffer pointers on all active PEs are reset. At this opportunity, a special event record is written which will later provide the means for correlating between all the local timestamps. The reset guarantees that no untransferred events remaining in the buffer will be mistakenly accepted as current events, ensuring the consistent representation of events by the data transferred. Although this prohibits processes from alternately enabling and disabling simultaneously both UGE and SGE monitoring, this can be achieved in separate system calls.

11.3.3 Event Log Access

In order to prevent event loss, each of the local event logs is periodically read and the indices set to point to the remaining unread events, if any. The event log resides in the kernel address space, so this area is not directly accessible to user processes. It therefore became necessary to create a new system call, named *collect(pe, cbuf, count)*.

Collect() retrieves events logged on a given PE. Its first argument, *pe*, indicates the processor from which the event is to be collected. The second argument, *cbuf*, is the address of the buffer in the user process' address space into which the event log is to be copied. (It is the user's responsibility to provide a buffer large enough to hold all the event records retrieved.) The third argument, *count*, is the number of events to be retrieved from the log. The *collect()* system call returns the total number of event records retrieved.

11.3.4 Correlating Events

The *collect()* system call allow user processes to read the kernel event log. Although user applications may invoke the call directly, one of the objectives of the DAEMON project was to avoid requiring extensive modification to user applications in order to use DAEMON's services. Correlating the various retrieved logs is not simple, so a system-wide daemon process, called **daemond**, was written to gather event records from each of the PEs. **Daemond** is a responsive dynamic process; when the rate of event generation drops, the length of time between successive polls is increased via a simple decay function. This serves to further reduce the overhead caused by polling, especially when few events occur or when no processes are monitored.

Event correlation proceeds in stages, using double buffering methods for collections. The first stage of.event correlation is time normalization. If the buffers have been reset, all the special event records are examined and a table of delta values for timestamps is created. If no special events have been located, then the previous delta values are used. If the special records chronologically follow other standard event records, then the previous records are normalized before the delta values are reset. Having calculated or authenticated the current deltas, all the timestamps are adjusted accordingly.

Once timestamps have been normalized they can be sorted. Unfortunately, due to the coarse granularity of the system clock, several events can sometimes occur within the same timestamp. As the kernel event buffer is FIFO, this can easily be solved when dealing with events generated at a single PE. When correlating events generated at different PEs, temporal logic (i.e., mathematical logic that is time-dependent) must be applied.

The rules used in conjunction with the data residing in each event record ensure that it is possible to correctly perform all the **meaningful correlations**. Meaningful correlations are defined as those in which two processes influence one another's execution, either directly or indirectly (by means of message resources). Only by possessing full knowledge of meaningful correlations can deadlocks and livelocks be identified.

DAEMON provides a non-intrusive software monitor capable of detecting both SGEs and UGEs. Because the event detection mechanism is implemented in the MOSIX kernel, it is readily available to any extensions or toolkits available on MOSIX. Performance measurements for DAEMON are given in Chapter 10.

11.4 Summary

This chapter presented the MPE language extensions for writing parallel programs. It then gave the performance results of several applications that were enhanced by MPE to run in the MOSIX multicomputer environment. The chapter concluded with a description of the monitoring toolkit of MOSIX.

Due to the efficiency of the MOSIX internal mechanisms, as shown in the previous chapter, all the applications, with the exception of the matrix multiplication, achieved almost a linear speedup. This demonstrates that both MOSIX and MPE have relatively small overhead. The deviation from a linear speedup, which is especially prominent in the matrix multiplication, can be attributed to:

1. The inefficiency of the "parallel" algorithm of the program due to the the use of fine granularity. For example, the parallel algorithm of the matrix multiplication with one subprocess was already 25% slower than the sequential algorithm.

2. The communication between the master and slave processes.

3. The difference in the completion times between the slaves at the end of each stage, due to an uneven allocation of work.

These factors depend mostly on the nature of the parallel algorithm, particularly on the granularity of the distributed tasks. In order to achieve low communication overhead, the amount of computation each slave performs should be as large as possible. The optimal grain size should be determined empirically for each algorithm.

On the other hand, increasing the granularity leads to a decrease in processor utilization due to differences in the completion times between the slaves at the end of each stage. When this happens, the master must wait for all the slaves to finish their tasks. If they do not complete at the same time, then some will probably have to wait idly until the others finish. This phenomenon is aggravated when the computation time of each job cannot be determined in advance, or when the number of slaves is not an exact multiple of the number of processors in the system. Even when all the slaves require the same CPU time, the influence of a multiprogramming environment and the nondeterministic load balancing mechanism of MOSIX will cause this phenomenon. As the granularity decreases, this period of unused processors shortens.

The communication time between the parent process and its subprocesses is determined by two factors:

1. A fixed delay time of the interprocessor communication mechanism in MOSIX

2. A time period relative to the message length

When the message is short, the first factor, which is typically in the range of 5 – 15 milliseconds, is dominant. Longer messages will increase the communication time because they also require CPU time for memory-to-memory copying.

The cost of communication is nicely illustrated by the matrix program. While the parallel CPU time in all the other programs is just slightly greater than the serial CPU time, Table 11.4 shows a significant increase in the CPU time of the parallel version. The reason for this is the relatively large data movement between the slaves and the master, which affects the efficiency factor.

The efficiency column clearly shows a descending function. Except for the the graph coloring program, the efficiency continues to decrease in the second interval (consisting of 9 – 12 slaves). This indicates that the slaves in these algorithms keep the processors constantly busy. As a result, the extra slaves do not improve the processors' utilization, but they do increase the system overhead. In the graph coloring program, the efficiency behaves somewhat unexpectedly as the number of slaves increases. This is due to the nature of the parallel backtracking algorithm, where the function causes irregular cutoff in the search tree.

Bibliography

[1] N. Alon, A. Barak, and U. Manber. On Disseminating Information Reliably Without Broadcasting. In *Proceedings of the 7th International Conference on Distributed Computing Systems*, pages 74–81, Berlin, September 1987.

[2] System V Interface Definition. AT&T, 1985.

[3] M.J. Bach. *The Design of the UNIX Operating System*. Prentice-Hall, Englewood Cliffs, N.J., 1986.

[4] M.J. Bach, M.W. Luppi, A.S. Melamed, and K. Yueh. A Remote-File Cache for RFS. In *Proceedings of the Summar 1987 USENIX Conference*, Phoenix, AZ, 1987.

[5] A. Barak and Y. Kornatzky. Design Principles of Operating Systems for Large Scale Multicomputers. In *Proceedings of the International Workshop on Experience with Distributed Systems, Lecture Notes in Computer Science, No. 309*, pages 104–123. Springer-Verlag, J. Nehmer (Ed.), September 1987.

[6] A. Barak and A. Litman. MOS: A Multicomputer Distributed Operating System. *Software-Practice & Experience*, 15(8):725–737, August 1985.

[7] A. Barak and A. Shiloh. A Distributed Load-Balancing Policy for a Multicomputer. *Software-Practice & Experience*, 15(9):901–913, September 1985.

[8] A. Barak, A. Shiloh, and R.G. Wheeler. Flood Prevension in the MOSIX Load-Balancing Scheme. *IEEE TCOS Newsletter*, 3(1):24–27, Winter 1989.

[9] A. Barak and R.G. Wheeler. MOSIX: An Integrated Multiprocessor UNIX. In *Proceedings of the Winter 1989 USENIX Conference*, pages 101–112, San Diego, CA, February 1989.

[10] A. Barel. NSMOS - MOS Port to the National's 32000 Family Architecture. In *Proceedings of the 2nd Israel Conference on Computer Systems and Software Engineering*, pages 3.1.1.1–3.1.1.8, Tel-Aviv, May 1987.

[11] D.L. Black. *Scheduling and Resource Management Techniques for Multiprocessors*. Technical Report CMU-CS-90-152, School of Computer Science, Carnegie Mellon University, Pittsburgh, PA, 1990.

[12] U.M. Borghoff. *Catalogue of Distributed File/Operating Systems*. Springer-Verlag, Berlin, 1991.

[13] D.R. Brownbridge, L.F. Marshall, and B. Randell. The Newcastle Connection- Or UNIXes of the World Unite! *Software-Practice & Experience*, 13(8):45–58, August 1982.

[14] D.R. Cheriton. The V Distributed System. *Communication of the ACM*, 31(3):314–333, March 1988.

[15] F. Douglis and J.K. Ousterhout. Process Migration in the Sprite Operating System. In *Proceedings of the 7th International Conferenence On Distributed Computing Systems*, pages 18–25, Berlin, September 1987.

[16] Z. Drezner and A. Barak. An Asynchronous Algorithm for Scattering Information Between the Active Nodes of a Multicomputer System. *Parallel and Distributed Computing*, 3(3):344–351, September 1986.

[17] Open Software Foundation. *Introduction to OSF DCE*. Prentice-Hall, 1992.

[18] A. Goscinski. *Distributed Operating Systmes The Logical Design*. Addison-Wesely, Sydney, 1991.

[19] S. Guday. DAEMON: A Monitor for Distributed Systems. Master's thesis, Department of Computer Science, The Hebrew University of Jerusalem, Jerusalem-Aviv, February 1992.

[20] H. Härtig, W.E. Kühnhauser, W. Lux, and W. Reck. Operating System(s) on Top of Persistent Object Systems - The BirliX Approach. In *Proceedings of the 25th Hawaii International Conference on Systems Sciences*, volume I, pages 790–799. IEEE Press, 1992.

[21] F. Herrmann, F. Armand, M. Rosier, M. Gien, V. Abrossimov, I. Boule, M. Guillemont, P. Leonard, S. Langlois, and W. Neuhauser. Chorus, a New Technology for Building UNIX-Systems. In *Proceedings of the Autumn'88 EUUG Conference*, pages 1–18, October 1988.

[22] R. Laor. MPE: A Parallel Programming Environment for a Distributed Memory Multicomputer. Master's thesis, School of Mathematical Sciences, Computer Science Department, Tel-Aviv University, Tel-Aviv, September 1990.

[23] S.J Leffler, M.K McKusick, M.J. Karels, and J.S. Quarterman. *The Design and Implementation of the 4.3BSD UNIX Operating System*. Addison-Wesley, Reading, MA, 1989.

[24] M.S. Manasse, L.A. McGeoch, and D.D. Sleator. Competative algorithms for server problems. *Journal of Algorithms*, 11(2):208–230, June 1990.

[25] U. Manber. *Introduction to Algorithms: A Creative Approach*. Addison-Wesley, Reading, MA, 1989.

[26] S.J. Leffler M.K McKusick W.N. Joy and R.S. Fabry. A Fast File System for UNIX. *ACM Transactions on Computer Systems*, 2(3):181–197, August 1984.

[27] J.H. Morris, M. Satyanarayanan, M.H. Conner, J.H. Howard, D.S. Rosenthal, and F.D. Smith. Andrew: A Distributed Personal Computing Environment. *Communication of the ACM*, 29(3):184–201, March 1986.

[28] S.J. Mullender and A.S. Tanenbaum. Immediate Files. *Software-Practice & Experience*, 14(4):365–368, April 1984.

[29] S.J. Mullender, G. van Rossum, A.S. Tanenbaum, R. van Renesse, and H. van Staveren. Amoeba: A Distributed Operating System for the 1990s. *IEEE Computer*, 23(5):44–53, May 1990.

[30] J.K. Ousterhout, A.R. Cherenson, F. Douglis, M.N. Nelson, and B.B. Welch. The Sprite Network Operating System. *IEEE Computers*, 21(2):23–36, February 1988.

[31] Proteon Inc. *Operation and Maintenance Manual for the ProNET Q-bus Local Network Interface*, August 1982.

[32] Proteon Inc. *ProNET Model p1580 VME Local Network System*, April 1986.

[33] K. Ramamritham, J.A. Stankovic, and W. Zhao. Distributed Scheduling of Tasks with Deadlines and Resource Requirements. *IEEE Transactions on Computers*, C-38(8):1110–23, 1989.

[34] A.P. Rifkin, M.P. Forbs, R.L. Hamilton, M. Sabrio, S. Shah, and K. Yueh. RFS Architectural Overview. In *Proceedings of the Summar 1986 USENIX Conference*, Atlanta, GA, 1986.

[35] R. Sandberg. *The Sun Network File System: Design, Implementation and Experience*. Sun Microsystems Inc., 1986.

[36] R. Sandberg, D. Goldberg, S. Kleiman, D. Walsh, and B. Lyon. Design and Implementation of the Sun Network Filesystem. In *Proceedings of the Summar 1985 USENIX Conference*, pages 119–130, Portland, OR, 1985.

[37] M. Satyanarayanan. A Survey of Distributed File Systems. Technical Report CMU-CS-89-116, School of Computer Science, Carnegie Mellon University, Pittsburgh, PA, February 1989.

[38] M. Satyanarayanan, J.H. Howard, D.A. Nichols, R.N. Sidebotham, A.Z. Spector, and M.J. West. The ITC Distributed File System: Principles and Design. In *Proceedings of the 10th ACM Symposium on Operating Systems Principles*, pages 35–50, Orcas Island, WA, December 1985.

[39] H. Scheidig. The Ten Laws Underlying the Design of the Distributed System POOL. Technical Report 33/1985, University of Saarland, Saarbrucken, 1985.

[40] M.D. Schroeder, A.D. Birrell, and R.M. Needham. Experience with Grapevine: The growth of a distributed system. *ACM Transactions on Computer Systems*, 2(1):3–23, February 1984.

[41] D.D. Sleator and R. Tarjan. Amortized efficiency of list update and paging rules. *Communication of the ACM*, 28(2):202–208, Febuary 1985.

[42] A.Z. Spector and M.L. Kazar. Uniting File Systems. *Unix Review*, 7(3):61–71, March 1989.

[43] C.H. Staelin. *High Performance File System Design*. Technical Report CS-TR-347-91, Department of Computer Science, Princeton University, Princeton, N.J., 1991.

[44] J.A. Stankovic and I.S. Sidhu. An Adaptive Bidding Algorithm for Processes, Clusters, and Distributed Groups. In *Proceedings of the 4th International Conference on Distributed Computing Systems*, pages 49–59, 1984.

[45] Sun Microsystems Inc. *Network Programming Guide*, March 1990.

[46] A. Tevanian and R.F. Rashid. Mach: A Basis for Future UNIX Development. Technical Report, School of Computer Science, Carnegie Mellon University, Pittsburgh, PA, June 1987.

[47] UNIX Time-Sharing System, Seventh Edition. Bell Telephone Laboratories Inc., Murray Hill, N.J., January 1979.

[48] D. Walsh, B. Lyon, G. Sager, J.M. Chang, D. Goldberg, S. Kleiman, T. Lyon, R. Sandberg, and P. Weiss. Overview of the Sun Network Filesystem. In *Proceedings of the Winter 1985 USENIX Conference*, Dallas, TX, 1985.

[49] W. Zhu and A. Goscinski. The Development of the Load Balancing Server and Process Migration Manager for RHODOS. Technical Report CS90/47, Department of Computer Science, University College, The University of New South Wales, Canberra, N.S.W., 1990.

Index

Springer-Verlag
and the Environment

We at Springer-Verlag firmly believe that an international science publisher has a special obligation to the environment, and our corporate policies consistently reflect this conviction.

We also expect our business partners – paper mills, printers, packaging manufacturers, etc. – to commit themselves to using environmentally friendly materials and production processes.

The paper in this book is made from low- or no-chlorine pulp and is acid free, in conformance with international standards for paper permanency.

Lecture Notes in Computer Science

For information about Vols. 1–595
please contact your bookseller or Springer-Verlag